On Second Language Writing

On Second Language Writing

Edited by

Tony Silva
Purdue University

Paul Kei Matsuda
Miami University

2001

LAWRENCE ERLBAUM ASSOCIATES, PUBLISHERS
Mahwah, New Jersey   London

Lawrence Erlbaum Associates, Inc., Publishers
10 Industrial Avenue
Mahwah, NJ 07430

Cover concept by Paul Kei Matsuda

Cover design by Kathryn Houghtaling Lacey

Library of Congress Cataloging-in-Publication Data

On second language writing / edited by Tony Silva and Paul Kei
   Matsuda.
             p.   cm.
Includes bibliographical references and index.
ISBN 0-8058-3515-6 (alk. paper)
ISBN 0-8058-3516-4 (pbk. : alk. paper)
1. Rhetoric–Study and teaching (Higher) 2. Second language
   acquisition.   I. Silva, Tony J.   II. Matsuda, Paul Kei.
P53.27 .O5 2000
808'.04'0711—dc21   00-039402
                                                      CIP

Books published by Lawrence Erlbaum Associates are printed
on acid-free paper, and their bindings are chosen for strength
and durability.

Printed in the United States of America
10 9 8 7 6 5 4 3 2

For Margie and Aya

Contents

Preface

Twenty five years ago, finding scholarship on second language (L2) writing would have been very difficult. Fortunately, this is no longer the case. In the last quarter century, the amount of scholarly work on second language writing has increased dramatically. L2 writing scholars have published literally hundreds of articles in a variety of composition studies and second language studies journals; similar numbers of papers have been presented at regional, national, and international professional meetings. More than 400 doctoral dissertations addressing second language writing issues have been written and defended. The field now has a journal and two book length annotated bibliographies devoted exclusively to second language writing. Recent years have seen the publication of a number of monographs, collections of original papers, and reprint collections addressing in whole or in part, in general and in particular, the area of L2 writing. And very recently, an online L2 writing research network has come into being.

A couple of years ago, believing that the scholarship on second language writing was reaching a critical mass, we felt a need to take stock of this large and increasing body of knowledge. Consequently, we decided to host a symposium on second language writing at Purdue University to which we invited a number of widely known and respected second language writing specialists to systematically address basic concerns in the field, to consider the state of the art at the end of the century (and the millennium) with regard to L2 writing teachers, students, theory, research, instruction, assessment, politics, articulation with other disciplines, and standards.

Given our institutional context, we thought such a symposium would work best as a small gathering—with about 100 participants. We felt, however, that there might be more than a hundred people interested in what our speakers had to say. So we asked our contributors to, in addition to preparing brief talks, write formal papers for a collection meant to be read rather than listened to. This they generously did, and this collection is the result of that work.

In Chapter 1, The Composition of a Life in Composition, Barbara Kroll presents an enlightening and entertaining autobiographical reflection on her life as a teacher of language and composition. In this reflection, she focuses on five episodes in her life that helped her to define herself as a professional. She punctuates her narrative with interpretive breaks—brief personal commentaries that reflect on and enrich her narrative. Barbara's message is that the personal is professional and that understanding student success or failure requires a pioneering spirit, a willingness to reflect on one's actions, and an openness to change.

Chapters 2 and 3 focus on student second language writers. In Hearing Voices: L2 Students' Experiences in L2 Writing Courses, Ilona Leki listens for the voices of students to get their take on what goes on in L2 writing classes. She does this by focussing on five qualitative studies (four done by other researchers and one of her own) that detail specific problems observed over the long term in L2 writing classes or described by the students who experienced them. The results of these studies, which reflect disjunctures between the goals and objectives of teachers and students, serve to give L2 writing professionals a better idea of the nature of students and educational systems and to stimulate further reflection. In On the Question of Power and Control, Pat Currie focuses on the evaluation of L2 students' writing in terms of the amount, nature, and use of power by teachers and institutions. Specifically, she considers the consequences of three policies: restrictions on the number of non-English for Academic Purposes (EAP) courses in which students are permitted to enroll, the evaluation of EAP writing, and the inclusion of EAP course grades in a student's grade point average. On the basis of this consideration, Pat calls for a careful and critical examination of the effects of these policies on L2 writers and teachers and urges teachers to advocate on the students' behalf to change policies that discriminate against or disadvantage L2 writers.

Chapters 4 and 5 address L2 writing theory from somewhat different perpectives. In Notes Toward a Theory of Second Language Writing, Bill Grabe argues for the need for a theory of writing to guide the work of second language writing professionals and sketches a broad theory that could usefully organize research, instruction, and assessment practices. In doing this, he examines theoretical work both in L1 and L2 writing and draws the conclusion that, since, at the current time, there exist no viable predictive models of writing, second language writing professionals might be better served at this point by a descriptive model of writing developed through the characterization of conditions on learning to write. The generalizations thus produced could serve as a foundation for more sophisticated theory building in the future. In Does Second Language Writing Have Gender?, Diane Belcher looks for signs of feminization (i.e., identification with innovative epistemological and pedagogical elements) in second language writing scholarship with regard to research paradigms, discourse style, and cultural (gender) sensitivity. More specifically, Diane examines the extent to which second language writing research does or does not practice traditional science, is or is not agonistic or adversarial in its theoretical stances, and does or does not treat gender as a salient cultural feature. After presenting her (nonadversarial) argument, Diane concludes that second language writing researchers are more progressive, postmodern, and feminized than their counterparts in some other areas of second language studies and that there is good reason to be optimistic that second language writing research will continue to move in this direction.

Chapters 6 and 7 address particular issues in empirical research with implications for inquiry in general. In For Kyla: What Does the Research Say About Responding to ESL Writers?, Lynn Goldstein examines the research on teacher-written commentary in L2 writing which focuses on rhetorical and content issues. In this examination, she asks what makes a particular body of literature (here, the research on teacher-written commentary) problematic, discusses how future research might be conducted so that sound and appropriate implications can be drawn by second language writing practitioners, and critically examines the research on teacher-written comments as a whole. On the basis of this examination, she suggests that the findings of studies in this area not be uncritically accepted; that studies in this area need to look at the elements of teacher commentary, student reactions, and student revisions simultaneously; and that researchers avoid conceptualizing the teacher-student interaction as linear in such studies. In Research Methodology in Second Language Writing Research: The Case of Text-Based Studies, Charlene Polio provides a taxonomy of measures and analyses for studying second language texts and highlights some of the methodological issues that second language researchers must contend with. She focuses her examination of these measures and analyses on gauging overall quality, linguistic accuracy, syntactic complexity, lexical features, content, mechanics, coherence and discourse features, fluency and revision, and discusses issues and problems that second language writing professionals need to be aware of when attempting to use a particular measure or critically evaluate empirical research that uses such measures and analyses. She concludes by calling for full and explicit reporting of methodology, for measuring and reporting reliability, and for conducting studies to validate measures.

In chapter 8, Fourth Generation Writing Assessment, Liz Hamp-Lyons sketches a brief history of the first three generations of writing assessment—direct testing, multiple choice testing, and portfolio based assessment. She then goes on to enumerate the key qualities that will characterize fourth generation writing assessment. She suggests that these qualities will be technological (drawing on advances in computer applications), humanistic (understanding writing as a complex set of processes), political (involving competing interests and differences in beliefs and values) , and ethical (ensuring fairness in the assessment of writing).

Chapters 9 and 10 focus on L2 writing instruction from different angles. In Instructional Strategies for Making ESL Students Integral to the University, Trudy Smoke, using examples and illustrations from her instructional context (the City University of New York), puts forth strategies that she feels have strengthened support for L2 writing throughout the college and community and have helped convince colleagues, friends, and students to advocate on behalf of ESL programs and support services. These strategies include linking ESL classes with discipline-specific courses (i.e., content based instruction), collaborating with teachers across disciplines (e.g., in block programs for entering students), obtaining grants for collaborative projects (which bring prestige and seed money for innovative programs and teaching), and developing writing assignments that help students gain political power (through the use of a critical-democratic pedagogy and theme based second language writing courses). In Advanced EAP Writing and Curriculum Design: What Do We Need to Know?, Joy Reid focuses on the implications of EAP writing research, on the development of multiple needs analysis to identity college and university writing demands, and on the issues that must be investigated if curricular integration is to be accomplished. More specifically, she sees curriculum design as based on students' needs, principles underlying theory and practice, and external expectations and constraints. She describes EAP writing curricula as involving collecting, describing, and assessing authentic information, and then integrating the results into course objectives that will structure classroom pedagogy.

Chapters 11 and 12 explicitly take up the issue of politics in L2 writing theory and practice. In Critical Pragmatism: A Politics of L2 Composition, Sarah Benesch, noting that, in recent years, greater attention has been paid to politics in language instruction and that this attention has been met by opposition from those with pragmatic views, sets out to show that L2 composition does not have to choose between pragmatism and critical thinking and argues for a critical pragmatism. She demonstrates how critical pragmatism might work in L2 composition and discusses both the theoretical underpinnings and practical possibilities. Specifically, she looks at how critical research addresses important issues overlooked by a strictly pragmatic stance; outlines the assumptions and goals of critical research and pedagogy; discusses current opposition to politics in English language teaching, L2 composition, and EAP; and concludes with an example of critical pragmatism from her own teaching. In The Place of Politics in Second Language Writing, Terry Santos focuses on the role of politics in L2 writing within the larger context of critical applied linguistics. To do this, she reviews the central concerns of critical theory, critical pedagogy, and critical applied linguistics to show how and why they constitute a major reassessment of the goals and practices of mainstream TESOL; considers the extension of this critical perspective to L2 writing, specifically, the theoretical positions and pedagogical recommendations of critical theory in relation to second language writing; offers her own critique of critical approaches to L2 writing; and concludes with her view of the future role of the sociopolitical in second language writing.

Chapters 13 and 14 take up the issue of articulation between L2 writing and other fields of study. In Second Language Writing and Second Language Acquisition, Joan Carson focuses on the interaction of second language acquisition (SLA) and L2 writing, noting that SLA and L2 writing differ in terms of central foci (competence vs. performance) and temporal perspective (diachronic vs. synchronic) as well as in terms of what fundamental questions each area asks. In addition, Joan sees an understanding of the development of second language competence as underlying L2 writing in a fundamental way. To consider how SLA theory might inform L2 writing models, she examines the notion of error in L2 writing and considers it from the perspective of four basic SLA research questions: What does learner language look like? How do learners acquire a second language? What accounts for differences in learners' achievements? What are the effects of formal instruction? In Dangerous Liaisons: Problems of Representation and Articulation, Carol Severino, a educator and advisor of rhetoric teachers, a writing lab director, and a liaison between the rhetoric and ESL communities at her institution, describes the perils of the go-between roles she plays. These include explaining ESL students to American teachers in an advocatory way, explaining American students and teachers to ESL students, introducing rhetoric professors and teaching assistants to the notion of contrastive rhetorics, mediating between the L2 writing and literature discourse communities, and explaining ESL students and their needs to university administrators. Based on her experience as a liaison, she suggests the following: prepare ESL students to be their own advocates and explainers; hire more international, immigrant, and bilingual students as rhetoric, composition, and lab teaching assistants; qualify explanations about culture and education; don't be afraid to say, "I don't know" or to refuse to be a liaison; and, when students ask about cultural issues, ask them to write about their observations.

In the final chapter, The Difficulty of Standards, For Example in L2 Writing, Alister Cumming takes a close look at the notion of standards with respect to two recent research studies. This examination led him to an awareness of four fundamental dilemmas that formulations of educational standards confront, particularly in terms of L2 writing. These include defining the construct of L2 writing; figuring out what students have learned; relating L2 writing to other abilities and modes of communication; and accounting for variability among language varieties, people, and situations. Alister identifies three senses of the term, "standards": norms of empirical inquiry; specific curricular formulations; and typical genres of texts, writing tasks, and teaching practices. He concludes that unless standards regarding L2 writing are articulated, studied, and justified, confusion and political manipulation are likely.

Some concluding remarks: First, as readers will see, difference abounds in the chapters that comprise this collection. Some papers are written in first person, others in third; there are personal narratives, logical arguments, and syntheses; some papers are shorter, some longer; some more formal, some less formal; some are global in perspective, others local; there are clear differences in political and ideological orientations; some authors are more optimistic, some less; and the papers reflect influence from a number of disciplines. We see this difference as a strength: while the papers differ, in our view, they complement each other. In addition, we feel that the diversity here is healthy and a reflection of the dynamic nature of current scholarship in second language writing. This is not an area that will march in lockstep into the new millennium. Second, we want to be up front about a limitation of our collection—for the most part, it addresses work done in North America with young adult second language writers. Given our financial and logistical contraints, this was perhaps inevitable. However, we do see this as a problem, and consequently, we are currently engaged in a number of projects designed to draw attention to work in second language writing done in other languages and contexts and to help make the field more inclusive. Stay tuned.

ACKNOWLEDGEMENTS

First and foremost, we would like to thank our contributing authors for making this collection possible. We very much appreciate their generosity in giving this project their time, effort, and expertise, and for their advice and cooperation. We would also like to thank Lawrence Erlbaum Associates in general and Naomi Silverman, Lori Hawver, April Montana, and Sarah Wahlert in particular for their enthusiastic support, guidance, and help in producing this volume. Finally, we would like to thank Jessie Moore for an outstanding job on the indexes.

Contributors

Diane Belcher directs the ESL Composition Program at Ohio State University. She is co-editor of the journal, *English for Specific Purposes,* and has co-edited several books, including (with George Braine) *Academic Writing in a Second Language* (1995), (with Alan Hirvela) *The Reading/Writing Connection: Perspectives on Second Language Literacies* (forthcoming), and (with Ulla Connor*) Reflections on Literacy in More than One Language* (forthcoming). She is also the former chair of the TOEFL Test of Written English Committee and a member of the TOEFL Committee of Examiners.

Sarah Benesch is Associate Professor of English at The College of Staten Island of The City University of New York. She has edited two collections: *Ending Remediation: Linking ESL and Content in HigherEducation* (TESOL) and *ESL in America: Myths and Possibilities* (Heinemann). She is currently writing a book on critical English for academic purposes.

Joan Carson is Associate Professor and Chair of the Department of Applied Linguistics and English as a Second Language at Georgia State University. Her primary research area is academic biliteracy, and she has published in a number of journals, including *TESOL Quarterly, Written Communication, Language Learning, Journal of Second Language Writing, Reading in a Foreign Language*, and *Reading Research and Instruction*. She is co-editor with Ilona Leki of *Reading in the Composition Classroom: Second Language Perspectives* (Boston: Newbury House, 1993).

Alister Cumming is Head of the Modern Language Centre and Professor in the Department of Curriculum, Teaching and Learning at the Ontario Institute for Studies in Education of the University of Toronto. He teaches graduate courses and conducts research on second language education, particularly in reference to English as a second/foreign language and in regards to curriculum organization and evaluation, second-language writing, and student assessment.

Pat Currie is Associate Professor of Linguistics and Applied Language Studies at Carleton University, where she teaches in the graduate, EAP, and CTESL programs. She has published in *TESOL Quarterly, Journal of Second Language Writing, English for Specific Purposes*, and several edited books. Her research interests include second language writing, academic literacy, the development of EAP materials, and L2 teacher education.

Lynn Goldstein is Professor of Applied Linguistics and TESOL at The Monterey Institute of International Studies where she also directs the writing program for matriculated graduate students. Her interests include teacher training as well as research in composition, feedback on writing, and sociolinguistics.

William Grabe is a Professor in the English Department at Northern Arizona University. His interests include reading, writing, and literacy—both L1 and L2, both child and adult, and both theory and practice. He is also interested in issues of literacy assessment, written discourse analysis, English grammar, language policy, teacher training, and content-based instruction. He co-authored with Bob Kaplan, *The Theory and Practice of Writing* (Longman, 1996), is editor of the *Annual Review of Applied Linguistics* (Cambridge University Press); and will be President of the American Association for Applied Linguistics during the 2001–2002 year.

Liz Hamp-Lyons is Chair Professor of English at the Hong Kong Polytechnic University, where she is also Director of the Asian Centre for Language Assessment Research. Her scholarly interests include second language writing pedagogy, especially response; second language and first language writing assessment, including portfolio-based assessment, web-based and other 'distance' performance assessment, as well as theoretical and philosophical issues in assessment, particularly validity theory and ethics. Her latest book is *Assessing the Portfolio: Principles for practice, theory, research* (with Bill Condon), Hampton Press, 1999.

Barbara Kroll, Professor of English and Linguistics at California State University, Northridge, is involved in training current and prospective teachers to work with both native and non-native English-speaking writers. Her publications have focused on issues in the teaching of writing, teacher training, and writing assessment, all from the ESL perspective. She has taught courses and presented workshops at several TESOL Summer Institutes and TESOL Summer Academies, and she has been a frequent conference presenter. She also worked with ETS on developing the TOEFL Test of Written English.

Ilona Leki is Professor of English and Director of ESL at the University of Tennessee. Her books include *Understanding ESL Writers: A Guide for teachers*, *Academic English*, and *Reading in the Composition Classroom* (with Joan Carson). She is co-editor (with Tony Silva) of the *Journal of Second Language Writing*. Her research interests center around the development of academic literacy, and she was the winner of the 1996 TESOL/Newbury House Distinguished Research Award.

Charlene Polio is Associate Professor in the English Department at Michigan State University, where she directs the MA TESOL program. Her primary interests in the area of L2 writing are research methodology and the relationship to second language acquisition. She has published in the areas of L2 writing, second language acquisition, and foreign language classroom discourse. She is Chair of TESOL's Research Interest Section and on the editorial board of the *Journal of Second Language Writing*.

Joy Reid is Professor of English at the University of Wyoming, where she coordinates the ESL support program and teaches writing, ESL methods, and linguistics. Her publications include an ESL writing textbook series (*The Process of Composition, The Process of Paragraph Writing, and Basic Writing*); teacher resource books, *Teaching ESL Writing* and *Grammar in the Composition Classroom* (with Pat Byrd); edited anthologies, *Learning Styles in the Second Language Classroom* and *Understanding Learning Styles in the Second Language Classroom*, and many articles on ESL writing, learning styles, discourse, discourse analysis, and the change process. Her current writing includes the third edition of her writing series and a co-authored linguistics book for non-majors.

Terry Santos, Professor of English at Humboldt State University in Northern California, teaches courses in TESOL training, second language acquisition, and ESL writing in the undergraduate and graduate programs in the English Department. She received her Ph.D. in Applied Linguistics at UCLA, and has published articles in *Journal of Second Language Writing*,

TESOL Quarterly, *TESL Reporter*, *Applied Linguistics*, and *The Kenyon Review*. Her interests include first and second language writing, grammar, methodology, and assessment.

Carol Severino, Associate Professor of Rhetoric and Director of the Writing Center at the University of Iowa, teaches and researches about the relationships between writing, literacy, culture, and pedagogy. She serves on the editorial or review boards of *Writing Center Journal*, *Journal of Second Language Writing*, *Learning Assistance Review*, *Composition Studies*, and the *Journal of Advanced Composition*. Co-editor of MLA's *Writing in Multicultural Settings,* she has articles forthcoming in *College English* and the Boynton/Cook collection, *The Politics of Writing Centers.* She also plays the drums in the rock band, "Rough Draft."

Trudy Smoke is Professor in the English Department at Hunter College, CUNY where she directs the Freshman and Developmental English Programs. She is the author of *A Writer's Workbook* published by Cambridge University Press, *Making a Difference* published by Houghton Mifflin, and most recently *Adult ESL: Politics, Pedagogy, and Participation in Classroom and Community Programs* published by Erlbaum. She is a frequent contributor to professional publications and a presenter at TESOL, 4C's and other conferences in our field. Dr. Smoke also co-edits the *Journal of Basic Writing.*

Editors

Paul Kei Matsuda is an Assistant Professor of English at Miami University, Ohio, where he teaches undergraduate and graduate courses in composition, rhetoric, and linguistics. He received his PhD from Purdue University, where he taught undergraduate and graduate writing courses for both native and nonnative speakers of English, and graduate courses for ESL writing teachers. With Tony Silva, Paul founded and chairs the Symposium on Second Language Writing, and has edited *Landmark Essays on ESL Writing*. At the Conference on College Composition and Communication, Paul chaired several workshops and the Special Interest Group on Second Language Writing, and currently serves as chair of the Committee on Second Language Writing. His articles have appeared in journals such as *academic.writing*, *College Composition and Communication*, *Composition Studies*, the *Journal of Second Language Writing* and *Written Communication*, as well as a number of forthcoming edited collections.

Tony Silva is Associate Professor of ESL at Purdue University, where he directs the Program in English Language and Linguistics and the ESL Writing Program and teaches undergraduate and graduate courses for ESL students and ESL teachers. With Ilona Leki he founded and edits the *Journal of Second Language Writing*; with Paul Kei Matsuda he founded and hosts the Symposium on Second Language Writing and edited *Landmark Essays in ESL Writing*; and with Colleen Brice and Melinda Reichelt he compiled the *Annotated Bibliography of Scholarship on Second Language Writing: 1993–1997*. He currently serves on the editorial boards of *Assessing Writing*, *Journal of Basic Writing*, *TESL Canada Journal*, and *Writing Program Administration*.

1

The Composition of a Life in Composition

Barbara Kroll
California State University, Northridge

In the summer of 1998, I ran into an old graduate professor of mine whom I had not seen for many years: Bill Rutherford, a well-known person in the field of second language grammar from the University of Southern California. I revealed to him that since assuming the mantle of teacher trainer myself, I passed along to many novice teachers a method he showed me more than 20 years ago for how to mark a variety of linguistic errors in student compositions.[1] He was gratified to hear that in training me, he had, in fact, trained numerous others as well. Later in our conversation, he mentioned that he regarded me as someone who had helped pioneer the field of teaching second language writing. If I was one of the pioneers, it is because I happened to find myself in circumstances that allowed me to participate in the field in its infancy. How exactly this pioneering unfolded is the subject of this chapter.

The topic of this chapter is in itself a kind of pioneering, for not much in the field of second language writing has been published in the area of personal reflection. So herewith, in true pioneering fashion, I want to stake my claim in the fairly new territory I call *autobiographical reflection*, a genre that seems to be emerging and fostered among first language (L1) writing teachers (see, e.g., McCracken, Larson, & Entes, 1998; McGann, 1997; Tompkins, 1996; White, 1999) but that has not gotten much exposure in our second language (L2) writing circles (although, see Spack, 1997, for a related discussion). In the "reading" of my life story as unfolded in this chapter, I believe I will be able to find important lessons not only for myself but for others as well. One of the most significant lessons I draw from my

1

own history is how strongly our personal stories shape our teaching on an ongoing basis. Further, as we grow in experience and continue to increase our knowledge, what also expands is our ability to reflect on our choices and decisions more insightfully, and our own autobiographies play a critical role in this.

In her case study on teaching styles in the composition classroom, Katz (1996) identified each of the four English as a Second Language (ESL) writing teachers she investigated by a metaphor that she selected to encapsulate each one's dominant style and classroom personality. What I see in the two assignments discussed in this chapter, and what is apparent in my teaching career as a whole, is that I have always been ready to try new ideas and to create materials and assignments when I come across something that lends itself to creative use. Thus, adding a new term to those in Katz' model, the metaphor I apply to myself is that of *teacher as improviser,* a term most appropriate for pioneers. Why I believe this is true for me will hopefully become clear as I recount my story.

I have been in this field a long time, and elsewhere I have spoken about some of the earlier practices and beliefs I now look back on with embarrassment in light of what we know and what we do today (Kroll, 1996). But it is also important to state that all of the things that I did in all of my writing classes (for both English-speaking and nonnative English-speaking students) 20 or 30 years ago, whether it was designing my syllabi, creating writing assignments, conducting individual classes, or responding to student writing—all of my practices were in keeping with what people believed at the time. It is just that—especially as regards to ESL writing—there did not seem to be that many people around who had an interest in both composition and in second languages, so there were few places or people to turn to for guidance, and people did not talk much then about what they believed anyway. (They just did it.) Thus, it was, in a sense, the perfect time for pioneering.

A Pioneering Assignment

Let me begin to tell you about my pioneer days by sharing with you an assignment that dates back to my early teaching. It is only through what I learned later in my career that I am able to interpret why this particular assignment worked out to be so successful in the classroom, but I present it now as a way to illustrate how some of my improvising manifested itself.

This assignment evolved from my response to an essay that was required reading for English majors I was teaching in Israel in the early 1970s. The essay was the introduction to a book on literature, and its purpose was to explain how literature differed from other types of texts and what the value of reading literature could be. The authors began by presenting a presumably simple fact about a murder: "A man murders a girl with whom he is in love" (Brooks, Purser, & Warren, 1952, p. 2). From this basic scenario the authors then created a variety of short texts: an autopsy report, a legal indictment, a newspaper account, and a "sob sister's" story. Later in the essay, the "facts" as embedded in these versions of the murder were revealed to summarize, more or less, Robert Browning's poem, "Porphyria's Lover," and the essay's authors explained what, in their view, made the literary text superior to the four other short texts they had written (Brooks et al., 1952, pp. 5–8).

What I lifted from this essay was the idea of presenting the students with a series of facts and then asking them to embed all of those exact facts in two completely different texts of their own invention. For the purpose of this assignment, I created the character of James Brandon, a college professor, and then listed five miscellaneous details of his biography. I quote for you the exact assignment I presented to my students in January, 1974:

Instructions
Incorporate all of the information contained in the five sentences below into two separate essays unified by two completely different themes. You may add as much information as necessary to get the point of view across, but you may not omit any of the details, except those contained in parentheses.

Facts
1. James Brandon was the youngest of five children.
2. He received his PhD in political science at the age of 25 (in 1962).
3. He was voted "Most Popular Teacher of the Year" by the student body of Clearview University (in 1967).
4. He was a Fulbright Professor (1969–70 at Aarhus University) in Denmark.
5. He played the violin and drove a motorcycle.

My Israeli students loved this assignment and really were inventive beyond my wildest dreams. Some examples of the texts they came up with included a newspaper article describing James Brandon's win in a local motorcycle race; a business letter from a matchmaker to a client about finding the perfect match for her daughter; an obituary from the school paper about his tragic death in a motorcycle accident pointing to the poignancy of finding his smashed violin case in the wreckage; and a personal letter from his wife explaining to her mother why she had decided to leave him (the revving of the motorcycle engine and the off-key violin had driven her over the edge).

As a class, we looked at examples of several of the texts produced and discussed how the same presumably objective fact could be embedded in a context that gave it a positive or negative connotation. One minute the man was a multitalented admirable fellow and the next he was an egotistical, self-centered philanderer. What did that tell us about truth and reality? What did that tell us about the writer's need to consider audience and purpose in shaping truth and reality? These were lessons that I did not have to teach because the students had taught themselves through their own writing. This was definitely an assignment to recycle.

In later incarnations because I did not remember the exact name of my character, he metamorphosed into David James. After giving the writing assignment to my international students as a teaching assistant (TA) at the University of Southern California, and again finding how much the students enjoyed the task, I distributed 150 copies of a version of this assignment at the teacher's resource swap at the Conference on College Composition and Communication in Minneapolis in 1979. More recently, in the early 1990s, when I served for several years as the TA trainer for the freshman composition program at California State University, Northridge, I passed along this assignment to a few dozen teachers in training, and I suspect that David James (or James Brandon) continues to live on in classrooms all around the world.

Interpretive Break: Although it would be many years before I could put a term to it, what this assignment served to create was a community of writers in the classroom. As the class progressed and we read additional texts and moved on to other writing assignments requiring practice in a range of skills, there were many occasions for us to refer back to James Brandon and the rhetorical and linguistic choices that had been made in shaping the written products about him. Somehow the students were all in this together, and long before I knew about peer collaboration or group problem solving, I witnessed it taking place spontaneously as a result of this assignment.

Building a Career

When I first started to think back on my teaching career, what struck me was that the *path* to how I got in that career was as significant as the career itself in shaping my classroom persona today. Although I was interested in writing and in languages ever since I can remember, it took me a long time to find the exact career that would combine both of these interests. Perhaps it is not surprising, then, that I think that the best-equipped ESL writing teacher must cross, at the very least, these disciplinary boundaries, a view shared by many in the field (Matsuda, 1998; Silva, Leki, & Carson, 1997). Still, that can only happen if one is aware that these disciplines exist, and I surely knew nothing about linguistics or about composition studies when I started my higher education.

I am very interested in the dynamics of our personal histories. I find this important because I have come to believe that a teacher is not only someone who must know both content and pedagogy, but also someone with a personal history that shapes his or her classroom in both subtle and overt ways. Each time I teach a class, my autobiography is in that classroom just as surely as are the textbook materials and the course assignments. If the personal is political, as so many feminists began to claim in the 1970s, I would like to make the claim that the personal is professional as well.

Let me share five episodes of my autobiography that contribute to who I am in my classroom today and that explain how I have come to devote my professional attention to the teaching of second language writing. A second assignment is also presented from my early teaching within the framework of discussing how I find the terms *pioneer* and *improviser* apply to me.

Episode 1: Early Language Learning

My multiple experiences with language learning have had an enormous impact on how I perceive and work with students who use English as an additional language. In fact, I wonder how anyone who has not engaged in the serious study of at least one other language can really understand the processes of second language learning at all, and without that understanding, I do not believe one is properly prepared to teach foreign or second language students.

My earliest exposure to working with a foreign language was when I was 9 years old. I talked my parents into letting me sit with my older brother during the private Hebrew lessons he received to begin preparing for his Bar Mitzvah. I found the Hebrew alphabet a mysterious and awesome set of markings, and turning those symbols into pronounceable words to me seemed not unlike the code breaking that one of my action heroes of the time, Captain Midnight, offered to help us do with his decoder ring (available with just a few inner seals from Ovaltine jars[2]). I became quite good at reading the very simple introductory Hebrew textbook, limited to about 75 words, and proved much better than my brother at eventually deciphering the complex Hebrew prayers in terms of being able to provide phonetic representation of the texts. My comprehension was definitely zero, but then again, so was the comprehension of most young kids in similar circumstances. In any case, my first round of Hebrew studies ended in about a year.

Episode 2: From High School Through Graduate School

By the time I graduated from high school at the age of 17, I had completed 5 years of studying French, 3 years of studying Spanish, and 1 year of studying Russian. In the summer prior to starting college, I enrolled in an intensive French language-immersion program in Montreal, planning to major in

French in college. I am certain that I did not know what the word *linguistics* meant at that time. Despite my best efforts and the efforts of Père Charbonneau, my pronunciation teacher, I could not learn to pronounce French in a way that satisfied anyone as resembling French, to say nothing of Quebeçois. To further illustrate my continuing lack of linguistic awareness at the time, by the end of my second year of Russian studies as a freshman in college and into our reading of Pushkin short stories, I still did not have a clue how to determine which case ending to put on Russian nouns and how to get the adjectives to match in gender, number, and case. It was becoming clear that majoring in foreign languages in college was out of the question.

Of course, at that time, no one explained the rationale or systematicity behind the concepts of case or inflection, and it would be decades before I would come to understand what it means to say that Russian is a language with six cases. However, I also must say that at their peak, my skills at decoding Russian were as strong as my skills had been at decoding Hebrew earlier; I was a whiz at reading, but there was near zero comprehension. It took me until I was about 38 years old to realize that many nonnative speakers of English could similarly decode English with great proficiency while experiencing very little comprehension of what they "read."

> *Interpretive Break:* On occasion, I have found myself back at the kitchen table with that Hebrew teacher or looking at the blue cover of that last Russian textbook when I see the eyes of my ESL students glaze over with incomprehension during their reading of a text beyond their capabilities. Such memories alert me quite viscerally to the need to change direction or methodologies in the curriculum I am teaching.

While I was experiencing these foreign language learning issues in college, my freshman composition teacher, Professor Miriam Heffernan, excited my interest in English by her terse but laudatory written responses to my weekly themes. Maybe English would work out as a major although I only scored a 2 on the Advanced Placement Test in English. Professor Heffernan, a Henry James scholar, required us to keep a journal, which she periodically collected and responded to in ways that resemble how teachers of writing would respond to journal entries in a freshman composition class today, some 36 years later: just a little marginal encouragement as proof that her eyes had moved through the pages.

I do not know what motivated her to ask us to keep journals, but I do know that it got me in the habit of writing regularly for several years, and I am able to look back at the now yellowing pages from my college and graduate school years and retrace some of the angst that accompanied my decisions regarding career choices. Stitched among the entries of adolescent ravings related to working out my relationship to parents and friends and the universe, the entries of naive but timely discussions related to such political events as the Cuban Missile Crisis, civil-rights demonstrations in Mississippi, and the assassination of President Kennedy are the entries deliberating about what I was going to do with my life. I wavered between a commitment to writing, with dreams of the Columbia School of Journalism; a desire to be a college teacher, working toward a PhD in American Studies; and law school, from which I was easily dissuaded because of my very mediocre grades. When I was a senior in college, in a burst of creativity that never revisited me in quite that way, I wrote a series of poems, mostly sonnets, about my concerns over whether or not I could write and what my role in the world might come to be. I would like to quote the first of those poems because it speaks to exactly how I envisioned what writing was supposed to be. It also probably influenced my very stern responses to student essays when I taught my first writing class because so few could fulfill what I would now recognize as my unrealistic expectations of the time:

EGO, 1964
I
July 6, 1964

If I could write my thoughts on life
In words of poets who spoke their truths
As if from golden strings their music flowed,
I would not hesitate to speak out loud
Of nineteen sixty-four in eyes and mind
So young, and yet so eager to absorb.
But, silenced by my only average prose,
Which, though it can be read and understood,
Remains as open strings on a violin;
I cannot write, I must not write at all.
When I arrange what deep within me lies,
What's etched upon the x-ray of my soul,
In language brilliant, beautiful, and bold,
You'll hearken to my thunder and my cries.

Episode 3: First Teaching Job

Let us move on to 1967, when I had my first teaching appointment. At the age of 22, I got a part-time job teaching a section of freshman composition at my alma mater, Brooklyn College. My primary qualification for this position—besides being a warm body who appeared in the chair's office just as he needed to find one of those famous teachers known as staff to fill a sudden vacancy—was that I had a master's degree in hand. This degree was in mass communications, a field that I was drawn to because of my interest in writing and my mistaken idea that such a degree would position me for a wider range of job opportunities than the journalism schools. My choice to attend the Annenberg School of Communications at the University of Pennsylvania for the MA degree evolved from the fact that there I would also be able to enroll in some graduate courses in American Studies and continue to hedge my bets about future career choices. Well, I hated the Annenberg School, and in my three semesters there, I never did learn exactly what mass communications meant. And I was way too intellectually immature to engage in the type of scholarly inquiry that the "real" graduate students in the American Studies program did. But I was not a quitter, so I slogged through the communications part until I had my master's degree in hand. Ironically, it was that master's degree in a totally unrelated field that had gotten me that first teaching job and that later would qualify me for additional English teaching positions in several other schools. If I had given up on mass communications, perhaps I would not be talking about my career in ESL writing at all.

> *Interpretive Break: It should not be surprising that I am sometimes impatient with students who want to see a direct connection between every specific thing they study and what they imagine their future career paths to be. My own experience shows we might be quite grateful to have studied anything at all in the pursuit of career choices we had no possibility of envisioning, and we have no idea how what initially appears to be irrelevant might prove more than vital at some future point in time.*

Several months after I completed my MA, and after some experience as a newspaper reporter for a weekly Jewish newspaper in Philadelphia, I moved back to my parents' house to take a job as a publications editor at the U.S. Navy Yard in Brooklyn. Now I was less than 1 year out of graduate school, and I was starting on my third full-time job, this time writing public relations materials for the New York City Board of Education. I still remember the thrill of hearing the words of my very own 10-, 20-, and 30-second public service announcements on the radio as presented by the radio personalities of their day. "Don't be a drop-out parent. Drop in to your child's open school week." I simultaneously took the part-time teaching job, again hedging my bets. Did I want to be a writer or a teacher?

I moved into my brother's old bedroom (he had already left home) and set up my former bedroom as a study by painting over the green wallpaper of my youth with yellow paint to cheer me up in my new adult life as teacher and worker. It was in that room that I sat reading the journal, *College Composition and Communication (CCC)* and looked for the teaching ideas that would keep my night students, almost all of whom were older than me, from discovering that I was completely unprepared to teach. I do not recall exactly how I knew such a journal existed, but as a research assistant in graduate school, I had worked on a project that had to do with professional journals in fields related to communication, and I suppose I knew enough to know how to research such things even though I did not know how to research American Studies. I would guess that not one of the full-time English faculty in Brooklyn College in 1967 would have suggested that reading such a journal could help me learn to be a teacher of writing, let alone become a better teacher.

At the end of the academic year, I sold my car and quit my public relations job to spend the summer in England, thinking I might try to find a way to move there. But I didn't yet have the courage to move abroad, so I went back to Brooklyn and became what is called in California *a freeway flyer*, taking two part-time teaching positions that required lengthy drives (in my new car) four nights a week. In addition to freshman composition, I was assigned one section of developmental writing—whatever it was called at the time. Some of my students in that course were nonnative speakers of English whose writing exhibited frequent and very noticeable grammar problems. Not only did I have no idea how to help these ESL students, but I suspect I had virtually no curiosity about why their English was so different from that of the "regular" students in the class. I made no connection between their struggles and my own previous struggles in French, Spanish, or Russian. After all, they spoke fluent-enough English, even if it was accented, and they were surrounded by English-speaking peers. I did not perceive them as language learners in the way I had been a learner.

Interpretive Break: Although 30 years have passed since this naive and uninformed (non-)response of mine, I worry that too many teachers in too many locations might be as lacking in linguistic awareness today as I was then. Remembering my obliviousness to these students' difficulties is one reason I believe so strongly that those who teach writing to even a single ESL student must have some background in the field of language learning as well as their own personal experiences to reflect on and inform their teaching.

Episode 4: the Israeli Connection

Parallel with these developments, I sat in my yellow study and daydreamed of escaping from my parents' house and influence. At that time in my life, I also developed a very strong interest in Israel in the wake of the Six Day War in June 1967; Israel's lightning victory had stunned and excited much of the Jewish world. When my very closest friend, Jane, decided to give up her own PhD studies in Greek and Latin to emigrate to Israel, I leapt at the chance to go with her and join the ranks of diaspora Jews looking for a new life there. My first-generation American family had brought me up in Brooklyn with virtually no ties to the Jewish religion but with very strong ties to the Jewish people; still they were shocked and horrified at my decision to travel on a one-way ticket so far from home under the auspices of an Israeli government program for new immigrants. Once again, I sold my car.

Based on the month of the year we had decided to travel, Jane and I were assigned to go to Beersheba, a small desert city of 75,000, which has since that time more than doubled in size. In January 1969, when we arrived, Beersheba was most definitely a frontier town. There we were housed and fed in what was called an "absorption center," and we attended on-site Hebrew classes all day long, Sunday through Thursday and half days on Friday, for 5 months in the "ulpan" program.[3] Our class of some 25 immigrants included adults from perhaps six or eight different language backgrounds, and our teacher claimed to know no English. I still did not know what the word *linguistics* meant, but I was quickly learning what it meant to try to function in a language that was not one's own both in and out of the classroom. It was no longer Hebrew as a Foreign Language (HFL) but Hebrew as a Second Language (HSL).

With my zeal for the victorious Israeli Army, I was thrilled to get hired by them for a part-time job after my Hebrew classes teaching a handful of soldiers who were preparing for some sort of state-sponsored low-level multiple choice English grammar and reading test. Now, instead of *College Composition*, I found myself reading an English grammar reference book that I had located in the hopes of finding out enough about how the English language worked to be able to answer the soldiers' questions. I had become, through total happenstance, an English as a Foreign Language (EFL) teacher; I had about as much training for that as I had to be a composition teacher 2 years before. But, for whatever reasons, I resisted seeking a fulltime teaching position, when, in the last several weeks of our Hebrew immersion program and stay at the absorption center, the goal was for the new immigrants to find jobs. Even Jane gave up the classics to become a high school English teacher in Haifa, which she remains to this day. As for me, I kept trying to get a job in public relations and informational writing.

Well, guess what? Despite my success in acquiring fluent spoken Hebrew in the domain of basic interpersonal communicative skills (BICS; Cummins, 1979), I had very limited Hebrew writing skills. My 27 job interviews in public relations firms and in nonprofit settings like hospitals all ended with pretty much the same message: "We can't hire you because your English writing skills aren't enough to meet our needs. We'd have to hire someone else to do work in Hebrew. Maybe you should consider English teaching." I'm not sure if it really sank in that I was not in an English-speaking country, and I was going to be as restricted in my employment opportunities as those immigrant students in New York had been by their less than optimal English skills.

Eventually I took a job as a typist for the public relations department at Tel Aviv University, from where I wrote a bitter letter (in English) to the Minister for Absorption Affairs on the eve of my 1 year anniversary in the country about how my education and talents were going to waste. Called in to meet with an ombudsman, I was told yet again that I had exactly the right background for English teaching. There were no more doors to knock on, and I reluctantly gave up my hope for a career outside of teaching. Using my practical research skills, I was able to make the right contacts at the right time to be offered a full-time teaching position in a virtually brand new school, which is now called Ben-Gurion University of the Negev. It was again my master's degree in hand that cinched the deal. I was happy at the opportunity to leave Tel Aviv and return home to Beersheba. I found Tel Aviv too much like New York at its overcrowded and grimy worst; Beersheba was a city of friendly people, and stark, near colorless, landscapes bordered by vast expanses of nothingness. Just living there as an urban-raised American made me a pioneer.

My first-year teaching assignment, which began in the fall of 1970, found me teaching courses to three populations of students. The first group consisted of Israelis required to take English courses because the textbooks in virtually all subjects that they could study at university were only available in English, something that remains largely true today, and that explains why many Israeli academics are in the forefront of foreign language reading research. The second and third groups that I taught were English majors.[4] The coursework for the English major was divided into the study of literature, linguistics, and language, and I was hired as a language teacher. One group I was asked to teach was a handful of English majors who were immigrants from English-speaking countries. These native English speakers were required to take a composition course. By virtue of my five composition classes taught on American soil, I was deemed to be the big specialist who could teach the native speakers how to write. The third group that I taught consisted of Israeli students majoring in English, to whom I was to teach language. It remained for the six or eight language teachers to discover and invent what that part of the curriculum should include, although it was clear that we had to include the teaching of writing because the students were writing papers in English on literature and on linguistics.

It was through doing this job for 4 years that I developed my desire to find out how to help nonnative speakers in their study of English.[5] Soon I was back to reading *CCC*, I was still plugging away at those grammar books, and I finally learned at least a little about what linguistics meant by sitting in on my students' required introductory linguistics course.

Assignment 2: Falling Into Student-Centered Learning

Let me interrupt my narrative here to report on one very specific class exercise I created for my Israeli students from my early reading in *CCC*. The assignment was suggested by Lutz (1971), which he reported to have taken from the freshman English syllabus at the University of North Carolina for 1968–1969. The exercise consisted of providing each student in the class an index card with precise instructions to engage in a specific activity for a period of 3 minutes. The activities appeared to have no connnection to each other except that the timing was interdependent. For example, one student would be asked to stand in front of the room, repeatedly count to five and on each count of five say the words "If I had the wings of an angel." Another student was instructed to clap every time the person at the front of the room said "angel." Other students either sat in their seats or walked about the room and engaged in a specified action. Following this chaotic classroom event, students were asked to describe in writing what had just taken place in the classroom and also to write about their reaction to it. Although none of the actions that the students engaged in were particularly meaningful, what held them together was that none of them were spontaneous and self-motivated. Many of them were triggered by the instructions that had been given to a different student. For example, without the counting that the first student was told to do, the next student would not get the word *angel* as a clue to clap, the next student would not use the clapping as a signal to turn the lights on (or off), the next student would not use the light signal to time standing up, and so on.

I adapted this activity to my own (EFL) classroom situation and to the number of students in class. Although Lutz' (1971) interpretation focused on the fact that the activity helped students to understand the importance of searching for order in their writing—because the classroom "happening" was ordered in a way not at first glance apparent—I saw this at the time as an exercise in point of view, and I added a third section to the writing for which they had to describe what another teacher might have reported to an authority figure if that teacher had glanced in our room while the activity was taking place. I remember that I continued to use this activity for years simply because of the laughter and enjoyment the students had both in doing the activity and then in trying to figure it all out afterwords.

> *Interpretive Break: What I could not have done then was to provide any "real" explanation of why this activity was worth engaging in. Even if my teaching philosophy at the time was consciously motivated by wanting learners to have fun, I had no conscious understanding that students often retain more when learning is enjoyable, and that making learning fun is cognitively appropriate. I certainly thought that deviations from the teacher-fronted classroom should be kept to a minimum, so I could*

not have appreciated then as I do now how empowered the students must have felt to be participants in their own learning. I would now also recognize that this activity is excellent for ESL/EFL students because the first part requires very little use of language. The active event unfolds in an extremely physical way and thus helps kinesthetic learners, who are frequently overlooked in more quiet classrooms. Additionally, because the writing task derives from the immediate context, it is more accessible and engaging than many topics that students are traditionally asked to write about. They are thus motivated to write well. I was probably also drawn to this assignment because the writing it produced seemed so much more real than the writing students produced when they followed the rigid formulaic patterns in the textbooks of the day; their writing, for all its flaws, looked so much more like mine than when they wrote in response to contrived topics typical at the time. This experience certainly taught me that I shouldn't hesitate to experiment with curriculum, a lesson that exemplifies the "improviser" metaphor.

Episode 5: Graduate School Redux

Now I certainly felt like a pioneer as well as an improviser in trying an assignment like this, but the more I read in *CCC* and whatever else I could get my hands on at the time, the more I felt inadequate to the challenge of teaching my students. It was becoming obvious to me that I simply did not know enough to help them in an ongoing and principled way. Thus, the more I read, the more I realized that I needed further education in order to learn what it meant to teach language and to teach writing to students who want or need to carry out academic tasks in a new language.

As it happens, simultaneously with my full-time teaching, I had spent 2 of my 4 years commuting to Tel Aviv University and taking a full program of graduate courses in English and American literature. By the time I had completed all the work for a master's degree at Tel Aviv University except for the thesis, I had not learned a single thing that would help me become a better language teacher. I wanted to go back to school to learn something applicable to my new career path, and I knew I needed to get a PhD. It meant leaving Israel. This time I did not sell my car. I removed the battery and tires and mounted it on blocks, thinking I would be back in 2 years ready to write a dissertation.

Interpretive Break: One of the requirements of my graduate studies at Tel Aviv University, undertaken primarily to preserve my job security as a possible path to a PhD, was to pass a Hebrew test for foreign students. I was proud of the Hebrew speaking skills I had acquired, at last experiencing what successful language learning felt like. But the course that I enrolled in to prepare for the exam taught me exactly how different academic language could be from daily language. I finally came to understand that for me to be employable as a writer of Hebrew would have required a very lengthy learning process I wasn't prepared to commit to. I would never again question why I had to change my earlier career plans.

In August 1974, I made the 8,000 mile journey from Beersheba to Los Angeles, to begin my studies in the relatively new Rhetoric, Linguistics, and Literature program at the University of Southern California (USC), under the directorship of Professor Ross Winterowd. But once again, graduate school and I did not get along that well. And it was not merely the demotion from full-time, high-status faculty to part-time, no-status teaching assistant that caused the problem.

I loved teaching my international students and learning from them about so many more cultures than I had been exposed to in Israel, and Ross had us reading nearly everything on composition that had been published to that point in time. But as others of my teachers saw it, I did not seem to have much of a head for literature. Studying the Transcendentalists yet again, as if for the first time, seemed utterly pointless in light of what had become my professional goals—especially in comparison to what I was studying in my linguistics courses, which gave me concrete tools of language analysis I could apply to dealing with my foreign students' essays. It was Jackie Schachter, another of my linguistics professors, and a close associate of Bill Rutherford's, who encouraged me to switch focus by observing that I seemed to fit in better with the degree students in applied linguistics than I did in the rhetoric program with its heavy literature component. In my studies as a newly declared graduate student in linguistics, I became quite committed to serious research in the scholarly pursuit of how to become a better informed teacher, especially of ESL and ESL writing. And with the advice and encouragement of two of my other USC professors, Steve Krashen and Bob Kaplan, as well as Ross, I determined to write my dissertation analyzing ESL writing samples (Kroll, 1982). In the space of a few years, I had moved from novice to expert, or at least as expert as it was possible to be at the time. I had finally found the way to combine in a single focus those two threads that had been sewn in my life story: writing and languages. It wasn't Brooklyn, it wasn't Beersheba, but I was "home" at last. I went back to Israel for the summer and sold my car.

CONCLUSION

There is a famous saying in biology that "ontogeny recapitulates phylogeny," referring to the concept that the development of an individual organism duplicates the process that accounts for the development of the species to which it belongs. This chapter has recounted the ontogeny of this very specific teacher of ESL writing; it is up to others in the profession to determine the extent to which my story parallels or diverges from theirs. But I strongly encourage my colleagues to tell their stories as well.

In sharing my autobiography, I tried to demonstrate that what we choose to do as teachers in our classrooms results not only from education and prior teaching experiences but from our life experiences as well. Is it ironic or somehow quite fitting that I became a teacher of writing to nonnative speakers of English because my own early change of career path resulted from my lack of writing skills in what, for me, was a second language? My early teaching experiences took place in what was at the time a frontier town, and I responded as all pioneers must: by being willing to improvise.

Although I do not often teach ESL writing now, I do teach a variety of linguistics courses—another irony given my having fallen into a PhD program in linguistics without so planning. In the linguistics courses I teach, I find myself still on the lookout for ideas that allow me to improvise classroom exercises that engage students and that make them active partners in their own learning.

As the years have passed, though, I have come to recognize that improvising needs to be coupled with serious reflection. And if there is a moral to my story, it is this: To understand how and why our students succeed in their learning requires not only constant willingness to be a pioneer but also ongoing willingness to examine our actions with insight and to maintain openness to change.

In the 1950s, there was a television series called *Naked City* set in my home town of New York. As each week's program began, an unseen narrator intoned, "There are 8 million stories in the Naked City. Tonight you'll see just one of them." Well, there are as many stories in our field as there are teachers dedicated to the teaching of ESL writing. This has been just one of them.

ACKNOWLEDGMENTS

I am grateful to Joy Reid for providing valuable feedback on an earlier written draft of this chapter and to Ed White for sharing a prepublication version of his own reflective piece on teaching (White, 1999), which helped me find a voice to tell my story.

ENDNOTES

1. The basic idea is simply to underline the word or words in two (or more) sections of the sentence that are syntactically connected but that are at odds with each other because of some sort of grammatical violation, such as inappropriate pronoun reference or singular–plural inconsistencies. A line is drawn between the two underlined sections as a way to draw the students' attention visually to the error that has been committed.

2. In the 1950s, Ovaltine, the brand name of a popular chocolate drink mixture, sponsored the children's television program featuring Captain Midnight.

3. The word *ulpan* is typically not translated. The origin of the word is related to the first letter of the Hebrew alphabet, *aleph*. As a new country with a steady stream of immigrants from all over the world, Israel was committed to setting up Hebrew immersion programs for adults as a way to help newcomers integrate to the country and culture. The result was the development of the very successful ulpan program.

4. The English majors were the students who were asked to read the essay on literature by Brooks, Purser, and Warren (1952) discussed earlier in this chapter.

5. Because I have taken the occasion elsewhere in this chapter to honor by name those who most strongly and positively influenced my professional life, let me state that I am profoundly grateful to Professor Alice Shalvi, formerly of the Hebrew University of Jerusalem, who founded the Department of English at Ben Gurion University and who took a chance on me by cohiring me (along with the EFL director) in the first place. In recognition of my evolving interests and strengths as a teacher, she also transferred my appointment to a full-time position in the Department of English after my first year there.

REFERENCES

Brooks, C., Purser, J. T., & Warren, R. P. (1952). General introduction. In C. Brooks, J. T. Purser, & R. P. Warren (Eds.), *An approach to literature* (3rd ed. pp. 1–8). New York: Appleton-Century-Crofts.

Cummins, J. (1979). Cognitive/academic language proficiency, linguistic interdependence, the optimal age question and some other matters. *Working Papers on Bilingualism, 19,* 197–205.

Katz, A. (1996). Teaching style: A way to understand instruction in language classrooms. In K. M., Bailey, & D. Nunan (Eds.), *Voices from the language classroom* (pp. 57–87). Cambridge: Cambridge University Press.

Kroll, B. (1982). *Levels of error in ESL composition.* Unpublished doctoral dissertation, University of Southern California, Los Angeles.

Kroll, B. (1996, March). *Did we know anything at all?* Introductory remarks presented to a colloquium: "What we certainly didn't know when we started," at the TESOL conference, Chicago.

Lutz, W. D. (1971). Making freshman English a happening. *College Composition and Communication, 22,* 35–38.

Matsuda, P. K. (1998). Situating writing in a cross-disciplinary context. *Written Communication, 15,* 99–121.

McCracken, H. T., Larson, R. L., & Entes, J. (Eds.). (1998). *Teaching college English and English education. Reflective stories.* Urbana, IL NCTE.

McGann, P. (1997). "Well, think again!": Remarking on grading, subject positions, and writing pedagogy. *Composition Studies, 25,* 19–31.

Silva, T., Leki, I., & Carson, J. (1997). Broadening the perspective of mainstream composition studies: Some thoughts from the disciplinary margins. *Written Communication, 14,* 398–428.

Spack, R. (1997). The (in)visibility of the person(al) in academe. *College English, 59,* 9–31.

Tompkins, J. (1996). *A life in school: What the teacher learned.* Reading, MA: Addison-Wesley.

White, E. M. (1999). On being a writer, being a teacher of writing. In D. Roen, S. C. Brown, & T. Enos (Eds.), *Living rhetoric and composition* (pp. 171–191). Hillsdale, NJ: Lawrence Erlbaum Associates.

2

Hearing Voices: L2 Students' Experiences in L2 Writing Courses

Ilona Leki
University of Tennessee

In a recent issue of *College English*, Miller (1998) cited work by James Scott who argued that:

> all social action involves the performance of a "public transcript" and a "hidden transcript." As Scott defines these two modes of discourse, the public transcript serves "as a shorthand way of describing the open interaction between subordinates and those who dominate" (2); . . . it is a text that rarely fails to "provide convincing evidence for the hegemony of dominant values, for the hegemony of dominant discourse" (4). If the public transcript is, by definition, always available for inspection, the hidden transcript describes the discourse "that takes place 'offstage,' beyond direct observation by power holders," and for this reason, Scott insists, "whatever form it assumes—offstage parody, dreams of violent revenge, millennial visions of a world turned upside down—this collective hidden transcript is essential to any dynamic view of power relations" (4, 9) (cited on pp. 15–16).

The task I set myself for this chapter was to review the professional literature looking for instances of those "hidden transcripts" of second language (L2) students' experience in their L2 English writing courses. I wanted to hear their voices talking about the problems and successes they encountered in their writing classes and their interpretation of why things went as they did. I hoped to find research studies that used in-depth case study, longitudinal, multiple interview, and/or observational methods focused on L2 students with names who would tell us in their own voices what happened to them for better or worse in L2 writing classes. I was not interested in the "public transcript" of what they did, how they did it, or whether a particular teaching method or technique improved their writing. Instead I hoped to learn how they reflected on what they did and how they did it, what they understood from their experiences, how they constructed what was happening to them in L2 writing classes, what they said amongst themselves.

Given the explosion of research on L2 writing since 1990, I found many examples of the public transcript, studies documenting a wide range of aspects of L2 writing classes: students' writing processes, their preferences for teacher feedback, their behaviors during peer review sessions, their revision practices, drafts of texts, analyses of texts, performances on writing exams, selections of writing exam topics—a great deal of this sort of thing. Although much of this material is very helpful in illuminating what goes on in L2 writing, I was struck by the fact that so many of these studies talked about the students but never gave evidence that the researchers spent any time talking to the students, never asked them one on one what all this (whatever feature of L2 writing was under study) meant to them. No doubt those conversations sometimes did take place, but for some reason they did not end up in the public record in any detail. For example, in Schneider and Fujishima's (1995) case study of Zhang, we learn that he did so poorly in his courses that he was eventually kicked out of graduate school. We read the words of two of his English teachers and a writing-center tutor analyzing what his problem was but almost no words from Zhang himself, except for a couple of journal entries that revealed a reflective, and anxious, student and his astute analysis of some of his difficulties but no sense of what he felt happened to him during his six courses focusing on English. I single this fine study out only because I was so struck by the varied voices given a hearing in this report and, by contrast, the striking absence of Zhang himself.

This gap, as it felt to me, in the reporting of research focused on students' work but not including the students' voices, recalled something a well-known L2 writing researcher once said to me. Commenting on my interview studies of L2 students' writing experiences across the curriculum, she advised me not to always believe what my research participants told me about their experiences. What they told me might not be true. Is that why L2 writing researchers were not reporting on what students experienced, because it might not be true? Such an idea seems particularly odd in a postmodern intellectual climate in which the existence of an uninterpreted empirical reality that would warrant "the truth" is seriously challenged.

Surely in any in-depth study undertaken in a postmodern context and that tries to (re)construct or (re)present human behaviors and motivations in order to understand them, the researcher and the reader of the report cannot help but be aware of the impossibility of telling the truth. We construct stories, not the truth, stories that we interpret on the basis of the details we select. The real question is, as Brodkey (1987) said, "what to tell and how to tell it" (p. 38). Furthermore, Brodkey said,

> One studies stories not because they are true or even because they are false, but for the same reason that people tell and listen to them, in order to learn about the terms on which others make sense of their lives: what they take into account and what they do not; what they consider worth contemplating and what they do not; what they are and are not willing to raise and discuss as problematic and unresolved in life. (p. 47)

The stories we tell are intended to help us make sense of the human condition. This chapter, then, is a review of a small, select group of studies that seem valuable in helping us understand the kinds of struggles our students face in L2 writing classes and the varying stances they adopt in relation to these obstacles. It becomes clear later that these studies focus on somewhat negative aspects of L2 writing courses. My intention was not to go looking for problems, but as Newkirk (1996) suggested, "bad news" is a part of the human context; we cannot hope to ignore bad news and still learn much. Stake (1995) described research of the type reviewed here not as a "fixation on failure" (p. 16) but rather a reflection of the "belief that the nature of people and systems becomes more transparent during their struggles" (p. 16). In addition, this type of focus often works to stimulate further salutary reflection. My point in selecting this topic for this collection is to see what we can learn from access to the hidden transcript that might stimulate such reflection. In each case I believe that what we learn comes as a result of extended observation and discussion with these students over time.[1]

This chapter focuses on five studies that detail specific problems observed over the long term in L2 writing classes or described by the students who experienced them. Before moving to those detailed accounts, however, I would like to mention more briefly several studies that also prominently include student voices. Silva's (1992) account of his students' perceptions of what it is like to write in an L2 should probably be required reading for every L2 writing teacher at the beginning of every writing class as a constant reminder that behind many of the papers we read is a person's felt sense of struggle, a population of writers well aware of how much more easily they could be themselves and communicate their thoughts with clarity, precision, imagination, and force in their L1s. Brice's (1995) research revealed not just what students did with teacher feedback but how they reacted to it. Holmes and Moulton's (1995) study documented one student's increasingly intense discomfort with journal writing in his composition class because he was receiving no grammatical feedback on his journal entries and believed deeply (my guess is, correctly) that it was his problems with grammar that had once again landed him in an English as a Second Language (ESL) class in college although he had graduated from a U.S. high school. Fu's (1995) *My Trouble is My English* renders a painful portrayal of the experiences of four Laotian students in high school ESL classes. Although Swain and Miccoli (1994), Currie (1998), Spack (1997), and Johns (1991) do not deal with L2 writing classrooms, they do consult with students directly and bring us some very revealing and useful hidden transcripts. Finally, two recent dissertations, by Villalobos (1996) and Malicka (1996), also get behind the scenes of an L2 writing class. In the latter work, we see the gradual fall from grace of the L2 writing class over the course of a semester, the decline from the students' initial enthusiasm and high hopes for the course into resentment, frustration, and crushing boredom, all hidden from the teacher, masked behind the enduring respect for teachers that the cultures of some of these students had inculcated in them or had at least required in the public transcript of their interactions.

As these five more detailed reviews will show, a great deal occurs in the hidden transcript. In Hyland's (1998) study of the effect of teacher-written response to student writing, we see an interesting misunderstanding between teacher and student. Samorn, one of the students in this study, was a graduate student from Thailand gone to New Zealand to study tourism. As an English learner in Thailand, she had prided herself on her command of English grammar, something she had been praised for throughout her English studies. Wanting to build on her strengths in English, when asked by her writing teacher in New Zealand which features of her writing she wanted the teacher to focus on in her written responses, Samorn said she preferred to get extensive feedback on her grammar. Her writing teacher complied. Unfortunately, what the writing teacher was unaware of was the effect that this requested focus on grammar had on Samorn. Instead of being praised for her command of language as she always had been before, she was now receiving the response she had requested, but it was one that pointed out areas where she lacked control. Because her teacher remained unaware of the discouragement that this focus on grammar errors caused and because Samorn never altered her instructions to her teacher, by the end of the term Samorn's confidence in her ability to write in grammatically correct English was so drastically undermined that she decided to switch majors to a subject that would require less writing in English. Samorn apparently never had, nor took, the occasion to express to her teacher the problems she was able to discuss in her deep and extended contact with Hyland.

Harklau's (1998, 1999) work focused on the kinds of transitions that permanent resident students face going from high school to college. Two of her findings were especially striking. First, Harklau juxtaposed the ways her four students had their identities constructed for them first by the high school and then by the college context they found themselves in. In high school, Claudia, Hanh, and Penny from Vietnam, and Aeyfer from Turkey were thought of and referred to by their teachers as model students; they were described as hard working, as really caring about their education, and as well-behaved and compliant in class. The academic successes they experienced were praised, particularly in light of the fact that they were doing it all with a "handicap," as one teacher said, that is, doing it in a second language. Their teachers could only wish that their L1 English students would be so diligent, so focused on real learning. The English L2 students were seen as struggling against adversity and succeeding. The second construction of the identities of these students came, however, as soon as they got to college. There they were, not model students, not academically successful students; they were first and foremost ESL students, students with deficiencies in spoken and written English who had to be separated out from their native English-speaking (NES) classmates from high school into special writing classes, although they had just been held up to those very same NES students as models to emulate. And now this sudden transformation of their very identities. Quite a shock.

A second finding of Harklau's (1998, 1999) research focuses on what happens next to these students in their college ESL classes. Despite the sudden transformation of their identities as they entered college, the four students in her study felt shaky enough about their written English that they did not mind too much being placed into ESL classes in college, thinking that they could use the extra help. What they did not bargain on was the continued assault on their identities that then took place. The teachers in these classes were used to dealing with visa students, not so much with permanent residents. The materials used in the courses and the teachers' entire orientation functioned to set the students' experiences in their home countries against those in the United States. Readings focused on cross cultural differences, and writing assignments asked for papers comparing home to here. But for Claudia, Hanh, Penny, and Aeyfer home was here. They had arrived in the United States long enough ago that they really did not have a foreign experience they were familiar enough with or cared enough about to relate in their writing. Although they continuously tried to maintain their self-definitions as young Americans, the teachers kept trying to slot them into the role of foreigners, visitors unfamiliar with the ways of the new land. These students became increasingly alienated in these L2 writing classes, and although they had started off thinking that these classes would help them with their writing and take off some of the pressure they might have experienced in a freshman composition class with NES students, they ended up finding the courses at best useless, at worst insulting and undermining of their senses of self. Not that something was wrong with these classes for an international audience but, as this research clearly shows, the experiences of Claudia, Hanh, Penny, and Aeyfer in their writing class in college ended up reducing these people to their language skills.

In Nelson and Murphy (1992) we see the progressive, again detrimental, construction of an L2 writer, this time by the student members of a peer-response group. Thanks to the longitudinal nature of this study, like the last, we are able to see the movement of the peer-response group members toward gradually assigning to Juan the role of "worst writer" although, by class standards, his writing was not the weakest in the group. We see how Juan becomes trapped in this definition of himself, imposed from the outside, and witness his resulting emotional and even physical withdrawal from the peer-response group and so also from whatever benefits he might derive from the input of his group mates. Had he been asked in a preference survey or even in a single interview how he liked peer-response groups, or had the drafts of his texts been studied for the effect of peer review on revision, for example, we would not have had access to the dynamic of the social situation that was to mold his preferences or his revision behaviors. It is quite possible that Juan himself may not have been aware of the core of the problem he appeared to be having with his peer-response group.

Losey's (1997) revealing book, *Listen to the Silences*, is an ethnography of a basic writing class, focusing on five focal students, all Mexican Americans who had done all their high school work in the United States. These students were attending a community college in a small town in California with a majority Mexican American population. All of them registered in the community college in order to eventually secure jobs better than their current ones of cutting celery, picking strawberries, or working at an industrial laundry or sewage treatment plant. They hoped to eventually find jobs as a bilingual teacher, a minister, an engineer, the owner of a beauty salon, or just a better, less grueling, less manual job. Losey explored the links between the community where this composition class was taking place, the students and their histories, the teacher and her history, and the set up and organization of the community college and of the composition classroom to produce a compelling document. One of the key conflicts Losey detailed, and one that I think is or should be at the core of a lot of thinking about L2 writing classes, ended up being the difference between what the composition teacher, Carol, felt should be the goals for the course and what the five students felt they needed to learn. Carol believed that although many of her students did not need to or intend to take any writing courses beyond this one at the community college, it was her duty to prepare them for academic writing at the 4-year college level, that anything less was insulting to their potential as learners. Why should their sights be set low, she reasoned, as they had been in the local high school, where two of the focal students, for example, had taken an English course called Sports English, where they watched films about sports figures and wrote about them by essentially filling in forms. So Carol did not want these students, as she said, to just have fun learning to write, writing "journals and poems and stories and have a wonderful time, enjoy writing" (p. 114). Instead she wanted their experience in her class to be such that they would never "get scared when they hear 'I want you to compare this to this,' or ... 'I want you to analyze, I want you to summarize,' 'cause teachers, their teachers in the future, ... they're going to say just that" (p. 114).

In Losey's (1997) research we get to see first hand the sources of some of the academic writing problems these students have. In some cases they are asked to write papers commenting on issues they have no familiarity with and so no well-formed, thought-through opinions about. For example, assigned to write a paper comparing essays by Maya Angelou and Frederick Douglass, Federico, one of the focal students in the study adjusted the topic from the Black experience, a topic that had "little [personal] meaning for him" (p. 139), to one he really knew and cared about, social justice for Mexican Americans, an alteration Carol commented on somewhat negatively as off the topic. Carol's focus was getting these students ready for the next level of English, school for school's sake.

The students' goals were not the same. They had personal goals and wanted this writing class to help them meet those goals, but, as Losey (1997) pointed out, "These highly motivated students receive little support for their personal goals in the classroom" (p. 119); "they received repeated messages throughout their academic careers that ... *their* [italics added] goals [like getting out of the laundry and the sewer] were unworthy" (pp. 119–120).

In the cases reviewed here, we see attempts at communication between these L2 writing students and their teachers that go awry for one reason or another. Sometimes the teachers did not know what the students needed; in other cases, the students thought they needed one thing, and the teacher thought they needed something else; sometimes even the students did not know what they needed. In each case, however, the picture we get is of everyone negotiating in good faith. In the next case from my own research, we get rather far away from the model student image, but I think Jan's case is important because it exemplifies our complicity as members of the educational community in creating a context that ultimately helped to create Jan.[2] This case may seem unusual, even unique, and so perhaps not instructive for us in our work with other students but, as Haswell (1998) said, when we start looking closely enough, we see that it does not matter because no one's experiences are generalizable; anyone we study closely turns out to be unique.

Jan participated in a case study of his experiences from his first arrival in college (1994) until his graduation in June 1999 with a degree in business. He immigrated from Poland in 1992 when he was 17, having never studied English before. Yet because of his academic training in Poland and because the high school in the United States demanded so little of its students intellectually, he was soon making As in his high school courses despite his limited proficiency in English. When asked if he understood the material in his senior-level English class, he replied:

> Not really. For quizzes [which were all multiple choice] you got four choices and the answer was so stupid you can pretty much figure out what's the best answer.... I got A average without speaking English.

While he was making As in senior English, he was also taking ESL classes, which he characterized as "baby stuff." Their only value was in the friendliness of the other "foreigners" in the class (whereas, to his disappointment, the U.S. students in his high school appeared to be uninterested in him). Despite their friendliness, he had little use for them or for the ESL class. As he said,

> Jan: I hate the class.
> Interviewer: Did you like the students in there?
> Jan: They got on my nerves. Ass-kissing. Oh professor! [imitating an ingratiating tone]. Shut up, just sit down and shut up. And the professor was just so sweet—just shut up, oh hell, I HATE this. They're like, I LOVE this country, I love you all. I was like, just shut up and teach. I just hate like people just being so sweet in class. So I was like, ech, I was just shaking [shudders]. I hate you being so sweet, you know.

Clearly, he found the overly Mr. Rogers-like ESL class frustrating, even enraging. It is anyone's guess what these other L2 students were thinking, as we are reminded by Malicka's (1996) dissertation and the other studies cited here.[3]

Jan's frustrations were to continue in college. Having been lulled into seeing schooling in the United States as entirely nontaxing, he experienced the difficulty of dealing with college-level work as overwhelming. Although by this time his oral English abilities (which he claimed he developed while working full time during high school, not in his ESL classes) were excellent, these strengths were not acknowledged in the academic English writing class that he placed into at the university. There he was told instead that the English language he had developed over the previous 2 years was only slang, street language that he needed to discard as soon as possible in order to learn the academic English taught in this class. His teacher's disdain for his English abilities was soon mirrored in his disdain for his college L2 writing class:

> Interviewer: What about the English class?
> Jan: It sucks. Boring, boring, boring.
> Interviewer: Boring? Why is it boring?

Jan: I don't know. Mostly people are so, like involved in discussing topics . . . discussing stupid topics, like abortion or something.
Who cares? . . . Discuss women in military. Who cares? . . . They love
to discuss, . . . you know, talking, comparing the story to [their] own
experiences in United States, and blah, blah, blah. . . . People sit for
like 45 minutes discussing how interesting it is, you know.

Jan appeared to find the work in this class pointless. Furthermore, when
the L2 writing teacher asked for development of ideas in his papers, he
heard a call for "b.s.," which increasingly summed up his sense of everything required of him in college. He soon began to see all his academic
experiences in college as nothing more than hoops to jump through, a great
game in which his job was to accumulate credits and a proper grade point
average (GPA), a game he felt the teachers played too, assigning busy work,
such as group discussions of what he considered meaningless topics like
"women in military." Yet none of his resistance was visible. Instead, for example, although he made a point of not actually reading the assigned texts
in his English class, he sat politely with his over-eager (in Jan's description)
discussion group and at least appeared to listen.

What he seemed to be learning to perfection was how to play this game,
how to get what you want from a bureaucracy, and what he wanted were
grades good enough to eventually get a degree, even if it meant subvert-
ing the educational system. When his international business course required
three papers, he used the same three for his English class, cheerfully confident that no one would discover what he assumed was a fraud.

Jan even managed to distort the role of the writing center to suit his
perceived need to jump the hoops. When he discovered that his L2 writing
teacher was a tutor in the writing center, he began to sign up regularly, even
relentlessly, for appointments with her. As he explained in interviews, he
reasoned that if she saw how hard he was apparently trying, evidenced by
the fact that he came in nearly every day, she would have to give him credit
in the writing class for his efforts, and because, as his classroom teacher,
she was the one who would be grading the papers he was working on at
the writing center, then as a writing-center tutor, she would be directing him
toward the revision that she wanted to see and so would again be likely to
give him higher grades. In his mind, writing papers was a matter of simply
giving teachers what they wanted because the reasons for why they wanted
one thing rather than another—four papers rather than three, five sources
rather than eight—were indecipherable and entirely arbitrary.

Jan spent four semesters in L2 writing classes. Later in his college career,
when asked what he was using from his writing classes in the writing he was
doing in other courses, he referred vaguely to some grammar, punctuation,
and organizing techniques he said he learned. Perhaps most interesting,

however, was the fact that in his major courses in business, nearly all the assignments, including writing assignments, were group projects to which Jan contributed his computer or other skills; he rarely wrote anything at all, leaving all the writing to other members of the group. In his bravado and talk about just doing the minimum to get by, Jan recalled Fairclough's (1997) comments on the discursive practices of institutions. He seemed to have instinctively understood that "projecting a settled and centred, rational self is a ground rule for success however unsure your institutional or individual sense of identity may be" (p. 12).

Jan may be unusual, maybe not, but I want to understand his experience not because I think that other students are like him but because I think that by trying to learn more about the contents of the hidden transcripts of Jan, and Samorn, Federico, Aeyfer, and Penny we get a better idea of the range of possible human responses to the human condition—or even just to the L2 writing class condition—a better idea of "the nature of people and systems" (Stake, 1995, p. 16) and perhaps of how to stimulate "further reflection" (p. 42) among ourselves. Reviewing this research on L2 students' experiences in their writing classes leaves me with three reflections in particular:

1. a sense of how instructive negative cases can be;
2. a sense of the importance and value of qualitative research of the type that might uncover students' experiences; and
3. a sense of the relatively small amount of work on how students experience L2 writing courses, that is, how dim our students' voices are in the literature about them.

ENDNOTES

1. A number of published accounts document successful curricular innovations and include testimonials from students. I excluded from this overview all accounts in which researchers reported on their own writing students if the entirety of the students' reactions to those classes was positive (even glowing, as was sometimes the case) and when the sole purpose of including students' voices appeared to be to support claims about the effectiveness of the technique, the teacher, or the course.

2. The discussion here of Jan's case is an excerpt from a more complete study of his experiences as an L2 learner and as a student in the United States (Leki, 1999).

3. The impact of the social relationships he encountered in high school, the way these relationships positioned him, and his attempt to position himself relative to the others' views of him surely had great consequences for his subsequent construction of himself that took place in college. The importance of such social relations has been not been sufficiently acknowledged in L2 studies. See, however, Toohey (1998) for an naturalistic study of children in first grade that highlights the children's negotiation of status with each other and Kanno (1999) for comments on high school relationships. See also Thesen (1997) for an analysis of new university students

in South Africa and their quite conscious negotiation of their own identities within competing discourses.

REFERENCES

Brice, C. (1995). *ESL writers' reactions to teacher commentary: A case study.* (ERIC Document Reproduction Service No. ED 394 312)

Brodkey, L. (1987). Writing ethnographic narratives. *Written Communication, 4*, 25–40.

Currie, P. (1998). Staying out of trouble: Apparent plagiarism and academic survival. *Journal of Second Language Writing, 7*, 1–18.

Fairclough, N. (1997). Discourse across disciplines: Discourse analysis in researching social change. *AILA Review, 12*, 3–17.

Fu, D. (1995). *My trouble is my English.* Portsmouth, NH: Boynton/Cook.

Harklau, L. (1998, March). *"In the U.S. and your country": Constructions of language minority identity in classrooms.* Seattle: AAAL.

Harklau, L. (1999). Representing culture in the ESL writing classroom. In E. Hinkel (Ed.), *Culture in language teaching and learning* (pp. 109–130). New York: Cambridge University Press.

Haswell, R. (1998). Searching for Kiyoko: Bettering mandatory ESL writing placement. *Journal of Second Language Writing, 7*, 133–174.

Holmes, V., & Moulton, M. (1995). A contrarian view of dialogue journals: The case of a reluctant participant. *Journal of Second Language Writing, 4*, 223–251.

Hyland, F. (1998). The impact of teacher written feedback on individual writers. *Journal of Second Language Writing, 6*, 255–286.

Johns, A. (1991). Interpreting an English competency examination: The frustrations of an ESL science student. *Written Communication, 8*, 379–401.

Kanno, Y. (1999). Comments on Kelleen Toohey's "'Breaking them up, taking them away': ESL students in Grade 1." The use of the Community-of-Practice perspective in language minority research. *TESOL Quarterly, 33*, 126–132.

Leki, I. (1999). "Pretty much I screwed up": Ill-served needs of a permanent resident. In L. Harklau, K. Losey, & M. Siegal (Eds.), *Generation 1.5 meets college composition: Issues in the teaching of writing to U.S.-educated learners of ESL* (pp. 17–43). Mahwah, NJ: Lawrence Erlbaum Associates.

Losey, K. (1997). *Listen to the silences: Mexican American interaction in the composition classroom and community.* Norwood, NJ: Ablex.

Malicka, A. (1996). Tasks, interaction, affect, and the writer's development: A descriptive study of an ESL composition class. *Dissertation Abstracts International 57*(3), 1061A.

Miller, R. (1998). The arts of complicity: Pragmatism and the culture of schooling. *College English, 61*, 10–28.

Nelson, G., & Murphy, J. (1992). An L2 writing group: Task and social dimensions. *Journal of Second Language Writing, 1*, 171–193.

Newkirk, T. (1996). Seduction and betrayal in qualitative research. In P. Mortensen & G. Kirsch (Eds.), *Ethics and representation in qualitative studies of literacy* (pp. 3–16). Urbana, IL: National Council of Teachers of English.

Schneider, M., & Fujishima, N. (1995). When practice doesn't make perfect: The case of a graduate ESL student. In D. Belcher & G. Braine (Eds.), *Academic writing in a second language* (pp. 3–22). Norwood, NJ: Ablex.

Silva, T. (1992). L1 vs L2 writing: ESL graduate students' perceptions. *TESL Canada Journal, 10*, 27–47.

Spack, R. (1997). The acquisition of academic literacy in a second language. *Written Communication, 14*, 3–62.

Stake, R. (1995). *The art of case study research*. Thousand Oaks, CA: Sage.

Swain, M., & Miccoli, L. (1994). Learning in a content-based, collaboratively structured course: The experience of an adult ESL learner. *TESL Canada Journal, 12(1)*, 15–29.

Thesen, L. (1997). Voices, discourse, and transition: In search of new categories in EAP. *TESOL Quarterly, 31*, 487–511.

Toohey, K. (1998). "Breaking them up, taking them away": ESL students in Grade 1. *TESOL Quarterly, 32*, 61–84.

Villalobos, J. (1996). Process-oriented approach to writing: A case study of a writing class in English as a second Language (ESL) at the college level. *Dissertation Abstracts International, 57(12)*, 5028A.

3

On the Question of Power and Control

Pat Currie
Carleton University

Whether we have read about them in the literature, taught them in our classrooms, or met them in our research, second language (L2) writers have contributed significantly to our field. As our collaborators in both research and pedagogy, they have enriched our lives, deepened our understandings, and improved our teaching. They have, for example, given us insights into their writing processes (e.g., Silva, 1992, 1993; Zamel, 1983); the complexities of peer response groups (e.g., Carson & Nelson, 1994; Connor & Asenavage, 1994; Nelson & Carson, 1998); their perceptions of our classrooms (Kanno & Applebaum, 1995; Leki & Carson, 1994, 1997) and their attempts to enter the academy (e.g., Casanave, 1992; Johns, 1992; Riazi, 1997; Schneider & Fujishima, 1995; Spack, 1997).

This collaboration has further shown that L2 writers are people with an impressive array of qualities. We have witnessed, for example, their creativity in the face of adversity, their ability to select and adapt strategies in ways appropriate to their particular personalities and situations. Time and again they have shown a dedication and perseverance that have enabled them not only to relocate to a new country and learn a new language but also to develop the pragmatic competence necessary for complex and sometimes even exclusionary settings (Johns, 1990). Some, like Tic (Johns, 1992) have persevered in the face of family expectations that they follow more traditional routes, whereas others, such as Yuko (Spack, 1997) and Diana (Currie, 1998) succeed despite still-developing language skills that greatly increase their already burdensome workload. In their pursuits, many pore over their professors' comments not only for ways to improve but also for signs of encouragement that they are, in fact, progressing. This characteristic is evident in the following e-mail letter entitled "I've Made It!" sent to me by a former student:

> Hi Pat,
> This is [name]. How are you there? I just want to say hello to you and also to tell you some good news on my study. I just got my first paper back a few hours ago, and it is great! I've got a C+ for it! This is my first university paper that I've ever done before. It was about law. How do I think about the grade I just get? It is so beautiful, Pat. Although C+ is not a good grade overall, it is quite promising, Pat; there is really a potentiality for me to get to a higher level (a better mark) later. With respect to the comment made on my paper, my weaknesses in terms of paper organization are fixable. I did not have much major drawback addressing and backing up my points. So, what I am going to do is I will invest more time on organization (citation, sentence structures, etc) to get a finer paper next time (I have one more to complete next month.). Anyway, I am SO GLAD that my effort pays off in the course. However, Law is the only class that I have having a lot a lot a lot trouble in terms of understanding the material (the prof's talk is so fast and so abstract). Other courses, I am doing allright. I have to log off now, Pat. You have a good time there. When I have some good news as well as the "bad" one, I will let you know. Cheers.

Still others, such as Virginia (Casanave, 1992), make principled decisions to leave academe to pursue goals they have decided are more attuned to their own sense of who they are and what they value.

Along with creativity and strength of character, L2 writers have also shown great insight into their own processes; for example, into the conflict between their real selves and the discoursal identities they are expected to present in Western academic writing. Some, such as Yuko (Spack, 1997), although aware of the tensions involved, cling tenaciously to their real selves, determined to manage the process of negotiating the two competing discourses (Canagarajah, 1993): "And certainly there are certain things that I don't want to get used to or be Americanized.... And while I'm adjusting to a new, American culture, I want to be myself and be confident for what I am, because I believe that no culture is right or wrong or better than the others" (Spack, 1997, p. 15).

For Shen (1989), another writer who struggled successfully with his discoursal identity, the route to managing the contradictory demands lay in consciously identifying the features of each of the two discourses and then envisaging himself crawling out of one identity and into another, adopting the appropriate features for each one. Although it is unlikely that such a solution would be available to all, or, I suspect, even to many L2 writers, it was particularly effective for someone schooled in the practice of *yijing*, "the process of

creating a pictorial environment while reading a piece of literature" (p. 463).
I took special delight in Shen's solution, which required not only self-knowledge but also a critical contextual knowledge and understanding not
always accorded Chinese students—even in our own L2 literature.

Other student writers have been less successful, some losing their past,
some destroying a family closeness. There are likely many writers such as
Lu (1987), torn between two worlds and two opposing discourses, who
may lose one or both in the struggle. Virginia (Casanave, 1992), a bright
young Puerto Rican woman, left graduate school because she could not
resolve the conflict between the identity and values she shared with the
groups and communities she hoped one day to work with and the nature
of the discourse she was expected to adopt. Similarly, Carla (Fox, 1994) felt
apprehensive about returning home to her native Chile: "and I thought, if I
adopt this American writing style, what might become of me on my return?
Will I be shunned by my own students? Or even worse, will I look down
on my own people so much that I deny them their ways of communicating,
their language, their way to write?" (p. 72). What we see in these writers,
and in our own students, are people with great insight into who they are,
their life circumstances, their goals, and the obstacles they must surmount
in order to achieve those goals.

Moreover, their understandings have extended beyond us and our research interests to reach another group of people: our graduate students. At
my university, I teach a graduate class in L2 writing, a course with between
12 and 20 people, of whom one third to one half are usually international
students. One aspect of L2 writing that we look at in this course is the experiences of novices attempting to write for the academy. For one class meeting
the students select four or five papers from a list that includes Ballard and
Clanchy (1991), Basham and Kwachka (1991), Lu (1987), Lea (1994), Currie
(1998), Spack (1997), Johns (1992), Riazi (1997), Schneider and Fujishima
(1995), Shen (1989), and Casanave (1992). According to the feedback I get,
the L2 writers in these papers have enriched my graduate students' education
in a number of significant ways. They have, for example, created not only
a sense of shared experience in terms of academic hurdles and hoops but
also the belief that if so many novices eventually make it through, they, too,
will likely succeed. And very importantly, they have instilled an appreciation
of what it takes to overcome the many hurdles, to bridge the gap between
disparate cultures and achieve one's academic goals. Here I am thinking
especially of the native English speakers (NESs), who, until they read these
papers, may not grasp how unfamiliar cultural assumptions and practices
can complicate and even threaten academic pursuits. Finally, their accounts
and experiences have acted as stimuli for term papers, research essays, and
even for doctoral studies in L2 writing. The following excerpt is taken from
the introduction to one master's research essay inspired by some of these

stories, especially those of Shen (1989) and Lu (1987), whose accounts not only provided the master's student with the texts to be analyzed but also helped him reflect on the identity struggles he, too, was experiencing:

> More particularly, I have experienced some difficulties in accurately interpreting the expectations, and in producing the "voice" (Ramanathan & Kaplan, 1996) which my reader wants to hear through the text. . . . It seems, however, that I have overcome the initial difficulties and have begun to produce a text in this new discourse community. This success may be partially due to my pragmatic understanding of my status in the new community. As Ivanič and Roach (1993) observe, I am the one in a less powerful position, the one who wants to get into the community and obtain the degree from my powerful reader, and thus ". . . it is not in a powerless student's interest to rock the boat" (p. 6). It seems that now I know the way of singing, and the readers are beginning to show their acceptance of my "voice." (Liu, 1998, pp. 1–2)

He then reflects on the potential implications of his success on his Chinese identity:

> I am wondering if this is a good thing. I have already witnessed one friend, an excellent writer in Chinese who has studied in one of the Ivy-League schools, recently write an essay in a Chinese newspaper in such a rigid and strange style that it has lost all the charm of her previous writing. I have also observed that some of my Chinese friends who had gone through the same situation have begun to attach English words in expressing their thoughts. I am wondering if such things will happen to me, and how I will deal with them. (*ibid.* pp. 3–4)

Indeed, his voice has been accepted: He has successfully appropriated the discipline's "way of singing" to accomplish his own rhetorical and academic purposes.

Such contributions to the field make it essential that we as researchers and practitioners examine our side of the collaborative equation and evaluate and see how well we are assuming our responsibilities toward our learners. Related issues have already been broached by researchers such as Schneider and Fujishima (1995), who ask us to consider the lengths to which our institutions should go to assure a student's success and by Silva (1997), who argued strongly and persuasively for the ethical treatment of L2 writers in the four areas of understanding, placement, instruction, and evaluation. It is this last area, evaluation, that I wish to address in this chapter, for it is through evaluation in both in mass and classroom contexts that, either as institutions or as individuals, we wield substantial power and control over our students' lives. It is the amount, nature, and use of that power that I would like us to examine critically in this discussion. My specific concern lies with three policies related to the evaluation of L2 student writing: restrictions in the number of content and subject courses[1] a student is permitted to enroll in, the evaluation of EAP writing, and the inclusion of EAP grades in a student's grade point average (GPA).

At most North American colleges and universities, incoming international students without a TOEFL are required to take an in-house proficiency test, the results of which determine the level (if any) of ESL/EAP course the student must take. At some of these institutions, the test results also determine the number of content courses the student is allowed to take concurrently with EAP. The purpose of restricting the number of courses is intended to prevent the students from assuming a workload that could cause them to fail or at least to get lower grades than might otherwise be the case. Put another way, then, the policy is in place to "save the students from themselves."

For L2 students, the policy can and often does have a number of other consequences. First, it usually prolongs students' studies, increasing the time and money required for them to graduate. Moreover, as they will probably have to take courses during the summer to try to speed up the process, they are frequently removed from the summer job market, a result that likely increases the expense or at least the opportunity cost. Thus it is not surprising that in a research project I am currently conducting, former students have voiced their dissatisfaction with the policy, as seen in the following suggestion that the restrictions be removed[2]:

> I also suggest that ESL student in [introductory], [intermediate], and [advanced] should be allowed to take more courses than now. Since student paying the courses it's their responsibility to decide whether they can efford taking more courses. If the university allowed me to take few more courses in first year I could have finished haft of my degree by now. Most of students complain about this.

Nor is this feedback coming through formal channels only. When I meet former students on campus and enquire as to where they currently are in their studies, many voice the same sentiments, pointing out that if they could have taken more courses, they would have been further along in their academic careers.

Although I can appreciate the good intentions behind such a policy, I can also see a number of problems with it as it is currently conceived. For one thing, the restrictions are applied universally, regardless of an individual student's grades prior to arriving at the university, of their performance in their content courses as they move through their programs, or the various writing demands of their other courses. No distinction is made, for example, between an introductory course in calculus and one in sociology.

Further, such a policy appears to ignore the language-learning possibilities in content courses, the value of input—especially of what might well be comprehensible input if the student has a background in the subject—and the opportunities for exposure to discipline-specific subject matter and discourse unlikely to be encountered in ESL courses. My EAP course, for example, will not include the chance to participate in a physics lab or to write a computer program. Nor does it offer the intrinsic motivation of a course in the student's major or the increased effort and engagement that could well result in greater language gains.

Perhaps my greatest reservation, however, lies in the paternalistic attitude implicit in such a policy, which seems to be suggesting that, given free rein, L2 students will not only overload their academic schedules but will also fail to drop courses they are doing poorly in. In short, such a policy appears to assume that international students, unlike domestic students, are uniform in their inability to make decisions in their own best academic interests; hence their need for greater protection from themselves.

I am not proposing that course restrictions be removed entirely but rather that they be managed in a more principled and reasoned way. I would like to see the universities take into consideration a number of factors, including but not limited to students' academic background prior to entering the university, their areas of strength and weakness (Haswell, 1998), and their achievement throughout the EAP program. To determine the allowable number of courses, it might make sense to use the students' GPAs instead of only their EAP grades. I would also endorse Haswell's proposal that if there is room for doubt, the student be given the benefit. Finally, I would like to see research that tracks L2 students and their choices, thus enabling us to continue to assess our policies and adjust them accordingly.

The second area involving our use of power and control again concerns evaluation of writing but in this case in a classroom context. In many of our ESL programs, we evaluate our students' writing based solely on what they write for our courses, ignoring any writing done in their content or subject courses. There are a number of suggestions in the literature, however, that their performance in EAP classes may not be an accurate indicator of their writing abilities in other areas. For one thing, as Haswell (1998) pointed out, ESL writing evaluation is characterized by a lack of agreement or consistency across various groups of readers. Further, current research has strongly suggested significant differences between the evaluative criteria of English and ESL faculty and those of other disciplines (e.g., Atkinson & Ramanathan, 1995; Currie, 1994; Faigley & Hansen, 1985; Leki, 1995). Thus it is at least possible that our expectations are different enough from those of our content area colleagues to disadvantage our students. One case in point, this time involving mass assessment, is described by Johns (1991), whose biochemistry student continued to fail the proficiency examination despite an A− average in his major and a B+ average overall.

I am especially concerned here with similar cases in classroom contexts in which students might be in danger of failing their EAP courses even as they are performing well in content courses that involve academic writing. If our mandate in EAP is to prepare the students for the academy, I believe we need to ensure that we do not exceed that mandate, jeopardizing our students in the process. As a teacher I would have considerable difficulty holding back such a student; at the very least I would be concerned that my own criteria might not reflect the students' real-world needs. For me to be fair and principled in my evaluation, as Silva (1997) urged, I need to have a sense of both the writing requirements in my weaker students' content courses and how well they are performing there. Nor does finding out this information have to be a formal or onerous task. We can, for example, simply ask the students how they are doing and if we could see some of their graded assignments, using what we learn both as a reality check for our own expectations and as a basis for discussion about academic writing. Despite the limitations described by Haswell (1998), we might even consider some form of portfolio that would contain assignments signed off by the professor in content courses these students are currently enrolled in.

The final area I would like to consider also concerns our responsibility to ensure as far as possible that our students' grades reflect their ability to meet more than our English teachers' sense of appropriate writing. This issue—one that has been brought to my attention by former students in our program—concerns the calculation of the GPA. In many of our institutions, the grade a student achieves in a credit EAP class is factored into other significant institutional indicators such as the GPA. The justification for this appears to be twofold. First, the practice is nondiscriminatory: If it is lower than a student's other grades, it will lower his or her GPA; if, on the other hand, it is higher, it will raise it. Second, credit EAP courses must carry a grade for the purposes of calculating the allowable number of content courses. Although I, like Silva (1997), believe that EAP courses should be offered for credit (and I am pleased that my own university has adopted this policy), I would prefer either a pass–fail grading system for our EAP courses, or as an alternative, a policy that excludes EAP grades from the GPA. In his questionnaire response, one business student pointed out that a student could be doing exceedingly well in his content courses, less well in his ESL courses, and because of the latter, fail to get a scholarship:

> I think it should be optional whether to count ESL grade toward GPA for ESL students since this university language requirement course which prepare ESL students for other courses. For example, [intermediate and advanced EAP course] grades are counted toward GPA for social science students; I have A− average in other course but I got B-s in both [intermediate and advanced]. In order to increase my average to A- I have to get 6 points—at least 3 A+s

in full credit. So when we apply for scholorships its unfavorable (counting ESL grade to GPA) but people don't aim for scholarship [will be in] favor of counting the grade. Therefore it should be . . . [up to] the student to decide whether they want grade to be counted or not.

I had not realized that this particular student had applied for a scholarship, although I knew of others who had. I was exceedingly pleased to learn of his good grades, however, because I had taught him at the introductory level and knew not only that he was a very bright young man and a very good language learner, but also that he had been formally identified as visually disabled. Although I would reject optional inclusion as an administrative nightmare, I can certainly understand his frustration: After all, for most students we are a service course, one whose mandate is not to assume content course status but rather to support their attempts to acquire sufficient academic literacy to succeed in achieving their own academic goals.

In reflecting on these three institutional and classroom practices, I would like not to be cynical, not to entertain any suspicions that perhaps one way to ensure that scholarships are more likely to go to domestic students might be to find ways to advantage them. I would like not to attend to the small voice that reminds me that more international students in EAP courses means more teaching jobs and higher tuition revenues.

At the very least, however, I do believe that at the institutional level we sometimes adopt policies without thinking through their implications for international students. Perhaps it is merely that large institutions look for ways to streamline procedures and that just as L1 students find themselves dealing with bureaucratic decisions they find discriminatory or offensive, so too will L2 students; in the interests of efficiency, perhaps, lies the policy of restricting courses according to ESL scores and grades; or perhaps not. Or perhaps the motivations differ at different institutions. What remains constant, however, regardless of motivation, is the potential for negative impact on our students.

I suggest it is up to us—as L2 teachers and researchers committed to our L2 students—to examine critically and carefully the effect all our policies have on them. Pennycook (1996) cautioned us regarding exclusionary practices in our own institutions. And Delpit (1988) reminded us that it is those who lack the power who can most easily see an imbalance, although those who have it may not even be aware that one exists. Should we take up this challenge, our students are perfectly positioned to tell us what impact institutional policies have on their academic careers and on their lives and how we might modify those policies in the interests of fair play and equality. Given that our positions as L2 teachers and researchers are usually in less jeopardy than those of our students, I further suggest that it is our task—especially those of us with tenured positions—to advocate on their behalf, to work within our systems to try to change those practices that either intentionally or unintentionally discriminate against or disadvantage those with whom our past collaboration has been so rewarding. Future productive collaboration depends on our continued commitment and sense of equity.

ENDNOTES

1. By content or subject courses, I am referring to nonlanguage courses, whether English as a Second Language (ESL), English for Academic Purposes (EAP), or L2 composition.

2. The questionnaire does not mention the policy explicitly but merely asks for comments not already included.

REFERENCES

Atkinson, D., & Ramanathan, V. (1995). Cultures of writing: An ethnographic comparison of L1 and L2 university writing/language programs. *TESOL Quarterly, 29*, 539–568.

Ballard, B., & Clanchy, J. (1991). Assessment by misconception: Cultural influences and intellectual traditions. In L. Hamp-Lyons (Ed.), *Assessing second language writing in academic contexts* (pp. 19–35). Norwood, NJ: Ablex.

Basham, C. S., & Kwachka, P. B. (1991). Reading the world differently: A cross-cultural approach to writing assessment. In L. Hamp-Lyons (Ed.), *Assessing second language writing in academic contexts* (pp. 37–49). Norwood, NJ: Ablex.

Canagarajah, A. S. (1993). Critical ethnography of a Sri Lankan classroom: Ambiguities in student opposition to reproduction through ESOL. *TESOL Quarterly, 27*, 601–626.

Carson, J., & Nelson, G. (1994). Writing groups: Cross-cultural issues. *Journal of Second Language Writing, 3*, 17–30.

Casanave, C. P. (1992). Cultural diversity and socialization: A case study of a Hispanic woman in a doctoral program in sociology. In D. Murray (Ed.), *Diversity as resource: Redefining cultural literacy* (pp. 148–182). Alexandria, VA: TESOL.

Connor, U., & Asenavage, K. (1994). Peer response groups in ESL writing classes: How much impact on revision? *Journal of Second Language Writing, 3*, 257–276.

Currie, P. (1994). What counts as good writing? Enculturation and evaluation. In A. Freedman & P. Medway (Eds.), *Teaching and learning genre* (pp. 63–79). Portsmouth, NH: Boynton/Cook Heinemann.

Currie, P. (1998). Staying out of trouble: Apparent plagiarism and academic survival. *Journal of Second Language Writing, 7*, 1–18.

Delpit, L. (1988). The silenced dialogue: Power and pedagogy in educating other people's children. *Harvard Educational Review, 58*, 43–61.

Faigley, L., & Hansen, K. (1985). Learning to write in the social sciences. *College Composition and Communication, 36*, 140–149.

Fox, H. (1994). *Listening to the world: Cultural issues in academic writing.* Urbana, IL: National Council of Teachers of English.

Haswell, R. H. (1998). Searching for Kiyoko: Bettering mandatory ESL writing placement. *Journal of Second Language Writing, 7*, 133–174.

Ivanič, R., & Roach, D. (September 1989). Academic writing, power, and disguise. Paper presented at the conference of the British Association of Applied Linguistics "Language and Power." Edinburgh.

Johns, A. M. (1990). Coherence as a cultural phenomenon. In U. Connor & A. M. Johns (Eds.), *Coherence in writing: Research and pedagogical perspectives* (pp. 211–226). Alexandria, VA: TESOL.

Johns, A. M. (1991). Interpreting an English competency examination. *Written Communication, 8*, 379–401.

Johns, A. M. (1992). Toward developing a cultural repertoire: A case study of a Lao college freshman. In D. Murray (Ed.), *Diversity as resource: Redefining cultural literacy* (pp. 183–201). Alexandria, VA: TESOL.

Kanno, Y., & Applebaum, S. (1995). ESL students speak up: Their stories of how we are doing. *TESL Canada Journal, 12*, 32–49.

Lea, M. (1994). "I thought I could write until I came here": Student writing in higher education. In D. Graddol & S. Thomas (Eds.), *Language in a changing Europe* (pp. 64–72). Clevedon: British Association of Applied Linguistics and Multilingual Matters.

Leki, I. (1995). Coping strategies of ESL students in writing tasks across the curriculum. *TESOL Quarterly, 29*, 235–260.

Leki, I., & Carson, J. G. (1994). Students' perceptions of EAP writing instruction and writing needs across the disciplines. *TESOL Quarterly, 28*, 81–101.

Leki, I., & Carson, J. G. (1997). "Completely different worlds": EAP and the writing experiences of ESL students in university courses. *TESOL Quarterly, 31*, 39–69.

Liu, Y. (1998). *Identity issues in entering the academic discourse community: Problems and solutions.* Unpublished master's research essay, Carleton University, Ottawa, Ontario.

Lu, M. (1987). From silence to words: Writing as struggle. *College English, 49*, 437–448.

Nelson, G. L., & Carson, J. G. (1998). ESL students' perceptions of effectiveness in peer response groups. *Journal of Second Language Writing, 7*, 113–131.

Pennycook, A. (1996). Borrowing others' words: Text, ownership, memory, and plagiarism. *TESOL Quarterly, 30*, 201–230.

Ramanathan, V., & Kaplan, R. B. (1996). Audience and voice in current L1 composition texts: Some implications for ESL student writers. *Journal of Second Language Writing, 5*, 21–34.

Riazi, A. (1997). Acquiring disciplinary literacy: A social-cognitive analysis of text production and learning among Iranian graduate students of education. *Journal of Second Language Writing, 6*, 105–138.

Schneider, M. L., & Fujishima, N. K. (1995). When practice doesn't make perfect: The case of a graduate ESL student. In D. Belcher & G. Braine (Eds.), *Academic writing in a second language: Essays on research & pedagogy* (pp. 3–22). Norwood, NJ: Ablex.

Shen, F. (1989). Culture: Identity as a key to learning composition. *College Composition and Communication, 40*, 459–466.

Silva, T. (1992). L1 vs L2 writing: ESL graduate students' perceptions. *TESL Canada Journal, 10*, 27–48.

Silva, T. (1993). Toward an understanding of the distinct nature of L2 writing: The ESL research and its implications. *TESOL Quarterly, 27*, 657–678.

Silva, T. (1997). On the ethical treatment of ESL writers. *TESOL Quarterly, 31*, 359–363.

Spack, R. (1997). The acquisition of academic literacy in a second language: A longitudinal case study. *Written Communication, 14*, 3–62.

Zamel, V. (1983). The composing processes of advanced ESL students: Six case studies. *TESOL Quarterly, 17*, 165–187.

4

Notes Toward a Theory of Second Language Writing

William Grabe
Northern Arizona University

GOALS FOR A THEORY OF WRITING

One of the first questions that might be raised by any effort to develop a theory of writing, whether for first or second language contexts, is to ask why such a theory might be needed. Most researchers and practicing teachers are reasonably comfortable with their own senses of what writing is, how is it used, how it is developed in given contexts and settings, and how it can best be taught. In many situations the goals for writing development are reasonably clear, for example, when needing to write business memos or lab reports. In fact, theories of writing, as all-encompassing views, can lead researchers and teachers away from the real examination of writing performances in well-recognized contexts and can lead to vague generalizations and confusion. These dangers are certainly real enough. However, there are a number of genuine benefits in engaging with the concept of the construct of writing, with trying to determine how writing should be defined, understood, analyzed, and developed. These arguments are discussed in this chapter; a broad sketch of a theory of writing that may usefully organize research, instruction, and assessment practices for both first language (L1) and second language (L2) contexts is provided as well. In developing the ideas in this chapter, I am exploring the territory and should not be held accountable to a higher standard than other thinking papers. The ideas outlined here are primarily an effort to suggest another way in to the problem of defining the construct of writing.[1]

If writing specialists are to take seriously the need for self-reflective practices and critical inquiry, one of the foundations will need to be a theory of writing that can be examined openly and publicly, that can be discussed as an agreed on focus of study, and that can build on, or perhaps withstand, many intuitive, unspoken assumptions about writing and its uses in various settings. An agreed-upon construct of writing practice (or practices) will allow for research results that achieve a greater degree of comparability, more opportunities for convergent research findings, and a set of common terminology and descriptors. Without such foundations, there is little likelihood that research and instruction will develop beyond the current and on-going history of personal preferences, socialized practices that work, and reinvented ideas. This need to develop a common set of terms, understandings, interpretations, and analyses is only a minimal goal for theories of writing.

A more rigorous goal for defining the construct of writing would be to develop theories that actually model and explain human-performance outcomes at a number of proficiency levels and across a number tasks and contexts. This is not likely to be a realistic goal at any time in the near future. A second goal that moves beyond a reflective definitional understanding would involve theories that are partially explanatory and predictive. At such a level, one could, perhaps, predict how well a group of writers would perform under certain settings, task constraints, topics, and so forth.

In fact, a few theories of writing might already do this on very basic level, if given considerable interpretive space. For example, the models of writing as knowledge telling and knowledge transforming, as described by Bereiter and Scardamalia (1987), would make a number of predictions that should hold up well across a number of student writing groups, tasks, and performance constraints. So, a writer who plans for no more than 10 seconds will write a predictable essay with less new information (and most likely a lower quality essay) than a student who plans for 4 minutes and jots down certain ideas for planning. Similarly, a writer who makes a set of notes and directly converts those notes to continuous prose is not likely to write as well as a writer who sorts through the notes, moves information and topics around, and reshapes the outline to a new linear form. However, this level of prediction is not sufficiently powerful to count as an explanatory theory of writing—one that would make strong specific predictions about how given individuals and groups will perform under a range of conditions and a specific set of tasks.

At the moment, a descriptive theory of the writing construct may be the best that can be hoped for, with the expectation that it will guide productive inquiry, assessment, and instructional practices. Only in this way will a theory eventually move from descriptive to explanatory. Such a descriptive theory would have the following benefits:

1. It would allow us to discuss and understand better how writing is carried out and judged as effective in a number of circumstances.
2. It would help explain why some people write better than others when in similar contexts and when addressing similar tasks and topics.
3. It would help us understand why certain students do not learn to write very well in certain circumstances with specific types of writing tasks.
4. It would help us understand how students develop writing abilities in varying ways and under varying circumstances.
5. It would help us to evaluate specific programs and educational contexts and understand better educational successes and failures.
6. It would help us to design better instructional curricula.
7. It would help us to teach better and respond better to student needs.
8. It would help us understand how to assess writing abilities more effectively and more responsibly.

To the extent that a descriptive theory of the writing construct can suggest productive research goals, valid assessment practices, and effective instructional implications, it is a goal that has major practical value and is worth pursuing. (It is possible, at the same time, that a more predictive model of writing could also emerge out of research agendas that refine and delimit the relative importance of many components of a model of writing and their interactions across a range of contexts, tasks, and writing purposes.)

Perhaps the concept of the writing construct can be restated in more basic terms. Simply put, the goal is to describe what writing is; how it is carried out as a set of mental processes; how it varies (both cognitively and functionally) across tasks, settings, groups, cultures, and so forth; how it is learned (and why it is not learned); and how it leads to individual differences in performance. Of course, such goals for a theory of writing radically minimize the complexity of the tasks involved, the processes undertaken, and the extraordinary variety of contexts influencing performance (the performance conditions). Whether discussed simply as writing or as the writing construct, a theory of writing must be built from foundational ideas that are consistent with other learned skills and socialized practices.

To begin a discussion of a theory of writing, we need, first, a set of anchoring ideas and first assumptions. These include a starting point for exploration, a set of basic concepts that are to be built into a theory (and are not simply consequences or predictions from a theory, although research can support the value of having chosen useful first assumptions). A first anchoring assumption is that a theory of writing can be best developed from examining and exploring the writing processes and products of expert writers for given tasks and settings. Although there are no obvious objective standards to refer to for expert writing, the writing of experts provides performance targets for other writers to achieve. To understand what writing is, in effect, requires that we understand first what good writing is and describe that as well as possible. Other supporting ideas include a set of underlying theories (knowledge bases and performance conditions) that will influence the construct of writing. Such supporting theories include the following six:

1. A theory of language.
2. A theory of conceptual knowledge and mental representations.
3. A theory of language processing (writing processes).
4. A theory of motivation and affective variables.
5. A theory of social context influences.
6. A theory of learning.

These supporting theories, discussed in more detail in Grabe (2001), Grabe and Kaplan (1997), and Hayes (1996), provide resources to describe and explain performance outcomes that can be observed whenever the individuals, settings, or contexts change from one writing occurrence to the next.

PAST EFFORTS TO CREATE THEORIES OF WRITING (AND DESCRIBE THE WRITING CONSTRUCT)

L1 Theories of Writing

The first coherent theories of writing in modern contexts began to emerge in the early 1980s. Graves (1984) and Flower and Hayes (1980, 1981) proposed competing views of writing, and in particular, writing processes, although with little consideration for social contexts, task variation, motivational factors, learning theories, language knowledge, or even variability in the language processes themselves. (There are many discussions and reviews of this work.) In the later 1980s, two further major contributions to discussion of the writing construct were published. North (1987) wrote a synthesis of the field of writing research from an L1 composition and rhetoric perspective in which he explored the territory of research assumptions, research goals, and the findings of key studies. This study generated a useful map of the composition discipline and of competing ideas for understanding the nature of writing; however, it did not offer a productive synthesis that could be a foundation for future inquiry.

In contrast, the work of Bereiter and Scardamalia (1987) produced a number of fundamental insights relevant to theorizing about the construct of writing. In their work, they proposed a model of writing processes (rather than "the process"), suggesting that differences among writing ability may be due to at least two qualitatively distinct sets of writing processes. They support this model with empirical research studies (both their own and those of others) that highlight the differences between skilled and less-skilled writers; the variable processing demands of writing; the importance of coordinating strategic planning and processing; the need for planning that moves beyond content generation; and the need to foster in writers self-regulation, evaluative abilities, and self-reflection.

In the 1990s, L1 writing research evolved and expanded ideas and concepts introduced over the previous 15 years. Flower (1994) took much more seriously the interaction of individual cognition and social context in writing, drawing in contextual factors that influence writing performance. Both Witte (1992) and Faigley (1992) expanded their views on writing to incorporate social context influences and theories of language knowledge as factors influencing the discourse framing of texts. Hayes (1996) and Kellogg (1994, 1996) expanded their processing explanation for writing to incorporate motivational factors, learning-theory concepts, and social context influences. In the former case, Hayes thoroughly revised the initial Flower and Hayes process model of writing.

Finally, L1 writing research began to explore the role of genre knowledge in writing, both as a discourse construct and as a social context influence (Berkenkotter & Huckin, 1995; Swales, 1990). This work, incorporating ideas of social setting and task variability in advanced writing contexts, allowed for renewed discussions of the role of language as cues for discourse structuring and also raised issues of socializing practices (both in schools and out of schools) as they influence writing development.

L2 Theories of Writing

Theorizing on the nature of writing in L2 contexts has developed from somewhat different sources, deriving primarily from the fields of English for Specific Purposes (ESP), contrastive rhetoric, written discourse analysis, functional language use, and English for Academic Purposes (EAP) in U.S. settings. For much of the 1970s and 1980s, theorizing about writing followed closely on English L1 views of writing and theories of the writing process. At the same time, major independent contributions from L2 settings included the attention to language in writing production, the nature of organizational structuring in writing, and the influence of cross-cultural variation on writing.

In the 1990s, the work of Swales, Johns, and Connor (summarized in part in Grabe & Kaplan, 1996; see also Johns, 1997) has been influential in generating theoretical perspectives on the nature of writing and writing instruction. In addition, a number of productive research studies carried out in L2 contexts have provided us with a better understanding of L2 writing development and writing constraints (Belcher & Braine, 1995; Carrell & Connor, 1991; Carson, Carrell, Silberstein, Kroll, & Kuehn, 1991; Cumming, 1998; Ferris, 1995, 1997; Kroll, 1990, 1998; Leki, 1995; Leki & Carson, 1994, 1997; Sasaki & Hirose, 1996; Silva, 1993, 1997; Silva, Leki, & Carson, 1997).

A series of articles by Atkinson and Ramanathan (Atkinson, 1997; Atkinson & Ramanathan, 1995; Ramanathan & Kaplan, 1996a, 1996b) highlighted a number of culturally driven English L1 assumptions that differentiate L1 and L2 academic writing experiences and instruction. These assumptions have a particularly strong impact in L1 instruction that emphasizes critical thinking and the logic of argumentation. Such assumptions include the high value placed in English L1 university cultures on originality, critical thinking, creativity, logic, insight, cogency, individual voice, audience, and so forth.

A further set of articles, by Leki and Carson (Leki, 1995; Leki & Carson, 1994, 1997), points out the problems that L2 students have when they encounter the academic curriculum beyond the ESL writing classroom. Although many advanced ESL students have good coping skills, there are a number of issues that specifically confront these L2 writers. Their ESL writing experiences are typically too easy, with too great an emphasis on success and security. Practice in writing often does not match up well with the writing demands that students must address in courses across the university curriculum. Thus L2 writers have less practice in the skills they need, they often are not challenged sufficiently, and they often engage in writing that is not valued in many later courses (e.g., they get little practice with text-responsible prose).

Other differences between L1 and L2 writing involve the influences of L1 rhetorical and cultural preferences for organizing information and structuring arguments (Connor, 1996, 1997; Leki, 1991, 1997). Students have many implicit frames for presenting information and arguments in their L1; these frames and formats may not transfer straightforwardly to many English L1 academic contexts. Johns (1997) makes the argument that a writer's knowledge of appropriate genres is constructed out of shared values at many different levels (shared communicative purpose, shared knowledge of roles, shared knowledge of formal features, shared knowledge of register use, shared intertextuality, etc.). Such combinations of shared knowledge is a hidden dimension for L2 writers to master.

English L2 writers also are disadvantaged in a very basic way. It is easy to develop the argument that people improve in activities that they regularly practice, particularly in cases of complex processing activities such as writing. ESL writers, then, simply do not have nearly enough practice in writing the types of English prose that will benefit them most in the

English university environments. Related to the issue of limited-practice differences over a lifetime, L2 writers also do not have the same command of English structure and vocabulary that most English L1 writers do (Sasaki & Hirose, 1996). Although this difference is obvious, it is sometimes forgotten in discussions of L1–L2 differences for writers. A related consequence of this proficiency difference is that many more L2 writers welcome specific overt feedback from teachers on the form and structure of their writing, and their writing improves as a result (Ferris, 1997). L2 writers are also able to benefit in a number of ways from the appropriate presentation and exploitation of model essays.

Most recently, specific research that draws attention to the distinctions between L1 and L2 writing have been synthesized into a set of influencing factors that are often invisible to many writing programs and teachers. In particular, the work of Carson, Leki, Matsuda, and Silva (Leki & Carson, 1994, 1997; Matsuda, 1998; Silva, 1997; Silva et al., 1997) pointed out fundamental differences between L1 and L2 writers in terms of writing processes, writing purposes, and constraints on writing performance.

Perhaps the most consistent effort to explore L1–L2 differences involves the ongoing work of Silva (1990, 1993, 1997; Silva, Leki, & Carson 1997). In earlier work, Silva pointed out the many ways in which L2 writers learn and produce texts under conditions quite distinct from L1 writers. In his more recent collaboration with Leki and Carson (1997), he argued that L2 writer differences may not only call for changes by L2 writers but also for changes by English L1 writing teachers. Thus, a share of the learning burden rests with teachers who need to understand the cultural dispositions they bring with them to the classroom as well as the legitimate values that L2 writers bring. In their article, the authors address concerns about fairness and cultural awareness, and raise many points of difference for the L2 writer:

1. Epistemological issues (distinct cultural socialization and belief systems).

2. Functions of writing (a wider potential range of legitimate functions for L2 writing).

3. Writing topics (personal expression and humanistic individualism as North American educational preferences).

4. Knowledge storage (L1-based knowledge creates complexities for L2 writers).

5. Writing from reading (adds reading-skills complexities for L2 writers).

6. Audience awareness (English L2 audience sense may be culturally different from English L1 students).

7. Textual issues (cross-cultural discourse patterns, contrastive rhetoric).

8. Plagiarism (ownership of words vs. honoring authors and their writing).

9. Memorization, imitation, quotation (trying out the L2).

10. Students' right to their own language (whose English is right?).

These differences do not suggest simply a need for L2 writers to accommodate; rather, they suggest that L2 writers are sufficiently different in nature—and they have legitimate rights to these differences—that teachers need to be appropriately prepared to teach them effectively and fairly. This list also supports Silva's ongoing call for a specific theory of L2 writing development.

The goal of this section is not to review all significant work on either L1 or L2 writing but to point out a number of major points along the way to the present time. And, although there have been many insightful discussion of L1 and L2 writing, it has nonetheless, been recently noted (Cumming, 1998) that there is still not a strong, clear, and useful explanatory model of the writing construct.

MODELS OF WRITING

Descriptive Models

At present, there are no specifically L2 theories of writing development nor are there strongly predictive models of writing for L1 contexts. Aside from the earlier models of writing noted previously (Flower & Hayes, 1981; Bereiter & Scardamalia, 1987), there are two more recent attempts at descriptive model building, by Hayes (1996), and by Grabe and Kaplan (1996). Although the two come from somewhat different perspectives, they are remarkably similar in attempting to combine concerns raised by underlying theories needed to support writing and by combining contextual influences, cognitive knowledge bases, and processes of writing production.

Hayes' (1996) model opens up the earlier Flower and Hayes (1981) model and incorporates a number of additional components in a composing model of writing. Context factors are added with specific consideration given to task, audience, and purpose for writing. These context factors influence cognitive processing first through goal setting, motivations for engaging, task assessment and task planning, and attributions for success or failure. The goal-setting and purpose-driven component then focuses the processing system for writing. The writing processes draw on a number of knowledge bases and carry out the processing and planning in working memory. In working memory, the processes for writing interact closely with the various processes engaged in reading because reading is now a central component for the processing model. The processes in working memory engage knowledge bases in a way similar to that proposed by Bereiter and Scardamalia (1987), with the capacity of the writer to engage in knowledge-transforming writing. The information to be produced is then evaluated and transcribed. The produced text offers another context resource for further planning.

Overall, the model incorporates the earlier research on the writing process while accounting for motivational factors, context factors, and reading processes. Hayes (1996) referred to a range of recent research studies to support the proposed model, and he suggested how this model grows in sophistication as writers increase their abilities. Perhaps the only strong limitation to the model is that it makes no effort to account for growing language proficiencies as part of the knowledge bases used in writing (although it is listed in the model). Because growing language proficiency is such a critical element of L2 writing development, the model may not be completely appropriate for L2 theorizing.

The Grabe and Kaplan (1996) model is remarkably similar to the Hayes (1996) model in most respects. However, because it evolves out of applied linguistic considerations, it gives much greater consideration to the linguistic knowledge base and particularly to an account of communicative competence as applied to writing. This model also accounts for context factors, perhaps to a greater extent than the Hayes model does. Like the Hayes model, it also begins cognitive processing through a planning component, one that incorporates attitudinal and motivational influences on goal setting (purpose for writing) and planning. The writing processes begin in working memory as the planning and goal setting activate the relevant knowledge bases and generate online information for writing. This online generating is evaluated with respect to plans and goals. The writing is then produced and becomes a part of the context for further reference. The Grabe and Kaplan model does not specifically address how reading would be incorporated in the writing process, but that would not be difficult to do.

Both the Hayes (1996) model and the Grabe and Kaplan (1996) model attempt to synthesize a good part of the writing research literature, but neither goes further than a current synthesis. Thus, there has been no research to manipulate various components systematically to determine difference in writing outcomes that might be predicted by the model. Moreover, neither model is specific to L2 writing contexts and L2 writing development.

Processes and Performance Conditions

Most models that have been offered to date do not indicate a hierarchy of writing outcomes and predictable performance outcomes. The Flower and Hayes (1981) model was a model of individual differences in performance, but it did not predict performance outcomes except as post hoc analyses.

It was very good at assembling research information and using protocols of writers thinking aloud to construct a plausible explanation of what writers were doing in terms of cognitive processes while writing. However, it does not have explanatory power. The more recent Hayes (1996) model and the Grabe and Kaplan (1996) also both tap research studies to assemble a plausible account of what is likely to be going on as a person writes, and how writing can vary as a reflex of many external influences, motivations, and processing constraints. Although these models are more complete in terms of the performance conditions that influence writing outcomes, they still are no more explanatory than the classical Flower and Hayes (1981) model.

The Bereiter and Scardamalia (1987) "models" not only open up the idea of multiple processing models but also introduce hierarchical predictions in terms of processing involved while writing. This approach represents a new way of theorizing about writing because it is based on hypothesized empirical evidence rather than logic or post hoc analysis. At the same time, the conceptual changes suggested by their models of writing have not been developed in any significant way. That is, no further work has been done on a hierarchy of process models for writing; nor has research been done on task types that specifically engage one processing model or another; nor has the idea of multiple processing models been expanded beyond the two that were proposed more than a decade ago. These limitations recently led Cumming (1998) to state that there does not seem to be a genuine predictive model of the writing construct available to us, one that would predict relative difficulty of performance based on task, topic, and writer knowledge and one that would predict general stages of writing development.

EXPLORING THE CONSTRUCT OF WRITING: A THEORY OF PURPOSES, PROCESSES, AND OUTCOMES

More Than One Construct

We have to recognize the correctness of the critique offered by Cumming (1998). There does not appear to be, as of yet, a predictive model of the construct of writing that would be directly and transparently useful for research agendas, instructional practices, curricular planning, and assessment efforts. One could spend several dozen pages more on why this is so. Instead, I would like to offer a set of suggestions for what might be a useful direction for developing such a theory of the writing construct. These suggestions begin with the idea of purposes for writing, the processes of writing that might vary predictably according to purpose, and the task performances (as outcomes of purposes for writing) that would constrain variability in writing outcomes and assist in explaining individual differences in writing abilities.

When one turns to the description of writing abilities from the perspective of purpose (albeit in an unusual interpretation of the concept of purpose), certain opportunities to connect with other lines of inquiry open up. The concept of purpose has linkages directly to problems with describing the construct of reading. Carver (1992, 1997, 1998) has argued in a number of his writings that reading may not be a single construct but a set of related abilities and consequent processes that vary systematically with purpose for reading. Thus, reading to understand is different from skimming or reading to learn.

A similar notion of multiple, related constructs has been proposed for writing, although it has not yet been developed extensively. Bereiter and Scardamalia (1987) argued that there is not likely to be a single writing process but that there are at least two writing processes and perhaps more. These different writing processes are revealed through writing tasks that vary in processing complexity, much as Carver (1992, 1997, 1998) argued for reading processes. In this way, Bereiter and Scardamalia manipulated task complexity and informational complexity and then noted the impact of changing tasks and task complexity on writing performance. This idea provides a key for pursuing a more effective description of the writing construct.

In the view of purpose in writing presented here, the point is to determine basic reasons why people write. This concept of purpose might include writing to plan, discover, understand, learn, synthesize, interpret, or critique; it could also include purposes that might be seen as aims of discourse more traditionally, such as to inform, entertain, and persuade. Such a view of purpose is on a different scale from, and does not address, immediate functional purposes for writing such as to apologize, invite, threaten, deny, complain, congratulate, compliment, invite, fire, reject, hire, and so forth; nor is the idea of purpose intended to equate specifically with traditional rhetorical aims and modes of writing.

The key concept is that a related set of writing constructs (all part of a larger family of writing uses) may be triggered by basic writing purposes. For example, certain tasks reflect a simple basic purpose for understanding information and concepts. These tasks may include summarizing a simple passage to remember essential information (as on a note card) or writing notes from a text being read. Such tasks, although they can be a source of variation among students, will, nonetheless, be simpler to carry out than tasks that require synthesis across multiple source texts, which require critiques of information, or that require theoretical transformation (as described by Grabe, in press; Kirsch & Mosenthal, 1990, 1991; Mosenthal & Kirsch, 1991, 1992).

Basic Purposes for Writing

One could argue that purposes for writing can be outlined as a hierarchy of composing and processing demands on performance. Certain types of writing require increasing levels of composing and make greater processing demands. One of the first tasks for establishing a general hierarchy of writing purposes would be to develop research that would confirm the hierarchy of composing requirements and processing demands. A certain amount of research is already available in this regard, although not specifically or directly for this purpose (Bereiter & Scardamalia, 1987; Kellogg, 1996). Increases in processing demands could also be readily established by the same family of research methodologies used to determine processing capacity constraints in working memory (Carpenter, Miyake, & Just, 1994; Just & Carpenter, 1992).

Outlined in this section are five broad levels of writing purpose that may have hierarchical status. This is not the same as saying that these purposes impose a strict continuum of difficulty in task performance. It is well known that very simple tasks can be made very difficult, and tasks that, in principle, should be difficult can be made much easier to perform. This observation is evident to anyone who constructs tests on a regular basis. The argument made here is that, given a large number of related tasks that address some purpose, covering the normal range of difficulty influences (performance conditions), a hierarchy of writing outcomes will follow the very general purpose hierarchy listed:

1. Writing to control the mechanical production aspect (motor coordination, minimal fluency).
2. Writing to list, fill-in, repeat, paraphrase (not composing, only stating knowledge).
3. Writing to understand, remember, and summarize simply, and extended notes to oneself (composing and recounting).
4. Writing to learn, problem solve, summarize complexly, synthesize (composing and transforming, composing from multiple sources).
5a. Writing to critique, persuade, interpret (privileging perspectives and using evidence selectively but appropriately).
5b. Writing to create, an aesthetic experience, to entertain (composing in new ways, figurative levels of composing, violating composing norms in effective ways).

One way to understand the embedded hierarchy in this purpose list is to consider the following general logic. Most things being equal, one needs to be able to have production fluency in order to list and paraphrase. One needs to be able to list, repeat, and paraphrase ideas well in order to write simple summaries, write to understand (e.g., take notes), and write to remember. One needs to be able to summarize simply, write to understand and remember reasonably well in order to be able to write complex summaries, engage in problem solving, learn from texts, and synthesize information.

And one needs to be able to summarize, synthesize, and learn from texts to be able to critique, persuade, and interpret. There are assuredly cases in which one might not see this hierarchy followed, but the argument is that an appropriate and useful pattern will emerge across a sufficient number of writers, tasks, and contexts. Further, the argument is that these levels of purpose difficulty can be manipulated to some extent to control for other factors and to generate variability in writing.

This view of writing hierarchy clearly privileges writing purpose and associated processing demands above other factors that influence writing. To say this, however, does not suggest that other factors are not important; it only argues that purpose and attendant processing can be systematically controlled if a range of writing tasks are considered. It can also open up a way to assess writing proficiency and address writing development more directly. (See also Grabe, in press; Kirsch & Mosenthal, 1990, 1991; Mosenthal & Kirsch 1991, 1992, for discussion of a related alternative approach.)

Aside from a need to establish the processing correlates of these purposes for writing, a number of other factors deserve attention. First, an array of tasks is needed that can be identified with each level of writing purpose. To the extent that this would be possible, one could explore the relations among and across tasks as they are predicted to implicate one purpose level or the next. This goal (of examining task correlates) runs well beyond the scope of this chapter, but it is certainly a research direction that could easily be explored. Second, consideration will need to be given to the role of background knowledge that a writer brings to a task and how the writer adopts a stance to that knowledge. Finally, there will be a need to determine what counts for expert performance for any writing purpose and for any set of tasks that correlates with the purpose hierarchy. This is a difficult problem to explore, but it is no more difficult than establishing expert levels of performance for any domain (e.g., history, architecture, medicine, reading), assuming that the purpose hierarchy can guide and constrain performance interpretation in some way.

Writing Processes and Performance Outcomes

One major implication of the use of writing purposes to develop the writing construct is that there may be processing models for each distinct level of writing purpose. This is precisely the argument made by Carver (1992, 1997) for the construct of reading. Drawing on already existing research and theory in the field of writing, it is possible that the purpose of the hierarchy outlined previously could be related to the arguments of Bereiter and Scardamalia (1987) that there may be more than one writing process. This argument would suggest that, as writing purpose generally involves greater writing complexity and performance demands, the actual writing processes alter somewhat in their component emphases and capacity constraints. This is the basic theory proposed by Bereiter and Scardamalia with their models of knowledge telling and knowledge transforming. One can use these two concepts along with the composing—no-composing distinction to achieve three levels of processing differences. (Bereiter and Scardamalia also discussed basic production skills but did not suggest a separate model for this level of development.) Whether it would be feasible to outline four or five processing models to account for a full range of writing purposes is an open question and certainly not one that can be answered in this chapter.

AN ALTERNATIVE TO A PREDICTIVE THEORY OF WRITING

Categorizing Conditions on Learning to Write

It is also possible that a predictive hierarchical scale for writing abilities cannot be derived from any general set of purposes and associated processing emphases. It may be the case that the many interacting factors that contribute to an individual's writing abilities cannot be integrated into a framework with some degree of predictive power. In such a case, there simply would be no consistent way to capture an underlying path of development. Instead, a descriptive model of the writing construct would be all that is possible. If this were to be the true limits of what can be theorized about writing, then a fitting alternative frame of reference would be to follow Spolsky's (1989) lead for second language acquisition and develop, and then categorize, conditions on writing development.[2] Taking a *conditions* direction, one would stipulate the major component factors that influence writing development, whether as a descriptive model or as a list, and then carefully categorize the major themes and findings under each heading. In some sense, the goal would be to create a taxonomy of research on various aspects of writing performance.

There is real merit in taking this alternative approach to theory building for writing. In many cases, a model does not seek to organize the full set of research information available but rather selectively emphasizes that research that builds to a coherent explanation. A taxonomic effort provides for more comprehensive coverage and allows for contradictions to exist together until further research resolves these issues. A conditions view also allows for certain constraining factors to emerge across a range of collected studies: It offers a way of noticing less obvious trends and patterns.

In the case of second language acquisition Spolsky (1989) considered his discussion as an account of all the factors that will lead to better learning or that will inhibit learning. It is a preference model in that learning will be enhanced to the extent that multiple supporting conditions exist in the environment of a particular learning context. He sees this approach as a much better reflection of the complexities involved in language learning than the specification of a single model for all occurrences of learning. As Spolsky stated, "My goal . . . will not be to establish a model of how language is learned, but rather to explore how to specify, as exactly as possible, the conditions under which learning takes place" (p. 5).

It is, in fact, possible to adapt Spolsky's (1989) own major categories for conditions on learning to a writing context. They would appear as follows:

1. Knowing the language,
2. Knowing how to use the language (communicative competence),
3. The human learner,
4. Individual abilities and preferences,
5. The social context,
6. Attitudes and Motivation,
7. Opportunities for learning and practice, and
8. Formal instructional contexts.

To these eight could be added further categories:

9. Processing factors,
10. Cultural variability,
11. Content and topical knowledge,
12. Discourse, genre, and register knowledge (specific to writing).

It would be possible to generate additional categories for organizing research information. The choice of which categories to retain would depend on the useful generalizations that can be derived from the research reviewed and sorted. For example, in Spolsky's (1989) research, the categories served to generate anywhere from 2 to 17 useful generalizing conditions, depending on the category.

A Performance-Constraints View of Writing

A conditions approach to theory building in writing, following the lead of Spolsky (1989), would produce a number of generalizing statements drawn from sets of research on writing performance under varying conditions. These generalizations would be a useful foundation for other types of theory building in that they create a set of facts to be accounted for by any future model. They also suggest constraints on writing performance because conditions inevitably suggest constraints in the absence of these conditions. And recognizing constraints on writing performance could be a very useful foundation for effective instruction under varying conditions. Such a performance-constraints view would also allow for a number of explicit statements specific to L2 writing, including the limitations due to weak proficiency in the L2 (e.g., Sasaki & Hirose, 1996).

There is, however, a serious limitation with a conditions approach to writing theory. Each condition, which is a synthesis from research studies, has equal status. There is no good way to establish hierarchical relations among the many conditions, and it is the ability to establish hierarchical relations among conditions that leads to better understanding of a complex phenomenon. Certain conditions may be implicational, that is, dependent on other conditions, but these implicational relations might never have been assessed, so the dependencies are not made apparent through listings of conditions. In addition, many conditions may interact in either supporting or conflicting ways, but these combinations may never have been assessed in research, so one does not know how multiple conditions interact in new combinations. The point would seem to be that a conditions approach is a good one to take as more information needs to be gathered and categorized. However, at some point, its limitations require that a maturing field of research would move on to a more hierarchical predictive model of the construct. Whether or not the field of writing is sufficiently mature to make such a jump is an open question.

CONCLUSIONS

This chapter explores a number of issues associated with developing a theory of writing and writing development. One issue that has not been directly addressed is how a theory of L2 writing might be different from a theory of L1 writing. The discussion in the third section of this chapter raises a number of differences between L1 and L2 writing that could lead to proposing a distinct construct of L2 writing. However, based on the arguments suggested in sections four and five, it is most likely the case that a distinct theory of L2 writing may need to wait until models of writing move beyond a basic descriptive stage of development. Instead, I suggest that the work done by Silva and others to categorize ways in which L1 and L2 writing differ and to assemble research to support these differences, is a key stage in theorizing a separate L2 writing model. However, it may not yet be possible to move beyond a conditions approach to L2 writing for reasons noted in this chapter. A conditions approach may be a good way to establish a large set of facts about L2 writing that will need to be accounted for. This database can then be the foundation for a distinct model of L2 writing in the future.

ACKNOWLEDGMENTS

This chapter benefited from a reading of an earlier draft and a discussion with Alister Cumming and Terry Santos.

ENDNOTES

1. The ideas developed in this chapter are most directly applicable to the academic writing of adolescents and adults. However, many of these ideas can be extended across the range of writing development, including children who are beginning writers.

2. A participant at the Symposium on Second Language Writing at Purdue University commented to me that my discussion of constraining factors on writing performance reminded her of Spolsky's (1989) theory. I am thankful to her for reminding me of Spolsky's volume, *Conditions for second language learning.*

REFERENCES

Atkinson, D. (1997). A critical approach to critical thinking in TESOL. *TESOL Quarterly, 31,* 71–94.

Atkinson, D., & Ramanathan, V. (1995). Cultures of writing: An ethnographic comparison of L1 and L2 university writing/language programs. *TESOL Quarterly, 29,* 539–568.

Belcher, D., & Braine, G. (Eds.). (1995). *Academic writing in a second language: Essays on research and pedagogy.* Norwood, NJ: Ablex.

Bereiter, C., & Scardamalia, M. (1987). *The psychology of written composition.* Hillsdale, NJ: Lawrence Erlbaum Associates.

Berkenkotter, C., & Huckin, T. (1995). *Genre knowledge in disciplinary communication.* Hillsdale, NJ: Lawrence Erlbaum Associates.

Carpenter, P., Miyake, A., & Just, M. (1994). Working memory constraints in comprehension: Evidence from individual differences, aphasias, and aging. In M. A. Gernsbacher (Ed.), *Handbook of psycholinguistics* (pp. 1075–1122). San Diego: Academic Press.

Carrell, P., & Connor, U. (1991). Reading and writing descriptive and persuasive texts. *Modern Language Journal, 75,* 314–324.

Carson, J. (1993). Reading for writing: Cognitive perspectives. In J. Carson & I. Leki (Eds.), *Reading in the composition classroom* (pp. 299–314). New York: Newbury House.

Carson, J., Carrell, P., Silberstein, S., Kroll, B., & Kuehn, P. (1990). Reading–writing relationships in first and second language. *TESOL Quarterly, 24,* 245–266.

Carver, R. (1992). Reading rate: Theory, research, and practical implications. *Journal of Reading, 36,* 84–95.

Carver, R. (1997). Reading for one second, one minute, or one year from the perspective of Rauding Theory. *Scientific Studies of Reading, 1,* 3–43.

Carver, R. (1998). Predicting reading levels in grades 1 to 6 from listening level and decoding level: Testing theory relevant to the simple view of reading. *Reading and Writing, 10,* 121–154.

Connor, U. (1996). *Contrastive rhetoric.* New York: Cambridge University Press.

Connor, U. (1997). Contrastive rhetoric: Implications for teachers of writing in multicultural classrooms. In C. Severino, J. Guerra, & J. Butler (Eds.), *Writing in multicultural settings* (pp. 198–208). New York: MLA.

Cumming, A. (1998). Theoretical perspectives on writing. In W. Grabe et al. (Eds.), *Annual Review of Applied Linguistics, 18. Foundations of second language teaching* (pp. 61–78). New York: Cambridge University Press.

Faigley, L. (1992). *Fragments of rationality: Postmodernity and the subject of composition.* Pittsburgh, PA: University of Pittsburgh Press.

Ferris, D. (1995). Student reactions to teacher response in multiple-draft composition classrooms. *TESOL Quarterly, 29,* 33–53.

Ferris, D. (1997). The influence of teacher commentary on student revision. *TESOL Quarterly, 31,* 315–339.

Flower, L. (1994). *The construction of negotiated meaning: A social cognitive theory of writing.* Carbondale: Southern Illinois University Press.

Flower, L., & Hayes, J. (1980). The dynamics of composing: Making plans and juggling constraints. In L. Gregg, & E. Steinberg (Eds.), *Cognitive processes in writing* (pp. 31–50). Hillsdale, NJ: Lawrence Erlbaum Associates.

Flower, L., & Hayes, J. (1981). A cognitive process theory of writing. *College Composition and Communication, 32,* 365–387.

Grabe, W. (2001). Reading–writing relations: Theoretical perspectives and instructional practices. In D. Belcher, & A. Hirvela (Eds.), *Reading and writing relations in L2 contexts.* Ann Arbor, MI: University of Michigan.

Grabe, W. (in press). Narrative and expository macro-genres. In A. Johns (Ed.), *Genre in the classroom: Theory, research, and practice.* Mahwah, NJ: Lawrence Erlbaum Associates.

Grabe, W., & Kaplan, R. B. (1996). *Theory and practice of writing.* New York: Longman.

Grabe, W., & Kaplan, R. B. (1997). The writing course. In K. Bardovi-Harlig & B. Hartford (Eds.), *Beyond methods: Components of second language teacher education* (pp. 172–197). New York: McGraw-Hill.

Graves, D. (1984). *A researcher learns to write.* Portsmouth, NH: Heinemann.

Hayes, J. (1996). A new framework for understanding cognition and affect in writing. In C. M. Levy, & S. Ransdell (Eds.), *The science of writing* (pp. 1–27). Mahwah, NJ: Lawrence Erlbaum Associates.

Johns, A. (1997). *Text, role, and context.* New York: Cambridge University Press.

Just, M., & Carpenter, P. (1992). A capacity theory of comprehension: Individual differences in working memory. *Psychological Review, 99,* 12–149.

Kellogg, R. (1994). *The psychology of writing.* New York: Oxford University Press.

Kellogg, R. (1996). A model of working memory in writing. In C. M. Levy & S. Ransdell (Eds.), *The science of writing* (pp. 57–71). Mahwah, NJ: Lawrence Erlbaum Associates.

Kirsch, I., & Mosenthal, P. (1990). Understanding mimetic documents. *Journal of Reading, 34,* 552–558.

Kirsch, I., & Mosenthal, P. (1991). Understanding process knowledge models. *Journal of Reading, 35,* 490–497.

Kroll, B. (Ed.). (1990). *Second language writing: Research insights for the classroom.* New York: Cambridge University Press.

Kroll, B. (1998). Assessing second language writing. In W. Grabe et al. (Eds.), *Annual Review of Applied Linguistics, 18. Foundations of second language teaching* (pp. 219–240). New York: Cambridge University Press.

Leki, I. (1991). Twenty-five years of contrastive rhetoric. *TESOL Quarterly, 25,* 123–143.

Leki, I., (1995). Coping strategies of ESL students in writing tasks across the curriculum. *TESOL Quarterly, 29,* 235–260.

Leki, I. (1997). Cross-talk: ESL issues and contrastive rhetoric. In C. Severino, J. Guerra, & J. Butler (Eds.), *Writing in multicultural settings* (pp. 234–244). New York: MLA.

Leki, I., & Carson, J. (1994). Students' perceptions of EAP writing instruction and writing needs across the disciplines. *TESOL Quarterly, 28,* 81–101.

Leki, I., & Carson, J. (1997). "Completely different worlds": EAP and the writing experiences of ESL students in university courses. *TESOL Quarterly, 31*, 39–69.

Matsuda, P. K. (1997). Contrastive rhetoric in context: A dynamic model of L2 writing. *Journal of Second Language Writing, 6*, 45–60.

Matsuda, P. K. (1998). Situating ESL writing in a cross-disciplinary context. *Written Communication, 15*, 99–121.

Mosenthal, P., & Kirsch, I. (1991). Extending prose comprehension through knowledge modeling. *Journal of Reading, 35*, 58–61.

Mosenthal, P., & Kirsch, I. (1992). Understanding knowledge acquisition from a knowledge model perspective. *Journal of Reading, 35*, 588–596.

North, S. (1987). *The making of knowledge in composition.* Portsmouth, NH: Heinemann.

Ramanathan, V., & Kaplan, R. B. (1996a). Audience and voice in current L1 composition texts: Some implications for ESL student writers. *Journal of Second Language Writing, 5*, 21–34.

Ramanathan, V., & Kaplan, R. B. (1996b). Some problematic "channels" in the teaching of critical thinking in current L1 composition textbooks: Implications for L2 student-writers. *Issues in Applied Linguistics, 7*, 225–249.

Sasaki, M., & Hirose, K. (1996). Explanatory variables in EFL students' expository writing. *Language Learning, 46*, 137–174.

Silva, T. (1990). Second language composition instruction: Developments, issues and directions. In B. Kroll (Ed.), *Second language writing: Research insights for the classroom* (pp. 11–23). New York: Cambridge University Press.

Silva, T. (1993). Toward an understanding of the distinct nature of L2 writing: The ESL research and its implications. *TESOL Quarterly, 27*, 657–677.

Silva, T. (1997). Differences in ESL and native-English-speaker writing: The research and its implications. In C. Severino, J. C. Guerra, & J. E. Butler (Eds.), *Writing in multi-cultural settings* (pp. 209–219). New York: Modern Language Association.

Silva, T., Leki, I., & Carson, J. (1997). Broadening the perspective of mainstream composition studies. *Written Communication, 14*, 398–428.

Spolsky, B. (1989). *Conditions for second language learning.* New York: Oxford University Press.

Swales, J. (1990). *Genre analysis.* New York: Cambridge University Press.

Witte, S. (1992). Context, text, intertext: Toward a constructivist semiotic of writing. *Written Communication, 9*, 237–308.

5

Does Second Language Writing Theory Have Gender?

Diane Belcher
The Ohio State University

In her essay on the "feminization" of composition (i.e., first language [L1] composition) Susan Miller (1991) calls attention to the "slipperiness" of the term *feminization*, that is, its concomitant positive and negative connotations. In Miller's view, feminization can be seen as positive insofar as it refers to certain "new intellectual and practical movements" (p. 39) but negative in that it also suggests the low-status cultural identity of composition as "women's work," a field with a marginalized service orientation and a huge part-time work force, predominately female. One could easily make a case for the relevance of the negative descriptor *femininization* to second language (L2) composition, but that is not the focus of this chapter. Instead, I consider feminization in what Miller calls its more positive sense, its identification with innovative epistemological and pedagogical developments, developments that feminists view as good for women, other marginalized people, and even mainstream men. The areas I look at in this chapter can be seen as pertaining to research paradigms, discourse style, and cultural sensitivity (with gender included under the category *culture*). More specifically, I discuss the extent to which L2 writing research does or does not practice traditional science, is or is not agonistic, or adversarial, in its theoretical stances, and does or does not treat gender as a salient cultural feature.

RESEARCH PARADIGMS IN SECOND LANGUAGE
ACQUISITION AND SECOND LANGUAGE WRITING

What is meant by "traditional science" is probably best explained by citing some notable commentary from the feminist critique of science, which is often seen as synonymous with the postmodernist critique (see Lutz, 1995). There are certainly many women who gladly and successfully practice traditional science. The feminist critique expresses the perspective of those who are feminists, or postmodernists, although they feel they speak for many less vocal others. This critique has been credited with, or blamed for, essentially expanding the paradigmatic playing field, not just in the human sciences but also in the natural sciences (Harding, 1986; Keller, 1984; Sullivan, 1992). Much of the feminist criticism of science derives from their objection, as Lutz points out, to the erasure of authorship and social context.

> Most graduate students learn early on that they must learn to speak the language of theory, to transform personal issues into theoretical forms, to erase authorship and context.... The feminist critique of traditional ideologies of science has taken on this issue squarely: by definition, theory has traditionally allowed for the erasure of the subject who writes and the human subjects who are written about. It allows the theorist to avoid the roots of statements in real-world encounters, to speak for or appear to speak for the whole, and to speak from a transcendental vantage point. (p. 259)

Although some see in the feminist critique of science a rejection of objectivity (including some feminists), many feminists see it as a call for a heightened type of objectivity, or what Sandra Harding (Hirsch & Olson, 1995) calls "strong objectivity," which goes hand in hand with "strong reflexivity." According to Harding, "objectivity is maximized not by excluding social factors from the production of knowledge—as Western scientific method has purported to do—but precisely by 'starting' the process of inquiry from an *explicitly social* location, the lived experience..." (Hirsh & Olson, 1995, p. 193). This interest in social location is most often pursued, by feminists and others, by means of nonpositivistic, qualitative, naturalistic research methods, such as participant observation, interviews, and other ethnographic thick description (see, e.g., Flynn, 1990, 1991; Kirsch, 1993; Olesen, 1994). Feminists, thus, have been at the forefront of the movement toward an alternative to traditional Western epistemology, which as Shotter and Logan (1988) put it, is viewed as:

> a general, decontexted kind of theoretical knowledge that can be possessed by individuals of their *external* world...expressed in a hierarchically arranged, closed system of binary oppositions...concerned with achieving a unity of

vision and thought, [while] feminist thought can be seen as different in every respect: as a practical, particular, contexted, open, nonsystematic knowledge of the social circumstances in which one has one's being, concerned with achieving a heterarchy of times and places for a plurality of otherwise conflicting voices. (p. 75)

Interestingly, recently Alan Firth and Johannes Wagner (1997), who never explicitly mention the feminist critique of science, put forth a call for a reconceptualization of second language acquisition (SLA) that would move away from the deficit approach to L2 learning (i.e., the view of the learner as a *deficient communicator*).[1] The feminist-style correction they call for would involve three major changes in the ontological and empiricist parameters of SLA, namely, (a) "significantly enhanced awareness of the contextual and interactional dimensions of language use," (b) "increased emic (participant-relevant) sensitivity," and (c) "broadening of the traditional SLA database" (p. 285). Firth and Wagner complain that SLA too often sees people in binary, native speaker/nonnative speaker (NS/NNS) terms, and privileges a research methodology given to:

coding, quantifying data, and replicating results . . . assign[ing] preference to (researcher manipulation of) experimental settings rather than naturalistic ones . . . endors[ing] the search for the universal and underlying features of language processes rather than the particular and the local . . . [and] at best . . . marginaliz[ing], and at worst ignor[ing], the social and the contextual dimensions of language.[2] (p. 288)

What is especially interesting about this plea for a more humanistic approach to SLA, in addition to its feminist–postmodernist stance, is not so much the controversy it has aroused, as evidenced by the plethora of responses (e.g., Hall, 1997; Kasper, 1997; Long, 1997; Poulisse, 1997) that appeared in the same issue of *The Modern Language Journal*, but rather the fact that there is no recognition in Firth and Wagner (1997) of the movement toward reconceptualization that has already taken place in L2 writing research and theory (because all research reveals a theoretical stance, my tendency is to conflate the two terms, *research* and *theory*), and in fact began around 1990 (Belcher, 1993). Certainly, many L2 writing specialists— whether cognitivists, expressivists, or social constructivists—have taken the qualitative or social turn, or at least tried their hands at it. To follow is a brief overview of the work of a little more than a handful of them. This group includes both women and men and is discussed in no particular order other than alphabetical.

In 1992, Christine Pearson Casanave and Philip Hubbard reported on the results of their analysis of 85 graduate faculty survey respondents,

representing 28 departments, in an effort to better understand the writing assignments and writing problems of doctoral students. They concluded very
confidently by remarking "it is our belief that ESL [English as a Second Lan-
guage] writing teachers who are preparing graduate students ... are obliged
to (a) help students with local as well as discourse-level writing problems;
(b) learn what the students need to write" (p. 47) and the list goes on.
Other studies by Casanave published in 1992, 1995 and then 1998, however, were naturalistic. In her recent publication in the *Journal of Second
Language Writing*, Casanave (1998) is notably more tentative, commenting
in her extensive list of background assumptions that "the portrayals [of the
informants]...are primarily my reconstruction of [their] stories.... I hope
[she adds] that readers will reflect on the issues in light of their own experience in different sociocultural academic contexts and make connections
and comparisons where appropriate" (p. 179).

Similarly, in 1988, Ulla Connor, with Janice Lauer, published a study that
looked at crosscultural variation in persuasive writing, using the Toulmin
model of informal reasoning to analyze 150 essays by high school students
in the United States, United Kingdom, and New Zealand randomly chosen
from a pool of thousands of International Association for the Evaluation of
Educational Achievement (IEA) essays. By 1996, Connor had published, with
Susan Mayberry, a case study of one Finnish graduate student. Likewise, in
1990, Alister Cumming reported on an analysis of the think-aloud protocols of 23 writers responding to two different prompts. "Units of decision-
making" (p. 489) were segmented, coded, and counted. By 1992, Cumming
had turned, at least momentarily, to a much more naturalistic approach, an
observational study of the instructional routines of three writing teachers.
The same type of movement toward the qualitative can be seen in Ann Johns'
work. In 1981, Johns was reporting on the 140 responses to her English
skills survey, and in 1990, with Patricia Mayes, the results of their analysis
of the summary protocols of 80 low- and high-proficiency ESL reading and
writing students. By 1992, Johns had published two cases studies, each of
a single student. At approximately the same time, 1991, Ilona Leki brought
out her report on 100 ESL students' responses to a survey on error correction preferences. Four years later, in 1995, Leki published an award-winning
article in *TESOL Quarterly*, a naturalistic study of five students' coping strategies. John Swales' early introduction "moves" research, with Hazem Najjar,
published in 1987, was based on a corpus of 110 article introductions from
two journals. In his 1990 book, *Genre Analysis*, Swales described his then
most recent research, case studies of three dissertation writers. And finally,
Vivian Zamel's (1985) well-known article *Responding to student writing*, reported on the responding behaviors of 15 teachers responding to a total
of 105 student texts. In 1990, Zamel published, *Through students' eyes*, a

naturalistic study of three students' progression from an ESL to a first-year (L1) composition class.

What can we say about this shift, which looks very much in step with the feminist critique of science? It is not my intention to imply that there is any difference in relative worth of the earlier and later works. Many of the earlier, nonqualitative works have been extremely influential in our field and made significant contributions.[3] Nor do I think it safe to say that L2 writing has moved away from such methods as surveys, verbal reports or protocols, and textual analysis. It may be safer to say that such indices are now more likely to be offered as one of a number of triangulated windows to the writers studied (but note the obvious: an increase in windows means a decrease in number of writers viewed). Certainly, quantitative studies still also hold an appeal (e.g., the work of Dana Ferris and the growing popularity of corpus linguistics). It is probably also not safe to draw any conclusions about the individual researchers whose work is aforementioned. Not all would identify themselves as converts to qualitative research, but a few would. Ann Johns (personal communication, April 18, 1997) once remarked that quantitative research was what she did before tenure. With tenure, she does the work that genuinely interests her, that is, qualitative studies. Johns warns junior faculty at her institution not to follow her lead until they reach a similar degree of security. What we can safely conclude, though, about the field of L2 writing (if not the institutions it may be found in) is that it has been very accepting of those who may not be comfortable with or entirely satisfied with the methods and goals of traditional science.

Discourse Style and Theoretical Pluralism

Yet, if methodologically we may be seen as feminized, or in step with the feminist critique, our discourse style, how we represent and communicate with each other, may not be. Although our field may be characterized by theoretical pluralism, it is not quite a peaceable kingdom. We may ask ourselves how far we have come since Tony Silva, in 1990, described L2 writing as having a "merry-go-round of approaches...generat[ing] more heat than light," and "not encourag[ing] consensus on important issues, preservation of legitimate insights, [or] synthesis of a body of knowledge" (p. 18). Perhaps we could go even further today and argue that not only is consensus not encouraged, but dissensus is relished and rewarded, especially with publication. In her latest best seller, on the argument culture, Deborah Tannen (1998) suggests (with no reference to Swales) that the standard way of opening any academic paper, "position[ing] your work in opposition to someone else's, which you prove wrong, actually creates a need to make others wrong" (p. 268). In a similar vein, Peter Elbow (1986, cited in

Tannen, 1998), observes that "we tend to assume that the ability to criticize a claim we disagree with counts as more serious intellectual work than the ability to enter into it and temporarily assent" (p. 273). Jane Tompkins (1988) has recalled, with some self-loathing, the pride and excitement she felt when composing the article that "made her career," remembering that a "sense of outrage" and "passionate conviction" at that time "fueled" her "frontal assault on another woman scholar": "I felt the way a hero does in a western" (p. 588). Tannen associates this type of gleeful aggressiveness with what she calls the masculine argument culture; many feminists, especially feminists in L1 composition, would agree with Tannen (e.g., Lamb, 1996).[4]

I too, (Belcher, 1997) have complained in print about adversarial academic discourse and the discomfort it causes some writers. In that article, mindful that pointing out and labeling discourse as *adversarial* seems itself an adversarial act, I only briefly touched on agonism in our own field. But at the risk of appearing contentious about contentiousness,[5] I would like to look at one illustrative sample of an agonistic interaction in L2 writing, Suresh Canagarajah's (1993) *David vs. Goliath* (see Tompkins, 1988) response to Ann Raimes' *Out of the woods* and her response to him. I have chosen this response or comment interaction partly because I doubt that Canagarajah would object to my characterizing his remarks as confrontational, comments with evaluative language such as "she fails," "get[s] away with," and, referring to Raimes's particular type of theoretical pluralism, "lacks ... complexity" and "resembles ... an escapist, indecisive, [and] stultifying relativism" (p. 302). Not surprisingly, these comments elicited a defensive reaction from Raimes, who reiterates in her response what she "thought [she] *had* indicated" about her own theoretical leanings, toward the process approach, defending her own distancing from a "focus on social context," the lack of social commitment in her article that Canagarajah had complained of, by noting that "social context has been usurped by a 'social constructionist' approach (Johns, 1990, p. 25), which has radically departed from its original (L1) ideological connections" (p. 307). Raimes' accusation that Canagarajah "misleads readers" (p. 307), which suggests that he addresses the anonymous *TESOL Quarterly* readership rather than Raimes herself, underscores, it seems to me, the monologic nature of this type of agonistic exchange, (i.e., the missed opportunity for genuine dialogue).[6]

A less agonistic style and stance may well be emerging thanks to the qualitative world views of some number of L2 writing researchers today. Casanave's (1998) previously cited, carefully articulated background assumptions are one example. Another noteworthy example can be found in Li Xiao-ming's (1996) *"Good writing" in Cross-Cultural Context*. Although Li's informants, Chinese and American high school writing teachers, basically fall into what James Berlin (1998) would term expressionist and social epistemic camps, she does not pit them against each other in her presentation of their views as in some grand debate, nor does she choose sides herself:

> Different narrators preside at different stages in the telling of the tale of 'good writing' in two countries. My own reading, as a researcher and an insider-outsider, comes at the end, not because it is final or conclusive, but as one of many possible readings. I hope such a tale will achieve what successful modern novels can achieve, that is, readers find it necessary to work out their own versions of the story, and they will start to reflect on their own criteria and ways of responding to student papers. Some conventional readers may feel uncomfortable with the lack of closure, focus, confidence, and authority in the report, as I still do with modern novels, but it is the author's intention to give all those privileges to the reader. (p. 9)

Gender as Culture

The third area of intellectual innovation associated with feminism that is examined in this chapter, cultural sensitivity, is one that we might expect L2 writing to be quite femininized in. For a field that has shown such great interest in the cultural context of the learner (e.g., all of the contrastive rhetoric research; see Connor, 1996), L2 writing has taken surprisingly little interest in the culture of gender. Stephanie Vandrick (1994) points out that ESL pedagogy in general would do well to begin to attend to feminist pedagogy as it "addresses gender as a critical factor in the learning environment" and hence "is important to all educators who are interested in equity and in opportunities for students to learn and flourish" (p. 69). But we should note that many postcolonial feminists have, in fact, been highly critical of earlier feminist conceptualizations of gender in that they largely ignored the interplay of gender with culture, race, ethnicity, and class (see, e.g., Anzaldua, 1990; hooks, 1990; Ong, 1995; Spivak, 1988; Trinh, 1989). Aihwa Ong (1995) argues, citing Kipnis (1988), that "if 'feminism seeks to be the paradigmatic political discourse of postmodernism,' it must stop being 'blind to the geopolitical implications of its own program' ... tied to First World privileges and declining Western hegemony" (p. 367). But just as feminism has begun to acknowledge, with the help of postcolonialist feminists, how culture complicates our view of gender, L2 writing research has begun to show signs of seeing gender as a factor worth noting as part of the cultural context of the writer.[7]

Although she does not identify herself as a feminist, in her case study of a Lao student, Ann Johns (1992) is quite attentive to her informant Tic's situation as a young Lao woman grappling with the demands of her family, home community, and new academic community: "During the semester in which she was my student, Tic was under considerable pressure from her mother to marry an established, older Lao, 'because they are calling me (at 18 years) a loose woman'" (p. 187). Johns suggests that Tic is no anomaly:

> Many of the diverse students at SDSU, particularly women, experience the ambivalence within families that Tic experienced; yet their survival in a new culture is often enhanced by the core values of their first cultures, values that may not be held by their immediate families but are passed down through the elders, the religious leaders, and the oral and written traditions of the community. (p. 188)

Casanave (1992) is equally, if not more, attentive to gender issues in her case study of a Puerto Rican graduate student who dropped out of her program in sociology. She cites more than one example of her informant Virginia's dissatisfaction with and eventual total alienation from the Anglo male culture of her department, which struck her as cold and uncaring, uninterested in her as a person.

> She eventually did complete the assignment, but concluded that grades were based less on hard work and creativity than on students' ability to complete the assignments according to what she called the recipes of the professors. These recipes, Virginia came to believe, were the products of a sociological world run by White middle-class European and American males, theorists, as she called them. (p. 172)

A number of gender-sensitive observations can also be found in Karen Ogulnick's (1998) account of her experiences as a Japanese (L2) language learner working with both male and female tutors. She insightfully describes the obstacle to learning posed by her own reaction as a Western woman to the pedagogical style of her male Japanese tutor (or to his traditional Japanese "maleness," as Ogulnick calls it):

> Although Keno's interest in helping me develop literacy skills had a positive effect on my motivation, in the end I actually made very little progress learning to read and write with him. In fact, later entries show considerable resistance to practicing these skills with Keno. My diary strongly suggests that the problem lay in the didactic role Keno played. . . . Rather than it being a collaborative and interactive process. . . . The categories Keno and I had available to us in our languages seemed to make it almost impossible for us to ever really speak the same language. Keno's maleness and the role he assumed as *sensei* when teaching me Japanese were dominant images for me; likewise my language, cultural identity, position at the university . . . must have represented powerful symbols to Keno. (p. 45)

What might we learn by looking more closely at gender? Some of the findings and observations in L1 writing research may suggest what we might discover in L2. Dale Spender (1989) has found, for example, that although American girls outperform American boys as writers in school settings, they often compete far less successfully as writers in professional settings. It has also been found that even in those fields where the majority of the doctorates granted have gone to women for a number of years, the lists of the most prolific writers in those fields has not changed and are still overwhelmingly male (Schneider, 1998; see also Sandler, 1986). Another study indicates that although men and women are equally subject to writing blocks, women may tend "to block for longer periods of time . . . [and] experience more prolonged and overt psychological distress over their failure to make progress" (Cayton, 1994, p. 149). One male-oriented study (Connors, 1996) has suggested the need to look at, among other things, male resistance to the preferred teaching style of female composition teachers and how this resistance affects the students' progress as academic writers (or lack thereof). Of course, we should be wary, as are postcolonial feminists, of the relevance of studies that do not consider the possibility of cultural difference as we do in L2 writing. But, at the same time, is there good reason to assume that because gender appears to matter in L1 writing, it is not likely to do so in L2 writing?

CONCLUSION

Returning again to the three areas foregrounded in this chapter, namely research methodology, discourse style, and gender sensitivity, it does indeed appear that in the first of these areas, L2 writing researchers are more progressive, postmodernist, or feminized than others involved in L2 knowledge construction. Perhaps our greater feminization has to do with the number of women in L2 writing. Certainly if one compares L2 writing researchers to SLA researchers, it appears that women are more active in L2 writing.[8] Perhaps another factor is the greater frequency of humanities, especially literary studies, backgrounds among L2 writing specialists. Yet another reason for our qualitative tendencies may be the nature of writing itself, which, unlike speaking, as Grabe and Kaplan (1996) have pointed out, is culturally rather than biologically transmitted.

As for discourse style and gender sensitivity, or why we are so contentious and so often oblivious to gender, I am less willing and able to speculate. It does seem, however, that we have reason to be optimistic, as suggested earlier, for our naturalistic studies do appear to be nudging us toward more tentative, permeable, and dynamic theoretical stances, and our increasingly thick description is likely to make us ever more aware that L2 writers do have gender.

ENDNOTES

1. One of the very few L2 researchers to speak explicitly of the value of feminist approaches to research is Suresh Canagarajah (1996). He finds especially praiseworthy feminist scholars' call for "a caring, reciprocal relationship with subjects in the research process" (p. 325), in other words, their insistence on seeing and treating research subjects as people.

2. Critical pedagogists have expressed similar views not just of SLA but of linguistics as a discipline. Alastair Pennycook (1994), for example, remarks that "there has clearly been a rejection of connections between language and its contexts in much of mainstream linguistics" (p. 25).

3. In L1 composition, however, Stephen North (1987) has asserted that quantitative research, or "experimental" (as he called it) research, has been far less influential than more qualitative studies. North observes that while approximately 1,500 quantitative studies were published between 1963 and 1985 in L1 composition, "the Experimental community has not exercised anything like a proportionate influence on the field" (p. 144) perhaps because it "spends its energy *disconfirming* possible explanations" (p. 145).

4. Feminists, however, have pointed out how aggressive feminists themselves can be, even with each other. bell hooks (1990) recounts a recurring thought she has had at feminist gatherings: "I am startled by the dichotomy between the rhetoric of sisterhood and the vicious way nice, nice, politically correct girls can deal with one another, do one another in" (p. 90). hooks argues that for the sake of feminist solidarity, women must develop a means of "meaningful critique and rigorous intellectual exchange, without brutally trashing or negating one another" (p. 94).

5. Catherine Lamb (1996), who has commented on her own adversarialness toward adversarialness, observes that "we [feminists] have not talked much about how it can be feminist to both at times be confrontational and at other times advocate approaches that minimize confrontation" (p. 260).

6. About this exchange, Canagarajah (personal communication, October 7, 1998) has remarked that, in fact, his comment was originally composed as a longer essay. During the truncating revision process, which took place while Canagarajah was residing in a war-torn Tamil section of Sri Lanka, he had no opportunity to see the response that would appear juxtaposed with his own commentary. Canagarajah additionally observed, "But I also thought that we were talking two different discourses (in a way) and didn't have a common meeting point."

7. Although not specifically focused on L2 writing, Alister Cumming and Jaswinder Gill's (1992) study of Punjabi women and the accessibility of formal literacy instruction in Canada should be noted for its appreciation of the potential significance of gender issues. Cumming and Gill conclude that their research "makes clear that gender is a fundamental consideration to be accounted for in conceptualizing adults' motivation or potential to learn a second language, a consideration which needs to be accounted for in curricula and policies of educational programs intending to serve adult minority populations" (p. 248).

8. In the 1995 through 1997 volumes of *Studies in Second Language Acquisition*, for example, approximately 60% of the contributors were men. In the *Journal of Second Language Writing*, on the other hand, according to Paul Matsuda (1998), 76% of the contributors over the first 5 years of the journal, 1992 through 1996, were women.

REFERENCES

Anzaldua, G. (1990). *Making face, making soul / haciendo caras: Creative and critical perspectives by women of color.* San Francisco: Aunt Lute Foundation.

Belcher, D. (1993, April). *Constructing relevant realities: The qualitative approach to L2 writing research.* Paper presented at the 29th annual TESOL convention, Atlanta, GA.

Belcher, D. (1997). An argument for nonadversarial argumentation: On the relevance of the feminist critique of academic discourse to L2 writing pedagogy. *Journal of Second Language Writing, 6,* 1–21.

Berlin, J. (1988). Rhetoric and ideology in the writing class. *College English, 50,* 477–494.

Canagarajah, A. S. (1993). Up the garden path: Second language writing approaches, local knowledge, and pluralism (Comment on Ann Raimes's "Out of the woods: Emerging traditions in the teaching of writing"). *TESOL Quarterly, 27,* 301–306.

Canagarajah, A. S. (1996). From critical research practice to critical research reporting. *TESOL Quarterly, 30,* 321–330.

Casanave, C. P. (1992). Cultural diversity and socialization: A case study of a Hispanic woman in a doctoral program in sociology. In D. Murray (Ed.), *Diversity as resource: Redefining cultural literacy* (pp. 148–181). Alexandria, VA: TESOL.

Casanave, C. P. (1995). Local interactions: Constructing contexts for composing in a graduate sociology program. In D. Belcher & G. Braine (Eds.), *Academic writing in a second language: Essays on research and pedagogy* (pp. 83–112). Norwood, NJ: Ablex.

Casanave, C. P. (1998). Transitions: The balancing act of bilingual academics. *Journal of Second Language Writing, 7,* 175–203.

Casanave, C. P., & Hubbard, P. (1992). The writing assignments and writing problems of doctoral students: Faculty perceptions, pedagogical issues, and needed research. *English for Specific Purposes, 11,* 33–49.

Cayton, M. K. (1994). What happens when things go wrong: Women and writing blocks. In G. Olson & S. Dobrin (Eds.), *Composition theory for the postmodern classroom* (pp. 49–65). Albany: State University of New York Press.

Connor, U. (1996). *Contrastive rhetoric: Cross-cultural aspects of second-language writing.* New York: Cambridge.

Connor, U., & Lauer, J. (1988). Cross-cultural variation in persuasive student writing. In A. Purves (Ed.), *Writing across languages and cultures: Issues in contrastive rhetoric* (pp. 138–159). Newbury Park, CA: Sage.

Connor, U., & Mayberry, S. (1996). Learning discipline-specific academic writing: A case study of a Finnish graduate student in the United States. In E. Ventola & A. Mauranen (Eds.), *Academic writing: Intercultural and textual issues* (pp. 231–253). Amsterdam: John Benjamins.

Connors, R. J. (1996). Teaching and learning as a man. *College English, 58,* 139–157.

Cumming, A. (1990). Metalinguistic and ideational thinking in second language composing. *Written Communication, 7,* 482–511.

Cumming, A. (1992). Instructional routines in ESL composition teaching: A case study of three teachers. *Journal of Second Language Writing, 1,* 17–35.

Cumming, A., & Gill, J. (1992). Motivation or accessibility? Factors permitting Indo-Canadian women to pursue ESL literacy instruction. In B. Burnaby & A. Cumming (Eds.), *Sociopolitical aspects of ESL education in Canada* (pp. 241–252). Toronto: OISE Press.

Elbow, P. (1986). *Embracing contraries: Explorations in learning and teaching.* New York: Oxford University Press.

Firth, A., & Wagner, J. (1997). On discourse, communication, and (some) fundamental concepts in SLA research. *The Modern Language Journal, 81,* 285–300.

Flynn, E. (1990). Composing "Composing as a woman": A perspective on research. *College Composition and Communication, 41,* 83–89.

Flynn, E. (1991). Composition studies from a feminist perspective. In R. Bullock & J. Trimbur (Eds.), *The politics of writing instruction: Postsecondary* (pp. 137–154). Portsmouth, NH: Boynton/Cook.

Grabe, W., & Kaplan, R. (1996). *Theory and practice of writing.* New York: Longman.

Hall, J. K. (1997). A consideration of SLA as a theory of practice: A response to Firth and Wagner. *The Modern Language Journal, 81,* 301–306.

Harding, S. (1986). *The science question in feminism.* Ithaca, NY: Cornell University Press.

Hirsh, E., & Olson, G. (1995). Starting from marginalized lives: A conversation with Sandra Harding. *JAC: A Journal of Composition Theory, 15,* 193–225.

hooks, b. (1990). *Yearning: Race, gender, and cultural politics.* Boston: South End Press.

Johns, A. (1981). Necessary English: A faculty survey. *TESOL Quarterly, 15,* 51–57.

Johns, A. (1990). L1 composition theories: Implications for developing theories of L2 composition. In B. Kroll (Ed.), Second language writing: Research insights for the classroom. (pp. 24–36). Cambridge: Cambridge University Press.

Johns, A. (1991). Interpreting an English competency examination: The frustrations of an ESL science student. *Written Communication, 8,* 379–401.

Johns, A. (1992). Toward developing a cultural repertoire: A case study of a Lao college freshman. In D. Murray (Ed.), *Diversity as resource: Redefining cultural literacy* (pp. 183–201). Alexandria, VA: TESOL.

Johns, A., & Mayes, P. (1990). An analysis of summary protocols of university ESL students, *Applied Linguistics, 11,* 253–271.

Kasper, G. (1997). "A" stands for acquisition: A response to Firth and Wagner. *The Modern Language Journal, 81,* 307–312.

Keller, E. F. (1984). *Reflections on gender and science.* New Haven, CT: Yale University Press.

Kirsch, G. (1993). *Women writing the academy: Audience, authority, and transformation.* Carbondale: Southern Illinois University Press.

Lamb, C. (1996). Other voices, different parties: Feminist responses to argument. In D. Berrill (Ed.), *Perspectives on written argument* (pp. 257–269). Cresskill, NJ: Hampton Press.

Leki, I. (1991). The preferences of ESL students for error correction in college-level classes. *Foreign Language Annals, 24,* 203–217.

Leki, I. (1995). Coping strategies of ESL students in writing tasks across the curriculum. *TESOL Quarterly, 29,* 235–260.

Li, X. (1996). *"Good writing" in cross-cultural context.* Albany: State University of New York Press.

Long, M. H. (1997). Construct validity in SLA research: A response to Firth and Wagner. *The Modern Language Journal, 81,* 318–323.

Lutz, C. (1995). The gender of theory. In R. Behar & D. Gordon (Eds.), *Women writing culture* (pp. 249–266). Berkeley: University of California Press.

Matsuda, P. K. (1998). *The first five years of the JSLW: A retrospective* [On-line]. Available <http://icdweb.cc.purdue.edu/~silvat/jslw/5years.html>.

Miller, S. (1991). The feminization of composition. In R. Bullock & J. Trimbur (Eds.), *The politics of writing instruction: Postsecondary* (pp. 39–53). Portsmouth, NH: Boynton/Cook.

North, S. (1987). *The making of knowledge in composition: Portrait of an emerging field.* Upper Montclair, NJ: Boynton/Cook.

Ogulnick, K. (1998). *Onna rashiku (like a woman): The diary of a language learner in Japan.* Albany: State University of New York Press.

Olesen, V. (1994). Feminisms and models of qualitative research. In N. Denzin & Y. Lincoln (Eds.), *Handbook of qualitative research* (pp. 158–174). Thousand Oaks, CA: Sage.

Ong, A. (1995). Women out of China: Traveling tales and traveling theories in postcolonial feminism. In R. Behar & D. Gordon (Eds.), *Women writing culture* (pp. 350–371). Berkeley: University of California Press.

Pennycook, A. (1994). *The cultural politics of English as an international language.* London: Longman.

Poulisse, N. (1997). Some words in defense of the psycholinguistic approach: A response to Firth and Wagner. *The Modern Language Journal, 81,* 324–328.

Raimes, A. (1993). The author responds (to A. S. Canagarajah). *TESOL Quarterly, 27,* 306–310.

Sandler, B. (1986). *The campus climate revisited: Chilly for women faculty, administrators, and graduate students.* Washington, DC: Project on the Status and Education of Women, Association of American Colleges.

Schneider, A. (1998). Why don't women publish as much as men? *The Chronicle of Higher Education,* A14–A16.

Shotter, J., & Logan, J. (1988). The pervasiveness of patriarchy: On finding a different voice. In M. Gergen (Ed.), *Feminist thought and the structure of knowledge.* New York: New York University Press.

Silva, T. (1990). Second language composition instruction: Developments, issues, and directions in ESL. In B. Kroll (Ed.), *Second language writing: Research insights for the classroom* (pp. 11–23). New York: Cambridge University Press.

Spender, D. (1989). *The writing or the sex? Or why you don't have to read women's writing to know it's no good.* New York: Pergamon.

Spivak, G. C. (1988). *In other worlds: Essays in cultural politics.* New York: Routledge.

Sullivan, P. (1992). Feminism and methodology in composition studies. In G. Kirsch & P. Sullivan (Eds.), *Methods and methodology in composition research* (pp. 37–61). Carbondale: Southern Illinois University Press.

Swales, J. (1990). *Genre analysis: English in academic and research settings.* New York: Cambridge University Press.

Swales, J., & Najjar, H. (1987). The writing of research article introductions. *Written Communication, 4,* 175–191.

Tannen, D. (1998). *The argument culture: Moving from debate to dialogue.* New York: Random House.

Tompkins, J. (1988). Fighting words: Unlearning to write the critical essay. *The Georgia Review, 42,* 585–590.

Trinh, M. (1989). *Woman, native, other: Writing postcoloniality and feminism.* Bloomington: Indiana University Press.

Vandrick, S. (1994). Feminist pedagogy and ESL. *College ESL, 4,* 69–92.

Zamel, V. (1985). Responding to student writing. *TESOL Quarterly, 19,* 79–101.

Zamel, V. (1990). Through students' eyes: The experiences of three ESL writers. *Journal of Basic Writing, 9,* 83–98.

6

For Kyla: What Does the Research Say About Responding to ESL Writers

Lynn Goldstein
Monterey Institute of International Studies

Kyla was a student in a course that I teach on writing for publication. She was also an experienced writing teacher and was at the time of the class teaching writing in a tutorial setting. Kyla decided to write a paper on the most effective ways to provide written feedback to English as a Second Language (ESL) writers for an "uninformed" audience of ESL teachers. She intended to review the current research on teacher written feedback for ESL student writers in order to extrapolate from the findings of such research so she could write this paper. She began this project with enthusiasm but was quickly daunted. We talked on several occasions, and on one I suggested that she try some different heuristics to get a handle on the complexity of the information she was uncovering. At this point, Kyla took on the burden of understanding, that is, she figured if she were having difficulty, this was because she was a novice, one who was struggling with the writing of "experts." On the last occasion, she came to my office with large pieces of paper covered with her attempts to understand the research. We looked at these pieces of paper for a while trying to make sense of individual studies and the literature as a whole. When she told me that she could see no concrete suggestions she could pull from the research, I had to agree. My agreement, however, was not with Kyla's perception that she might somehow be at fault. On the contrary, in her attempt to write her paper, she had discovered a body of research that had many problems that mitigated against establishing concrete pedagogical suggestions, and her heuristics had led her to this absolutely correct perception. Kyla never wrote her paper, which I believe was an appropriate response to an impossible task.

Now I find myself writing this chapter, a critical review of research on teacher written commentary to ESL writers. Because I agree with what Kyla uncovered, I do so not in an attempt to discover pedagogical implications. My purpose here is to explore what makes this body of research problematic and to suggest ways that future research might be carried out so practitioners such as Kyla can eventually come away from these studies with sound and appropriate pedagogical implications. In addition, my intent is to examine the body of research as a whole rather than to critique individual studies per se. As such, I critically examine, in places, certain studies, to illustrate particular problems, but my intent is not to critique any one study in its entirety.

The body of research that I examine here is defined as research that looks at teacher written commentary in the English as a second or foreign language context and that looks at teacher written commentary that focuses on rhetorical and content issues as opposed to research that focuses on sentence-level issues of grammar, lexicon, and mechanics. In addition, in recognition that many scholars and teachers do not have ready access to unpublished manuscripts or the funding to purchase copies of dissertations through services such as University Microfilms International (UMI), I have only reviewed research that is readily available to other researchers and teachers through published journals, books, and edited volumes and through ERIC.

The scope of this chapter has been limited for a number of reasons. First, we need to move away from an over reliance on research about first language writers because first and second language writers may differ in crucial respects (see, e.g., Ferris, Pezone, Tade, & Tinti, 1997). I will, however, bring in first language research where I believe this research might inform us about sound research methodology. Second, learners of languages other than English in a foreign language setting (e.g., French at a university in the United States) may also be crucially different from learners of English as a second or foreign language. Hedgcock and Lefkowitz (1994), for example, found that learners of French, German, and Spanish as a foreign language in an American university setting had responses to teacher-written commentary that differed from the responses of the ESL subjects. They speculated that some of these differing responses might be explained by differences in the teachers' emphases on sentence level concerns versus rhetoric in these two contexts. Finally, there is an evident tension in the field of second language writing between those who believe that teachers should avoid commenting on sentence-level concerns and rhetorical/content concerns simultaneously (see, e.g., Raimes 1983) and those who believe that students can attend successfully to both types of comments at the same time (Fathman & Whalley, 1990). There appears to be no definitive answer to this question. As Kyla (Stinnett, personal communication, April 1998) discovered in her attempt to write her paper, studies that examine both rhetoric–content and sentence-level feedback take place in a wide range of instructional contexts, employ a wide range of feedback techniques to respond to both error and content–rhetoric, use a wide range of methods for determining success of revision or accuracy, contain a wide range of definitions of error, employ fundamentally and sometimes theoretically unfounded methods for examining error, and exhibit a pattern of not looking at error within a sound second language acquisition perspective (see Carson, this volume, for a discussion of the SLA perspective). Additionally, no matter which approach the research might support, how students handle teacher written commentary on rhetoric and content alone is a fundamentally important question that needs to be answered.

This chapter therefore focuses on four questions:

1. How much research has been carried out that specifically addresses teacher written commentary to ESL and English as a Foreign Language (EFL) writers on rhetoric/content?

2. What questions have been addressed by this body of research, and what questions might be addressed in future research?

3. What types of problems and issues are evidenced in the research methodology that need to be addressed in future research?

4. How might we conceptualize the process of responding to content–rhetorical concerns in the papers of ESL and EFL students and the process of writers revising in response to written commentary to aid in developing a body of sound research?

HOW MUCH RESEARCH

Research examining teacher written commentary on rhetoric–content is relatively new. In 1985, Zamel reported on how one group of teachers responded to their ESL students. However, with the exception of Zamel's study and Radecki and Swales' (1988) study, the investigation of teacher-written commentary on rhetoric–content in ESL and EFL settings did not really begin until the early 1990s. In addition, an exhaustive search of the ERIC and Language Learning and Behavior Abstracts (LLBA) databases uncovered only 15 published studies that look specifically at teacher written feedback on content and rhetoric (Cohen alone and with colleagues has written several papers that address this topic; only one of these papers is included here as these papers all address the same body of data and employ the same research methodology).

The 15 studies can be divided into three major areas of inquiry. The largest group of studies (nine) examines students' perceptions of and attitudes toward teacher-written commentary and students' self-report of how they use teacher-written commentary when revising (Arndt, 1992; Brice, 1995; Cohen

& Calvacanti, 1990; Enginlarlar, 1993; Ferris, 1995; Hedgcock & Lefkowitz, 1994, 1996; Radecki & Swales, 1988; Saito, 1994). (Although some of these studies also look at teacher-written commentary on sentence-level concerns or at foreign language learners, the research is reported in a way that it makes it readily feasible to look only at the results pertaining to rhetoric and content). Only two studies examine how teachers actually comment on student papers (Ferris et al., 1997; Zamel, 1985), and only four studies look at the relationship between teacher-written commentary and either subsequent student revision (Chapin & Terdal, 1990; Ferris, 1997) or student essay scores (Fathman & Whalley, 1990; Lipp, 1995). Although there is not a lot of research in any area, particularly noteworthy here is that the questions of how teachers comment and the relationship between teacher-written commentary and student revision have been largely unexplored.

It is also important to note that, in looking within any one area of inquiry, the studies are spread across different instructional contexts. In the studies that examine student perceptions, attitudes, and self-reports, two looked at writing classes in English for specific purposes and in intensive English language institutes (Radecki & Swales, 1988; Saito 1994), three looked at writing classes in an EFL context (Arndt, 1992; Cohen & Calvacanti, 1990; Enginlarlar, 1993), and five looked at writing classes for students matriculated at an American university (Brice, 1995; Ferris, 1995; Hedgcock & Lefkowitz, 1994, 1996; Radecki & Swales, 1988). The two studies that focus on how teachers comment both took place in a university ESL setting. The studies that look at the relationship between teacher commentary and student revision took place in a university ESL setting and an Intensive English Language Institute (IELI) while the two studies that examined the relationship between teacher commentary and student scores took place at an IELI and an unspecified setting (It is not clear from Fathman & Whalley whether the study took place in an IELI or in classes for matriculated university ESL students).

In sum, the examination of teacher-written response to rhetoric and content is a fairly new area of inquiry that has not received much attention and has not been examined with any depth (i.e., across a number of studies) within any one instructional context. In addition, although we have at least a developing understanding of student perceptions/attitudes, we know almost nothing about the nature of teacher written commentary or how students use this commentary in revision.

WHAT QUESTIONS HAVE BEEN ADDRESSED IN THE RESEARCH AND REMAIN TO BE ADDRESSED

Studies that examine student reactions and attitudes largely examine what students say they do with teacher feedback, how much they attend to this feedback, how much of this feedback they understand, and what they do when they do not understand a comment. Some of the studies examine these questions across students of different proficiency levels, across students with different levels of receptivity, and in different settings. Research that focuses on students' perceptions of teacher commentary has looked at how much students feel student commentary helps, students' attitudes toward types of feedback, and students perceptions of their teachers and their own priorities for teacher-written commentary.

One of the two studies that looked at how teacher's comments addressed the questions of whether comments were text specific, whether they appropriated students' meaning, and whether teachers comments appeared to be confusing (Zamel, 1985) whereas the other study (Ferris et al., 1997) asked how teacher commentary was constructed in terms of its syntactic form and pragmatic intent, text specificity, and hedging, and how these characteristics varied across different students, texts, and points in a term.

The studies that looked at the relationship between teacher-written commentary and student revision examined the degree to which students addressed the teachers' comments, the relationship between the type of comment and either the degree to which revisions were enacted and the degree of revision success, the degree to which revisions were related to teacher written commentary or to other factors, or the relationship between specific types of teacher-written commentary, and changes in student essay scores.

This review helps us see how much has not yet been examined in the research to date. This is not a criticism, for as pointed out previously this is a field very much in its' "infancy." Nonetheless, it is important to assess what we need to know in light of what has been looked at. First, all of the questions that have been addressed still need to be further researched. In part this is due to methodological problems that are discussed in the next section. It is also due to the fact that each study tends to be fairly unique, in which uniqueness is defined by a combination of the research questions asked, the methodology employed, and the context of the study. Without examining the same questions with comparable research methodology across different contexts, it is difficult to create a comprehensive picture of the relationship between teacher-written commentary and student revision. In addition, without examining a variety of questions within comparable contexts, it is also difficult to learn about the complexity of factors that interact as they influence the relationship between teacher-written commentary and student revision.

Secondly, a number of very important questions and issues have not yet been addressed. As discussed further later in this chapter, the research has largely been noncontextual and nonsocial, focused largely on texts (i.e., teacher comments as text or student revisions as text) and conducted within a linear model of teacher respond and student revise. However there are a good many factors that probably play an interactive role in how teachers comment, how students perceive and react to teacher commentary, and how students use such commentary when revising. These include student factors such as previous experience with commentary, gender, first language background and proficiency, as well as teacher factors such as attitudes toward a particular student, experience and training, ideology about commenting, text factors such as topic, genre and draft, and characteristics of the instructional context, including the actual pedagogy of the classroom and the support of and uses of writing in the class and the institution as a whole. These factors remain largely unexamined.

The following lists some questions that research could explore. This is not intended to be an exhaustive list but simply a list of unaddressed questions that I believe are the most compelling. Most of these questions call for a more contextualized view of the processes and products of teacher response and student revision, allowing us to view these processes and products not just as cognitive ones but as social ones. The questions are:

- What role does teacher commentary play in helping students become more effective writers over time (as opposed to the role it plays in revision immediately following commentary)?
- How are the roles teachers adopt as readers such as editor, audience, expert, peer, or gatekeeper reflected in how they comment and how students perceive these comments and use these comments? What determines what role the teacher adopts?
- What is the relationship between sociolinguistic norms such as politeness and the manner in which teachers comment and the manner in which students respond to and use commentary?
- How can we differentiate between comments that direct and are authoritarian and those that facilitate and are authoritative?
- How do students react to and use comments of an authoritarian versus authoritative nature?
- What are students' underlying motivations for using or not using teacher-written commentary?
- What factors interact to influence how successfully a student uses teacher-written commentary?
- How do individual students revise (as opposed to groups of students) in response to feedback?
- What is the relationship between the manner in which teachers actually comment and students' perceptions and reactions?
- What is the relationship between students' attitudes and reactions to teacher commentary and how they actually revise?
- How do different teachers across and within differing contexts define revision success?

- What kinds of information do we obtain when coding teacher commentary using different types of coding schemes?
- How do the factors of teacher, student, text and context interact, and how do these interactions affect how teachers comment, how students perceive and react to comments and how students' employ comments.

A CRITIQUE OF THE RESEARCH METHODOLOGY

Thus far we have seen a field just beginning the complex exploration of teacher-written commentary and student revision. Much research remains to be done that further explores those questions already asked and begins to explore important questions yet to be asked. Here then I turn a critical eye to the quality of the research that has been conducted thus far, not for the purposes of critiquing for its own sake but so that future research might be informed by and avoid the problems and issues identified here.

Supplying Adequate Information

The first issue to be addressed is how the research is reported. To be able to understand a study, critically examine its validity and reliability and compare findings across studies, certain information must be provided. As in any body of research, studies need to describe fully and account for their research methodologies, including the nature of the data collected and how the data was collected and analyzed. Then, specific to the study of teacher-written commentary, studies must fully describe the context and the text. Context is critically important to the understanding of the research results, but as Ferris (1997) notes "most research on teacher response has failed to consider adequately the larger context of the writing classroom and teacher-student relationships" (p. 315). Furthermore, as Matison-Fife and O'Neill (1997) state, there is a "standard interpretation of the classroom and the response situation instead of studying these complex contexts they give rise to" (p. 274). Contexts, however, are anything but standard. They are uniquely defined by the complex interactions of characteristics of the institutional setting (e.g., how writing and a particular student population is viewed by and treated by the institution as a whole; see Smoke, this volume, for an example of the politics of a particular institutional setting), the instructional setting (e.g., the type of program, where a course fits in the overall curriculum, or the degree of support for particular pedagogical approaches), the classroom setting (e.g., the teacher's methodological approach, the relationship between instruction and feedback), the teacher (e.g., the teacher's experience, ideology of feedback, attitudes toward different students) and the students (e.g., proficiency, course expectations, gender, attitudes toward the teacher). How teachers provide commentary and how students react to and use commentary takes place in this complex web of factors that defines each context. In addition, our concern with student texts, that is how teachers respond to them and how students construct and revise them, requires that studies provide sufficient information about these texts as part of a complete description of the context. We must have information about the topics, the content, the genre, the intended audience, and the intended purpose for the text in general and the draft in particular. All of these factors create the context and potentially affect not only how and what students write but teachers' expectations and what they respond to and how they respond, as well as students' expectations for, responses to and uses of teacher-written commentary.

Table 6.1 displays the 15 studies reviewed in this chapter and examines whether these studies provide a full description of context, texts, research methodology, and data analysis. It is striking that no study provided sufficient information in all four areas and that only four studies came fairly close to doing so. Furthermore, three studies supplied little or no information in all four categories.

Five of the studies lack a full description of the research methodology and data analysis, making it impossible to judge whether or not the findings of these studies are warranted because it is impossible to judge their reliability and validity. Furthermore, it is impossible to compare the results of these five studies to other studies. How the data was collected and analyzed affects research results; so whether we find similar results across studies or differences in findings across studies, we have no way of knowing whether the findings are really comparable and no way to explain differences.

Critically important information about context and texts is also missing from a substantial number of these studies. Only 6 of the 15 studies give adequate if any description of the text. No study fully discusses context as I have defined previously, and only 6 studies have fairly comprehensive descriptions of context. The abundance of missing information about context and texts makes it difficult to compare across studies. For example, take a case where an apparent conflict of findings exists between one study that finds that students have a negative reaction to teachers focusing on rhetoric and another that finds that students prefer rhetorical commentary to sentence-level commentary. Yet, imagine that the context of the first study was in part defined by a curriculum that largely focused on sentence-level concerns, an institutional disregard for how content is communicated rhetorically, a teacher's expectation that accuracy must precede content, and student expectation that learning does not happen if accuracy is not the primary focus of the teacher's commentary. And imagine that the context within which the second study occurred is defined in part by a curriculum

TABLE 6.1
Description of Context, Essays, Research Method and Method of
Data Analysis

Study	Context	Texts	Method	Data Analysis
Radecki and Swales	−	−	−	−
Arndt	−	+/−	−	−
Hedgcock and Lefkowitz	−	−	+	+
Hedgcock and Lefkowitz	−	−	+	+
Cohen and Calvacanti	−	+	+	+
Enginlarlar	+/−	−	+	+
Ferris	+/−	−	+	+
Brice	+/−	+	+/−	+/−
Saito	+/−	+	+/−	+/−
Zamel	−	−	−	−
Ferris et al.	+/−	+	+	+
Lipp	+/−	+/−	+/−	+/−
Chapin and Terdal	−	+	+	+
Fathman and Whalley	−	+	+	+
Ferris	+/−	+/−	+	+

Key: + full description.
   +/− some aspects fully described; other aspects not described.
   − description absent.

that gave weight to students ideas and rhetorical strategies without ignoring sentence-level concerns, institutional support for writing as a means for
discovering and learning content, a teacher's expectation that content and
rhetoric must precede accuracy, and a student's expectation that ideas and
the rhetorical strategies for presenting these ideas should be the primary
focus of teacher-written commentary. Now the findings of the two studies
are not in conflict but reflect the unique characteristics of the context within
which the writing, teacher commentary, and student revision took place.

Missing information about the students' texts also makes it impossible
to compare across studies or even data within one study. For example,
two teachers might comment in a seemingly different manner that might
be explained by the topic of the texts in which in one case the teacher
expected students to have good control of the content needed to write the
essay and in the other had the opposite expectation or might be explained
by the genres of these texts where one teacher might have an expectation
that expository writing is relatively difficult for his or her students, and the
other might have an expectation that narrative writing is relatively easy for
his or her students.

Future reports of research must include full descriptions of methodology, data analysis, context, and text. This crucial information allows consumers (i.e., other researchers, teachers, reviewers, and editors) on the one hand to judge the reliability and validity of any one study and decide if the findings are warranted and on the other compare studies and develop a comprehensive understanding of teacher-written commentary and student response across contexts and texts.

Problems With Methodology

These studies also exhibit a number of methodological problems and highlight a number of methodological issues that are instructive for future research. First, a number of studies in all three areas of inquiry contain confounding variables. Some studies compared students in different conditions without taking these differing conditions in account. Thus, students who wrote about different topics, who wrote in class versus out of class, who were in different pedagogical contexts, had different assignments and different genres, or were at different stages of drafting were treated as comparable. Clearly this is problematic when any one of these factors can affect student perceptions and attitudes, the way in which teachers comment, and how students process and use teacher-written commentary.

A review of the studies that focus on students' perceptions, reactions, and attitudes shows a number of other methodological problems and issues. Some of these studies seem to suggest, first of all, that what students say they do with commentary might correspond to what they actually do. However, research to date has not looked at the fit between student reports and what students actually do when they process and use teacher commentary when revising. In addition, most of these studies do not report anything about how the teacher commented, making it impossible to see whether there is any connection between the manner of commenting and students' perceptions, attitudes, and reports of how they would use the feedback (Brice, 1995, and Cohen & Calvacanti, 1990, are notable exceptions). Brice, for example, examined the relationship between actual teacher commentary and student perceptions' of what they understood or did not understand and what they found useful and not useful in the teacher's commentary. One caveat to her approach, however, is her unexamined finding that students received differential treatment. Although this is true, what is missing is a comparison between what the teacher actually commented on with what the teacher could have commented on. It is not surprising that students receive different feedback as they, along with their texts, are different. What is important to ask, however, is whether this different treatment is caused by unsystematic and perhaps biased responses or whether something in the text (e.g., one text having an abundance of errors that interfere with meaning and another text that is "clean" but lacks adequate support for the writer's claim), or the student (e.g., the student's approach to revision or knowledge of a particular content) calls for responding to these students in different ways.

An additional problematic area is that many of these studies only examine one text, some only examine the first text of the semester, and the few studies that examine more than one draft do not necessarily differentiate between the drafts. It could be expected, however, that characteristics of the text (content, topic, genre, audience, purpose, which draft) as well as the point in the semester when the students are working on that text could affect how students react to teacher commentary, what preferences they have for commentary, and how they use teacher commentary.

Methodological problems are also found in the two studies that address how teachers comment. As shown in Table 6.1, one study (Zamel, 1985) contains no information about the texts the students wrote, the characteristics of the context, teacher or students, and no information is given about how the data was analyzed. This missing information makes it impossible to judge the validity of the research methodology and to interpret the claim that ESL teachers focus largely on sentence level concerns, appropriate students' texts, and are unsystematic in their responses. The other study (Ferris et al., 1997) supplied almost all the necessary information to understand the research and findings (see Table 6.1). My concern here lies with the pragmatic coding of the comments. Comments are coded according to pragmatic intention (i.e., the teacher's intention) but this intention is not directly assessed. We need to avoid surmising teacher intention no matter how well we may know the teacher because we may be incorrect; instead teachers themselves need to help code their comments for intention.

Some other issues that we can learn from arise when we examine the first-language research on teacher written commentary. Some studies have had teachers respond out of context (e.g., see Sommers, 1982) to essays written by students they do not know. This is problematic because it is reasonable to expect that how teachers comment is influenced by contextual factors, including knowledge of each student. Thus teachers responding to essays written by unknown students are responding in an unnatural, acontextual manner. Another issue is the coding of teacher commentary on student texts or the determination of success of revision within students' texts. Typically raters do not always completely agree. Researchers tend to deal with such disagreement by either throwing out the data where raters have disagreed or calling on a third rater as a kind of arbitrator (see, e.g., Beason, 1993). Doing so, however, sweeps an issue under the rug that is inherently important to examine and understand, namely, where and why do raters disagree and what does this tell us about how teachers respond to student writing.

Methodological problems in the second language studies that examine the relationship between teacher commentary and student revision or essay scores are also instructive. First, studies that look at the relationship between teacher-written commentary and student scores on their texts implicitly assume that changes in such scores reflect the treatment (i.e., the teacher's comments). However, because the texts are not examined in any way, including what revisions students made, there is absolutely no way to determine how or to what degree teacher commentary affected these scores. Scores tell us nothing about revision—they are merely measures of improvement that could be influenced not only by teacher commentary but by many other factors.

Another issue, one also raised previously, is the relationship between what was commented on with what could have been commented on. Studies do not examine this relationship nor do they look at the students' total revisions but instead focus the analysis on where teacher commentary calls for revision. Yet, many teachers select out certain features of a text for commentary rather than commenting on everything, and some student revisions may not be the result of teacher commentary, or there may be places where teacher commentary is not used. When we examine only what teachers comment on rather than all that they might have commented on, we miss how teacher commentary is constructed. When we only analyze students' texts in the places where teacher' commentary would call for revision, we miss an opportunity to understand how teacher commentary is used within the whole process of student revision.

Worth noting here also is the need to understand teachers' processes as they comment on student texts and students' processes of using teacher commentary for revision. Most studies look at the products, that is, the actual teacher commentary and student revision, however few look at the processes that underlie the construction of these products. Some instructive exceptions (i.e., studies that look at processes not just products), asked students to do think-aloud protocols as they revised. First language studies include Dohrer (1991), Ziv (1982, 1984), and Onore (1984), and ESL studies include Brice (1995). Some studies on second language writers included interviews with students about their revisions (Chapin & Terdal, 1990; Hedgcock & Lefkowitz, 1996). Some second language researchers have also had teachers do think-aloud protocols (Cohen & Cavalcanti, 1990) as they comment. It is important to realize that studies that examine only the products can not inform us about the processes of reading and commenting on student papers and the processes of reading and using teacher commentary when revising.

Another consideration is that the four studies above that examine the relationship between commentary and student revisions do so by looking at the students as a group. Group behavior, although worthwhile to examine, masks the individual and thus does not allow us to see what each student brings to revision and the use of commentary. Conrad and Goldstein (1999) found, for example, that each of the three students brought a unique combination of factors that influenced how they used the teacher's comments, factors that could not be revealed by only looking at the three students as a group. Studies that focus on groups may be able to tell us some things about the effect of types of comments on the whole, but they cannot reveal how individual students interact with comments when they revise.

Finally, of interest as well is the diversity of coding schemes that researchers use to examine teacher-written commentary. Some code the form of the comments, looking at factors such as the syntactic form and pragmatic intention, text specificity, and hedging (e.g., Ferris et al., 1997); others examine whether the comments are implicit or explicit and whether they direct, correct, point out error as well as the type of problem they focus on (e.g., Chapin & Terdal, 1990). Interestingly, both of these approaches treat teacher commentary as a text and thus conduct a type of textual analysis on the comments. I would not argue against doing so because the form of the teacher's comments may play a role in student reaction to and student use of the commentary. However, we can learn from the research in first language writing that also examines commentary and revision as social interaction. When teachers comment on student papers, they assume stances or roles—they may be a gatekeeper, an editor, a proofreader, a friendly reader, a hostile reader, a peer, an audience interested in the ideas, to name a few. And when students read and subsequently use such commentary, it seems reasonable to expect that they read the teacher's comments within their construction of what role they believe the teacher has taken on and what that role implies for the teacher's attitude toward the student and the student's text. As Sperling (1994) states

> During the past few years, writing research has turned increasingly on the notion that writing and learning to write are social acts . . . . According to recent theory, students learn to write by addressing the responses that their writing evokes in others. In doing so they develop and hone expectations about the perspectives that readers bring to texts. (p. 175)

She continues later:

> research on written comments has tended not to question the ways teachers' expectations influence their reading of different students' writing and different writing types . . . the likelihood is strong that student writers and their writing are nevertheless shaped, for better or for worse, by teachers' expectations as projected to them through the many-faceted classroom social processes, including the comments that teachers write on students' papers. (pp. 177–178)

Sperling made these comments in her report on a study in which she examined one teacher's responses across a number of students and writing types. Because she was concerned with the social processes of "teacher as reader," she focused on what she called *orientations*. Briefly, these orientations allowed her to code the commentary in terms of whether or not the teacher responded to aspects in the students writing related to hers or her students' prior knowledge and experience; whether the teacher assumed the institutional role of teacher or something other than that, such as a peer, or expert reader; whether the teacher responded emotionally or analytically; whether she expressed if the writing worked for her or did not work for her; and whether and how she used her comments to teach. Sperling's results show that the teacher responded to each student with a unique combination of the above orientations, that is, she reconstructed her "teacher as reader" for each student. Whether we use Sperling's coding or some other, second language research must broaden its perspective, moving from analysis of teacher commentary and student revision that is largely textual to one that is additionally social.

RECONCEPTUALIZATION

In concluding, I would like to go further than pointing out what kinds of information are crucial for understanding, judging and comparing studies, suggesting questions that have yet to be addressed in the research, and discussing methodological problems and issues present in the current research. Taken as a whole, this body of research seems fundamentally problematic in a larger sense for three reasons. First, when reading the research, one sees a widescale and overwhelming uncritical acceptance of the findings of these studies. These findings are frequently cited as definitive in literature reviews or when a researcher compares his or her findings to others. In a sense they are becoming canonized. What we have seen from this critique, however, is that the findings need to be examined critically either because too much information is missing for us to judge or understand the findings or because we need to make sure that there are not methodological problems that call the findings to question.

Next, we need to consider two larger concerns for conducting future research. The first comes about because, in the current research, the areas of inquiry tend to be separated from each other. Yet, our common goal is an understanding of how student writing, teacher commentary, and student revision mutually shape each other. Because teacher commentary, student reactions to commentary, and student revisions interact with each other, research needs to look at all three simultaneously in any one context. Only then can we see their mutual influences and come to understand why teachers comment the ways that they do, why students perceive comments in the ways that they do, and why students use comments in the different ways that they do.

Third, what seems to underlie much of the research to date on teacher-written commentary and student revision is a conceptualization of the process as a linear one in which students write, teachers respond with commentary, and then students revise. This conceptualization ignores a process in which multiple factors interact in very complex ways that may in fact be unique for each study. As Fig. 6.1 shows, we need to consider characteristics of the institutional, programmatic and methodological context, the teacher, the student, the text the teacher comments on as well as the revised text, and the teacher's commentary. What remains unknown is how these characteristics uniquely define each setting, how they interact, and how this interaction influences the construction of teacher commentary, student reaction to commentary, and student use of commentary for revision.

Ten years from now, I would like to have another "Kyla" in my writing for publication class. I envision her wanting to write a paper for writing teachers

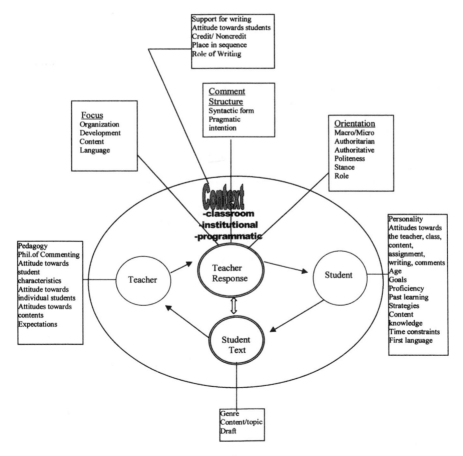

FIG. 6.1.

in which, based on research findings, she discusses effective teacher commentary and the relationship between commentary and student revision. Only this time, she is able to do so because there are numerous studies, thoroughly discussed and soundly conducted, across a wide array of contexts defined in all their complexity. The intent of this chapter is to push us in a direction that will make this possible. I look forward to seeing an increasing number of studies, ones that look at teacher-written commentary and student revision in sound and complex ways and that answer the many questions that remain to date.

REFERENCES

Arndt, V. (1992). Response to writing: Using feedback to inform the writing process. In M. Brock & L. Walters (Eds.), *Teaching composition around the pacific rim: Politics and pedagogy* (pp. 90–116). Cleveland, Philadelphia and Adelaide: Multilingual Matters.

Beason, L. (1993). Feedback and revision in writing across the curriculum classes. *Research in the Teaching of English, 27*, 395–422.

Brice, C. (1995). *ESL writers' reactions to teacher commentary: A case study.* (Eric Document Reproduction Service No. ED 394 312)

Chapin, R., & Terdal, M. (1990). *Responding to our response: Student strategies for responding to teacher written comments.* (ERIC Document Reproduction Service No. ED 328 098)

Cohen, A., & Cavalcanti, M. (1990). Feedback on compositions: Teacher and student verbal reports. In B. Kroll (Ed.), *Second language writing: Research insights for the classroom* (pp. 155–177). New York: Cambridge University Press.

Conrad, S., & Goldstein, L. (1999). ESL student revision after teacher written comments. *Journal of Second Language Writing, 8*, 147–180.

Dohrer, G. (1991). Do teacher's comments on students' papers help? *College Teaching 39*, 48–54.

Enginarlar, H. (1993). Student response to teacher feedback in EFL writing. *System, 21*, 192–203.

Fathman, A., & Whalley, E. (1990). Teacher response to student writing: Focus on form versus content. In B. Kroll (Ed.), *Second language writing: Research insights for the classroom* (pp. 178–190). New York: Cambridge University Press.

Ferris, D. (1995). Student reactions to teacher response in multi-draft composition classrooms. *TESOL Quarterly, 29*, 33–53.

Ferris, D. (1997). The influence of teacher commentary on student revision. *TESOL Quarterly, 31*, 315–339.

Ferris, D., Pezone, S., Tade, C., & Tinti, S. (1997). Teacher commentary on student writing: Descriptions and implications. *Journal of Second Language Writing, 6*, 155–182.

Hedgcock, J., & Lefkowitz, N. (1994). Feedback on feedback: Assessing learner receptivity to teacher response in L2 composing. *Journal of Second Language Writing, 3*, 141–163.

Hedgcock, J., & Lefkowitz, N. (1996). Some input on input: Two analyses of student response to expert feedback in L2 writing. *Modern Language Journal, 80*, 287–308.

Lipp, E. (1995). Training ESL teachers to write effective feedback on composition drafts. *Journal of Intensive English Studies, 9*, 50–66.

Mathison-Fife, J., & O'Neill, P. (1997). Re-seeing research on response. *College Composition and Communication, 48*, 274–277.

Onore, C. (1984). The student, the teacher, and the text: Negotiating meanings through response and revision. In C. Anson (Ed.), *Writing and response* (pp. 231–260). Urbana, IL: National Council of Teachers of English.

Radecki, P. M., & Swales, J. M. (1988). ESL student reaction to written comments on their work. *System, 16*, 355–365.

Raimes, A. (1983). Anguish as a second language? Remedies for composition teachers. In A. Freedman, I. Pringle, & J. Yalden (Eds.), *Learning to write: First language/second language* (pp. 258–278). London: Longman.

Saito, H. (1994). Teachers' practices and students' preferences for feedback on second language writing: A case study of adult ESL learners. *TESL Canada Journal, 11*, 46–70.

Sommers, N. (1982). Responding to student writing. *College Composition and Communication, 33*, 148–156.

Sperling, M. (1994). Constructing the perspective of teacher-as-reader: A framework for studying response to student writing. *Research in the Teaching of English 28*, 175–207.

Zamel, V. (1985). Responding to student writing. *TESOL Quarterly, 19*, 79–102.

Ziv, N. D. (1982). *What she thought I said: How students misperceive teachers' written comments.* (ERIC Document Reproduction Service No. ED 215 361)

Ziv, N. D. (1984). The effect of teacher comments on the writing of four college freshman. In R. Beach & N. Bridwell (Eds.), *New directions in composition research* (pp. 362–380). New York: Guilford.

7

Research Methodology in Second Language Writing Research: The Case of Text-Based Studies

Charlene Polio
Michigan State University

Researchers of second language (L2) writing, working in a variety of paradigms, focus on a range of factors including: the writing itself (i.e., the text); how the writers produce the writing (i.e., the writing process); the attitudes, practices, and beliefs of those involved in learning and teaching writing; and the social context, including what happens inside the classroom as well as goals outside the classroom. At this point in the history of L2 writing research, it is useful to step back and examine the methods and techniques that we have for investigating these factors. I begin such a discussion of research methodology by focusing on research that measures or analyzes some feature of L2 writers' texts. The purpose of this chapter is to provide a comprehensive, yet brief, taxonomy of measures and analyses for studying L2 texts and to highlight some of the methodological issues that L2 writing researchers must contend with.

The empirical studies[1] focused on in this chapter are works that examine L2 writers' writing for a variety of reasons. Most of this research uses relatively large sample sizes; one benefit of research on written texts is that it allows us to study of a large number of writers. A small portion of this research presents case studies, however, and the benefit of that research is that we learn more about one individual writer; analyses of written texts in such qualitative research provide an additional piece of evidence for triangulation. Although, most of the research discussed in this chapter claims to measure some particular construct, some of the studies simply describe a feature of L2 writers' texts and thus I am using the terms *measures* and *analyses*.

The various features of L2 writers' texts examined by researchers are divided into nine categories: overall quality, linguistic accuracy, syntactic complexity, lexical features, content, mechanics, coherence and discourse features, fluency, and revision. Most of categories are broken down into more specific categories. For each, examples of the various measures and analyses[2] are given, followed by a description of the research questions asked in the various studies. Each section ends with a discussion of the issues and problems that we need to be aware of when we attempt to either use such a measure or analysis, or to critically evaluate empirical research using the method.

OVERALL QUALITY

This category includes studies that for various reasons assess the overall quality of an essay as opposed to being concerned with any one particular component of it. The range of ways to assess quality, as shown in Table 7.1, includes holistic scales, analytic-scale composite scores, and less commonly, ranking. Studies using holistic scales often rely on published tests, most commonly the Test of Written English (TWE) or the Michigan English Language Assessment Battery (MELAB), as well as others written specifically for a study. All of the studies that used an analytic scale chose what is commonly called the Jacobs scale (Jacobs, Zinkgraf, Wormuth, Hartfiel, and Hughey, 1981) A small number of the studies did not give raters guidelines but rather had them rank the essays or place them in groups.

The purpose of assessing overall writing quality is varied. Some research attempts to correlate overall writing quality with components of what is considered to be good writing, such as Engber (1995), who examined measures of lexical quality and their correlations with scores on the TWE. Henry (1996) simply had raters put the essays in four groups without any guidelines and

TABLE 7.1
Overall Quality

Holistic scales	Test of Written English	Engber (1995)
	MELAB	Hamp-Lyons & Mathias (1994)
	Task specific	Braine (1996)
	Others	Kern & Schultz (1992)
Analytic scale composite score	Jacobs scale	Pennington & So (1993)
No guidelines/ranking		Henry (1996)

examined various qualities such as accuracy and complexity in relation to the overall quality. Some of this research attempts to use overall quality scores to show the effects of a program level treatment such as Tsang (1996), who used the Jacobs scale. Braine (1996) examined the differences in essays of students taking English as a Second Language (ESL) classes and those in mainstream university-writing courses. His holistic scale was tailor made to fit the writing assignment, which required students to refer to a reading. Other studies have examined certain characteristics of the writers in relation to the overall quality of their essays. Hamp-Lyons and Mathias (1994), for example, examined the relation between scores on the MELAB and topic choice.

One crucial issue for researchers should be choosing the most appropriate of these measures. Logistic considerations include how quickly the essays can be rated and whether or not the raters are familiar with the scale; however, the overriding consideration should be for the reliability and validity of the measure. Reliability needs to be determined so that significant group differences will not be masked by poor reliability. Lack of significant findings may be caused by poor reliability of the measure for the particular group of writers or essays. Using an established scale for a task or population for which it is not intended could be one cause of poor reliability. Using the TWE, for example, on a homogeneous group of beginning writers may not result in reliable scores.

Validity is more complex and difficult to show psychometrically in a single small-scale study. If we find a significant difference among groups, then the measure is probably measuring something. It is doubtful, however, that all of the measures reported here are tapping into the same construct. How then does a researcher choose a scale? One benefit of using an established scale such as the TWE or an in-house placement test is that there is some real-life implication for certain points of the scale. What if a reliable scale constructed for the study shows a statistically significant difference, but the difference is very small, for example between groups placed in two different programs? This scenario makes the results more difficult to interpret. One also has to look at the descriptors on the holistic scale or the components of the analytic scale to see if they are favoring one possible component of quality over another. A task-specific scale may be called for if the descriptors in the published scales do not address all the features the researcher wants to assess.

We need also to consider a study such as Henry's (1996) that used no guidelines but in which the raters ranked the essays by placing them in four groups. Henry explained that raters can be trained to achieve reliability but that in real life, that is not how readers process texts. She reported that the poor reliability (0.31) in her study should not be cause for alarm but rather as a phenomenon for further study. It is no doubt interesting what raters look for when they evaluate texts without criteria, but the low reliability could be a reason that the ratings did not correlate with the years of foreign-language study in her research.

And finally, we need to be concerned with how the research is reported. As standard practice, all studies should reproduce the scale used and explain the rating procedure including who the raters are and how many were used, whether or not they were trained, and what the interrater reliability was.

LINGUISTIC ACCURACY

Linguistic accuracy is a broad term that generally has to do with the absence of errors. The scope of the term varies from study to study and may or may not include word choice, spelling, or punctuation errors. Accuracy, as shown in Table 7.2, can be measured using a holistic scale that may or may not be a component of an analytic scale or can even be binary, acceptable or not. In addition, error-free units (clauses or T-units) can be counted as can individuals errors, with or without classification of those errors. Furthermore, two studies looked at accuracy qualitatively.

The most common reason for measuring accuracy is to assess the effects of some specific intervention or program. For example, Hedgcock and Lefkowitz (1992) examined the effects of peer versus instructor feedback using the grammar portion of the Jacobs scale and Robb, Ross, and Shortreed (1986) looked at the effect of feedback types using various measures of error-free units including ratio of error-free T-units and words in error-free T-units as a percentage of total words. The second reason for examining

TABLE 7.2
Linguistic Accuracy

Holistic scales	Jacobs scale	Hedgcock & Lefkowitz (1992)
	Other scales	Tarone et al. (1993)
	Binary classification	Devine et al. (1993)
Error-free units	Error-free clauses/total clauses	Ishikawa (1995)
	Error-free T-units/total T-units	Robb et al. (1986); Polio et al. (1998)
	Words in EFT/total words	Robb et al. (1986); Polio et al. (1998)
Number of errors	Without classification	Carlisle (1989)
	With classification	Frantzen (1995)
Qualitative analysis		Shaw & Liu (1998); Valdes et al. (1992)

accuracy is to compare two different kinds of writing or different task variables. Kobabyshi and Rinnert (1992), for example, looked at differences in accuracy on students' translation and direct writing by counting and classifying different kinds of errors. Third, researchers have studied how accuracy differs in the writing of different groups of writers. Tarone et al. (1993) looked at age of arrival as an independent variable and measured accuracy using a holistic scale. Fourth, some researchers have examined accuracy as part of a study that examines the reliability and validity of a language test (e.g., Fischer, 1984; Wesche, 1987). And finally, some research has examined writers' change in accuracy over time (e.g., Casanve, 1994; Henry, 1996).

In Polio (1997), I addressed the problem of reliability related to measures of accuracy as well as the importance of explicit reporting of the measures. Particularly, I suggested that researchers report their scales or guidelines, report interrater reliability, and have more than one coder or rater for every essay so that mistakes (i.e., missing an error) are not as significant.

In addition, we need to consider whether these various measures are measuring the same thing, and it is doubtful that they are. Number of errors certainly does not take into account the severity of the error or how it affects comprehensibility. It is possible that a number of errors count may pick up change more easily than error-free T-unit counts. Wolfe-Quintero, Inagaki, and Kim (1998) even argue that words in EFT units is not measuring accuracy at all, but rather fluency. Furthermore, some scales or counts may or may not take into account spelling, punctuation, or lexical errors.

Another issue is whether or not accuracy should be studied qualitatively. Valdes, Haro, and Echevarriarza (1992) described writers in different levels of Spanish classes as a preliminary step in comparing them to the ACTFL guidelines, and this seems appropriate for their study. Shaw and Liu's (1998) study of language development is more problematic in that they said accuracy was studied "impressionistically" (p. 231) whereas other discourse features were quantified. Later in their paper they stated, "when we carried out counts of error per T-unit or errors per line on samples, we could find no improvement [over time]" (p. 244). This is certainly possible, but it is a strong and important claim that measures of accuracy do not change over time; it should be shown using statistics.

With measures of accuracy, we need to consider how important it is to have a real-life equivalent. For example, if significant differences in accuracy are found on a measure, but that difference is so small that it would probably not show up on a scale used in a real-life testing situation, as was the case in Polio, Fleck, and Leder (1998), I would argue that from a theoretical perspective, the findings are interesting and can add to a model of L2 writing.

Another important question is whether or not accuracy in L2 writing is interesting at all. Accuracy can certainly add to the quality of a text, but are the measures related to second language development? It could be that there is no relation between accuracy and development and, in fact, after reviewing several measures, Wolfe-Quintero et al. (1998) were not able to give a clear picture of the relation. Developmental models of L2 speaking such as Picnemann, Johnston, and Brindley (1988) specifically pay little attention to error. Accuracy, however, can certainly be a reflection of a writer's attention to what he or she is doing as well as a reflection of the scope of his or her explicit knowledge. Differences in accuracy on two different tasks, such as the studies by Zhang (1987) and Kobayashi and Rinnert (1992), can give us some indication of the processes involved in doing those tasks regardless of whether or not development or quality is being measured.

COMPLEXITY

Wolfe-Quintero et al. (1998) stated that grammatical complexity means "that a wide variety of both basic and sophisticated structures are available and can be accessed quickly, whereas a lack of complexity means that only a narrow range of basic structures are available or can be accessed" (p. 107). She cited Foster and Skehan (1996) as defining development in grammatical complexity as use of more elaborate language and a greater variety of syntactic patterning. However, the various measures of complexity presented in Table 7.3 indicate that variety does not enter in the equations. I found no holistic scales that measured complexity exclusively, yet the terms *complex sentences* and *variety of structures* often appear as part of other components on analytic scales (e.g., Fischer, 1984; Jacobs et al., 1981).

There are three ways that complexity is measured in the literature: average length of a structure, specifically words in a T-unit, frequency of a structure such as passive sentences or dependent clauses usually within a certain

TABLE 7.3
Syntactic Complexity

Average length of a structure	Words per t-unit	Cooper (1981)
Frequency of a structure	Passive	Kameen (1979)
	Dependent clause	Homburg (1984)
Complexity ratio	Clauses/t-unit	Bardovi-Harlig & Bofman (1989)
	Coordination index	Bardovi-Harlig (1992)
Qualitative analysis	Syntactic profile	Coombs (1986)

period of time, and complexity ratios, the most common being clauses per T-unit. In addition, one study (Coombs, 1986) provided a syntactic profile of two writers, describing the kinds of structures used and their frequencies.

The purposes for studying complexity are quite similar to the reasons that researchers study accuracy. The first is to examine the effect of some treatment on writing. Cooper (1981), for example, looked at the effect of sentence-combining activities on complexity, calculating words per clause, words per t-unit, and clauses per T-unit. Second, researchers may want to look at differences between certain groups of students. Bardovi-Harlig and Bofman (1989) compared the syntactic complexity of students' writing that received scores of pass and no pass on a placement exam using clauses per T-unit. Third, researchers may want to determine the effect of task differences (e.g., Zhang, 1987). Fourth, researchers may want to study change over time (Casanave, 1994; Ishikawa, 1995) or, finally, simply describe a group of writers' products (Coombs, 1986) to aid in pedagogy.

Reliability may not be a problem for measures of syntactic complexity because some of the components, such as T-units, are relatively easy to define, at least with more advanced writers.[3] Nevertheless, some of the components, such as clause, are not defined consistently. Wolfe-Quintero et al. (1998) listed the various ways that clause has been defined in the literature. Although, such definitions may not make a difference in the results, it is another decision that the researcher has to make and should be explicit about.

Validity may be more of a problem as compared to accuracy. Although researchers may not agree on what an error is, they seem to agree that accuracy is the absence of it. The ways to measure complexity are more disparate. What, for example, is the relation between words per T-unit and clauses per T-unit?[4] What does more complex syntactic structures mean? Furthermore, more complex sentences may be indicative of something, probably development, but not necessarily quality; at an advanced level, too many complex sentences may be a problem and thus at some point, variety may be important to quality.

As with a few studies that have used accuracy measures, some do not seem to be measuring either development or quality. If we consider a study such as Kobayashi and Rinnert (1992), we see that there is a difference in complexity for lower level writers on a translation task versus direct writing. The study did not examine change over time but instead may have shed some light on the cognitive processes involved in different kinds of writing. However, it seems best that we measure complexity with some theory of language development supporting that measure, such as Pienemann et al.'s (1998) work on stages of development in spoken language. If we can show how written language develops over time, we can use that information, for

example, to compare how groups of writers progress afer a specific intervention. This is not an easy task. Wolfe-Quintero (1998) made some progress in
this area studying relative clauses as an indication of development, but most
would agree that an ideal way to examine development is through a longitudinal study of writers at different levels from different L1 backgrounds. She
also reviewed many studies (Wolfe-Quintero et al., 1998) and determined
which measures of complexity correlated best with development and found
that it was average number of clauses per T-unit.

And finally, we cannot necessarily use the same measures in all studies.
Ishikawa (1995) specifically tried to find measures that showed change for
low-level writers with regard to complexity. Bardovi-Harlig (1992) argued
that clauses per T-unit analyses were intended for studying the writing of
children and that not looking at the sentence as a unit ignores distinctions
that adult writers intended to make. She argued for using a coordination
index and showed change with respect to proficiency level.

LEXICAL FEATURES

Examining the lexicon as one of several components of a text seems to be
less common than measuring accuracy or complexity, and yet there have
already been two excellent discussions of measure choice (Engber, 1995;
Laufer & Nation, 1995). Many of the measures claim to measure lexical richness. Lexical richness has less of a clear norm than accuracy and probably
exhibits more variation among native speakers as well as more topic and
task-related variation. Laufer and Nation (1995) claimed that the purpose of
measures of lexical richness is "to quantify the degree to which a writer is
using a varied and large vocabulary" (p. 307). Some measures that focus on
the lexicon may not deal only with size and variation but also with error. A
writer's lexicon can be measured by quantifying the following and probably
related constructs identified in Table 7.4: overall quality, lexical individual-
ity or originality, lexical sophistication, lexical variation or diversity, and less
commonly, lexical density, lexical accuracy, and diversity of form classes.

The first way to measure lexical quality is using a holistic scale. The vocabulary component of the Jacobs scale has been use by Hedgcock and
Lefkowitz (1992), Pennington and So (1993), and Tsang (1996). Lexical indi-
viduality or originality is calculated by dividing the number of tokens unique
to a writer by the total number of tokens. This measure looks at an individual writer in relationship to a group. Lexical sophistication is measured
by looking at the ratio of so-called advanced tokens to the total number
of words as done in Engber (1995). Laufer and Nation (1995) advocated
their Lexical Frequency Profile that takes in account writers' use of words
on several different lists, not just a set of advanced words. Lexical variation

TABLE 7.4
Lexical Features

Holistic	Jacobs scale	Hedgcock & Lefkowitz (1992), Tsang (1996)
Lexical individuality/ originality	Ratio of tokens unique to a writer/number of tokens	Laufer (1991)
Lexical sophistication	Advanced token/total tokens Lexical Frequency Profile	Engber (1995) Laufer & Nation (1995)
Lexical variation/ diversity	Different types/total tokens Type/token with error	Frantzen (1995) Engber (1995)
Lexical density	Lexical words/total words With error	Laufer (1991) Engber (1995)
Lexical errors	Number of lexical errors Lexical errors/total errors	Kobayashi & Rinnert (1992) Chastain (1991)
Diversity of form class	Five ratios for nouns, verbs, adjectives, adverbs, modifiers, each in relation to total number of lexical words	McClure (1991)

or diversity is measured doing a type:token ratio (e.g., Laufer, 1991). Lexical density is measured by dividing the number of tokens by the number of lexical tokens (e.g., Engber, 1995). Several of the aforementioned measures may or may not take into consideration whether the words are used correctly. And finally two less commonly used measures include the number of lexical errors as in Kobayshi and Rinnert (1992) and the diversity of form classes as counted in McClure (1991).

Researchers have examined the lexicon of L2 writers' texts to examine how L2 writers' quality differs on writing tasks (Chastain, 1990; Kobayshi & Rinnert, 1992), how a program or classroom-level intervention affects the written product (Hedgcock & Lefkowitz, 1992; Tsang, 1996), and whether we see a change in measures of lexical quality over time (Laufer, 1991). In addition, Harley and King (1989) studied how young L2 immersion learners differed from L1 children, and Pennington and So (1993) studied how learners' quality compared in their L1 writing and their L2 writing. Some studies have focused more specifically on critically evaluating the measures. Engber (1995) studied which measures correlated best with overall quality and Laufer and Nation (1995) showed how their measure correlated better than other measures with an independent test of productive vocabulary as well as showing differences across proficiency levels.

Because most of the lexical measures must be carried out on a computer, interrater reliability is not an issue unless one is concerned with eliminating words that are not used correctly or identifying lexical errors, in which cases reliability should be reported. And this is the first choice that the researcher has to make, whether or not to consider error in the measures. Engber (1995) found that lexical variation minus error correlated best with raters judgments of overall quality. This is certainly not surprising, and it emphasizes the need to identify misused words before completing the calculations if one is concerned with quality.

With regard to the other measures, lexical originality is the measure of an individual against a group and thus a mean group score is meaningless. Lexical variation can be affected by essay length. As Engber (1995) pointed out, the longer the essay, the more likely that lexical items will be repeated. She dealt with this problem by analyzing segments of the same length. With regard to lexical density, Laufer and Nation (1995) argued that this measure is related to structural properties of an essay, not the lexicon, as is probably diversity of form classes. For lexical sophistication, the researcher has to identify a set of advanced words and this is obviously problematic. Laufer and Nation examined the proportion of words on frequency lists and a university word list. Because they show both concurrent validity and construct validity, in addition to reliability (similar scores across two essays from each participant), this is probably one of the better measures to use.

With the lexical measures, we need to be concerned with which ones are measuring quality and which development. Laufer and Nation's (1995) profile appears to measure change over time, and they found that their subjects used increasingly more sophisticated words. Risk takers who use advanced words incorrectly may actually detract from the quality of an essay but will score higher on the Lexical Frequency Profile. None of these measures seem to be based on a theory of lexical acquisition, other than more is better, but the lack of theory of lexical acquisition in second language acquisition (SLA) seems to force a data-driven approach.

CONTENT

Measures of content, as shown in Table 7.5, include holistic scales and other objective measures. Judgements about the quality of an essay's content are most often made through a holistic scale with a trait called simply *content* as on the Jacobs scale (e.g., Tsang, 1996). Primary trait scoring was used by Carlisle (1989) to evaluate the rhetorical effectiveness of writing, but the traits are not given. Hamp-Lyons and Henning (1991) used scales for mulitiple traits related to the content of a text including: interest, referencing, and argumentation. Fischer (1984) used scales for pertinence and communicative value. Others have tried to quantify features such as Kepner (1991) who counted the number of higher level propositions whereas Friedlander (1990)

TABLE 7.5
Content

Holistic scales	Jacobs scale	Hedgcock & Lefkowitz (1992); Tsang (1996)
Primary/multiple trait scoring	Specific traits not given Interestingness, referencing, argumentation	Carlisle (1989) Hamp-Lyons & Henning (1991)
Higher level propositions	Analysis, comparison & contrast, inference & interpretation, evaluation	Kepner (1991)
Number of details		Friedlander (1990)
Qualitative analysis	Topics included in essay Commentary on task	Valdes et al. (1992) Henry (1996)

counted the number of details. And finally, Henry (1996) and Valdes et al. (1992) simply presented a qualitative description of the content including a list of topics the writers covered and whether or not they commented on the task itself.

The research questions that have been asked with regard to essay content include: How does students' writing differ under different planning conditions? (Friedlander, 1990); how does students' writing change over time? (Henry, 1996; Valdes et al., 1992); what is the effect of a particular treatment on the content of students' writing? (Carlisle, 1989; Tsang, 1996); and, can traits related to content be reliably and validly measured? (Hamp-Lyons & Henning, 1991).

Ordinal scales are used to measure and evaluate quality. Of course, the scales should be reported in the study as well as interrater reliability. The scales are all intended to evaluate the quality of the content. One needs to determine whether they fit the demands of the writing task and whether they can distinguish among writers in a given population. In order to determine the construct validity of the scales, more studies such as Hamp-Lyons and Henning's (1991) are needed.

We need to consider also the less commonly used content-related measures and what exactly they are targeting. Kepner (1991) attempted to count the number of higher level propositions that included "propositions or propositional clusters within the student text which exemplified the cognitive processes of analysis, comparison/contrast, inference/interpretation/ and/or evaluation"[5] (p. 308). It seems that these might be difficult to identify, but Kepner reported a reliability of 0.84 on the counts. This measure may simply correlate well with length, as the counts were not reported as a function of number of words, and thus high-interrater reliability was achieved. Friedlander (1990) said that he counted the number of details, but he did not operationalize this feature; this too would simply increase with the number of words. One possible related measure that I did not find used in the L2 writing literature is the counting of idea units. Idea units come from work by Kintsch and Keenan (1973), and have been used in psychology with high reliability reported (e.g., Snowdon et al., 1996). This might be a measure worth exploring through which one can quantify the density of content.

MECHANICS

Only a few studies have attempted to quantify mechanics, as shown in Table 7.6. This term comes from a component of the Jacobs scale that includes descriptors on spelling, punctuation, capitalization, and indentation. Studies that have used other scales include descriptors related to what Jacobs et al. (1981) called mechanics listed under linguistic accuracy (e.g., Hamp-Lyons & Henning, 1991; Wesche, 1987).

The studies that have measured mechanics all have used the Jacobs scale, but mechanics was not the focus of any of the studies; it was used in evaluating several components to answer various questions regarding a program-level treatment (Tsang, 1996) or feedback (Hedgcock & Lefkowitz, 1992). In addition, Pennington and So (1993) reported a mechanics score when studying how writers' products differed with regard to quality in their L1 and L2.

The fact that statistical significance is not shown on this component in any of these studies, but is shown on other components of the scale, could indicate that the scale may not be reliably distinguishing quality regarding mechanics.

A second issue is whether or not mechanics is a construct at all. Are capitalization, indentation and punctuation related? Punctuation, it could be argued, is more closely related to syntax. There does not seem to be any theoretical motivation for grouping these features together or even measuring them at all; the motivation seems to be that mechanics is part of widely used scale that may be appropriate for measuring other traits. If in fact any of these components are interesting, there is probably a more precise way to measure them. It seems, however, that this area is of little interest to

TABLE 7.6
Mechanics

Jacobs scale	Pennington & So, (1993); Tsang (1996)

researchers of L2 writing, and thus no one has explored it extensively. In fact, in studies measuring accuracy, spelling is often explicitly disregarded (Polio, 1997).

COHERENCE AND DISCOURSE FEATURES

The category coherence and discourse features covers a diverse group of studies that do not fall into any of the other aforementioned categories. They fall into two sets. As shown in Table 7.7, the first set uses some type of scale to evaluate the overall coherence or organization of a text. This includes studies such as those previously mentioned that used the Jacobs scale and others that have used their own measures of coherence (Devine et al., 1993; Tarone et al., 1993). The measures in these studies are relatively straightforward and have examined the effects of a treatment or difference among groups of writers. They are all concerned with the quality of the text's organization.

The remainder of the studies are more varied in what they are examining but seem to have a similar purpose; they are concerned with how native speakers' (NS) and nonnative speakers' (NNS) texts differ or how low- and high-rated essays differ. Of this second set of studies, some, such

TABLE 7.7
Coherence and Discourse Features

Holistic scales	Jacobs scale – organization	Tsang (1996)
	Coherence	Tarone et al. (1993)
	Others scales	Devine et al. (1993)
Overall organization	Qualitative description	Henry (1996); Kaplan (1966)
	Classification using specific categories	Kubota (1998)
	Location of main idea	Kubota (1998)
	Topic structure analysis	Schneider & Connor (1990)
Metadiscourse features	Several features	Intaraprawat & Steffenson (1995); Mauranen (1993)
	Semantic and grammatical analysis of statements of doubt and uncertainty	Hyland & Milton (1997)
	Qualitative analysis of assertions	Allison (1995)
Cohesive devices	Repetition	Reynolds (1995); Bartelt (1993)
	Conjuctions, prepositions	Reid (1992); Schleppegrell (1996)
Register features	Many features related to register	Shaw & Liu (1998)

as Kaplan's (1966) early work, simply provide a description of the overall organization of L2 writers' texts with the goal of showing how writers from different cultures organize their texts differently. Others have given more precise descriptions such as Kubota (1998) who examined discourse patterns of Japanese students writing in both English and Japanese. She developed a classification system to code each essay's overall organization as well as where in the essay the main topic was located. Schneider and Connor (1990) used topical structure analysis to study the flow of topics throughout essays of low- and high-rated TWE exams.

Several studies have examined metadiscourse features, which Intaraprawat and Steffensen (1995) defined as "those facets of a text which make the organization of the text explicit, provide information about the writer's attitude toward the text content, and engage the reader in interaction" (p. 253). They coded features such as hedges, emphatics, and attitude markers in low- and high-rated essays. Hyland and Milton (1997) examined markers of doubt and uncertainty in native and nonnative essays. Allison (1995) gave a qualitative description of NNSs' use of assertions pointing out problem areas that might be addressed through pedagogy.

Various studies on cohesive devices have been completed. Bartelt (1992) provided a qualitative description of repetition in the texts of Apachean English writers. Reynolds (1995) in a comparison of NS and NNS essays, quantified repetition by coding the type of repetition and the density of links and bonds (as defined by Hoey, 1991). Others, such as Reid (1992) studied cohesion in native and nonnative texts by quantifying pronouns, conjunctions, subordinate conjunction openers, and prepositions.

Shaw and Liu's (1998) study is unique in that it examined a group of features considered to reflect register, including some syntactic features. They analyzed essays from students who were studying in 2- and 3-month programs and found significant change from the beginning to end of instruction. Statistically significant changes were found for various features including the use of contractions, first person singular, connectives, and passive voice. They argued that their subjects' writing became less like speech and more like written language over even a relatively short time.

Validity is not an issue with most of the studies here in that many of them, except those using holistic scales, do not claim to be measuring a construct, but rather are describing NNS texts or poor texts, probably to improve pedagogy. Shaw and Liu's (1998) work claimed to measure register features and is based a substantial amount of previous work in that area.

Ironically, most of these studies, unlike many of those previously discussed, do not examine the effect of teaching on the written product. One could argue that these types of features are more susceptible to instruction than interventions that target accuracy or complexity, for example. Madden and Myers (1998) examined writers' changes in certain metadiscourse features after instruction including hedging, summarizing, and highlighting. Because they did not have a control group, it is difficult to draw precise conclusions, but they did show an awareness that this may be an interesting area of study to examine the effects of instruction.

Detailed reporting in studies of discourse features is very important. Schneider and Connor (1991), in their study of topic progression, pointed out that inconsistent findings may be due to differences in coding and lack of information on reliability. They provided detailed descriptions of their analysis, including an example of their coding system on a complete essay. Reynolds' (1995) study is another from this category of research that provided a precise description and examples of his coding scheme. Such reporting is very helpful to other researchers who may want to examine the same features.

FLUENCY

Much has been written about fluency in L2 speaking (e.g., Lennon, 1990; Schmidt, 1992), but with the exception of Wolfe-Quintero et al. (1998)'s study, it has not been addressed directly in the L2 writing literature.

The term *fluent* may not mean how quickly the writer writes but rather how native like the writing sounds. This point is reflected in one of the holistic scales of fluency (Tarone et al., 1993) whose scale refers to "nativeness, standardness, length, ease of reading, idiomaticity" (p. 170). Other scales may include the word *fluent* under other components such as organization (e.g., Jacobs et al., 1981; Wesche, 1987) but do not claim to measure it as a separate component. In addition, other studies have included measures under fluency that are generally used for either complexity or lexical richness (Chastain, 1991; Frantzen, 1995).

There are two ways that have been claimed to measure fluency, as shown in Table 7.8. The first, and least common, is through the use of a holistic scale as referred to above. The second is by counting the amount of production according to some unit, generally words, but occasionally clauses or T-units. In addition, other measures more commonly used for complexity or lexical quality have been called *measures of fluency* such as clauses per T-unit, average length of T-unit, and type–token ratio.

Measures of fluency have been used to examine the effect of various interventions, such as Robb, Ross, and Shortreed (1986), who used total number of words and total number of clauses to look at the performance of groups who received different types of feedback. Henry (1996) studied the

TABLE 7.8
Fluency

Holistic scales		Tarone et al. (1993)
Amount of production	Words	Henry (1996); Robb et al. (1990)
	T-units	Ishikawa (1995)
	Clauses	Robb et al. (1990)
Other measures generally	Type/token	Frantzen (1995)
not considered fluency	Average length of t-units	Frantzen (1995); Chastain (1991)
	Clause per t-unit	Frantzen (1995)

essays of learners of Russian as a foreign language and quantified change over time. Zhang (1987) studied performance on different writing tasks. In addition, Intaraprawat and Steffensen (1995) examined how highly and poorly rated essays differed with regard to number of words.

The important issue here is defining fluency. Wolfe-Quintero et al., (1998) concluded the following:

> In our view, fluency means that more words and more structures are accessed in a limited time, whereas a lack of fluency means that only a few words or structures are accessed. Learners who have the same number of productive vocabulary items or productive structures may retrieve them with differing degrees of efficiency. Fluency is not a measure of how sophisticated or accurate the words or structures are, but a measure of the sheer number of words or structural units a writer is able to include in their writing within a particular period of time. (p. 25)

If we accept this definition, the measure becomes trivial. We should measure fluency by counting the number of words produced in a given time. Counting T-units or clauses would penalize writers who wrote longer structures thus reducing the raw numbers of T-units or clauses. Even reliability becomes somewhat trivial. Although there may be some discrepancy over what constitutes a word (e.g., contractions), such arbitrary decision will most likely be of no consequence.

Should we care about fluency as part of the writing process? Fluency may have no relation to quality or, possibly, a negative one. If, however, L2 writers can write more quickly, particularly if quality does not suffer, as a result of an intervention, then we can say that development has taken place. If we find that writers are more fluent on one writing task as opposed to another then that may tell us something about the cognitive processes of completing the different writing tasks.

REVISION

Studying revision by examining the written product is a limited way to look at revision in that we can study only what kinds of changes were made from one draft to the next and not what changes were made on an individual piece of writing. Furthermore, we cannot find out why the writer made the revisions, as we can with other methods that probe the writing process. However, being able to classify changes a writer makes without having to actually observe the process is potentially very useful in that a large number of essays can be examined; process studies using techniques such as think alouds and stimulated recall are so time consuming that they are restricted to a few subjects.

Table 7.9 shows four ways that revision can be coded. Ferris (1997) was the only one who used an ordinal scale (from 1 to 6) to code the revisions; she coded only those parts of the essays on which the teachers made comments on the first draft; thus the scale reflected the quantity and quality of the change in relation to the teachers comments. Mendonca and Johnson (1994) also coded changes in relation to comments, but rather peer comments, and they used a categorical classification system determining whether a peer comment prompted revision and whether a revision was prompted by a peer comment. Other studies have used more complex classification systems. Hall (1990) coded revision with regard to level, type, and purpose. Connor and Asenavage (1994) and Phinney and Khouri (1993) both used Faigley and Witte's (1981) hierarchical system.

Researchers coded revision to find out how students revised in response to either peer (Connor & Asanavege, 1994; Mendoca & Johnson, 1994) or teacher comments (Ferris, 1997). Two other questions that have resulted in researchers coding revision are: Do writers differ in how they revise in their

TABLE 7.9
Revision

Ordinal scale	Score from 1 to 6 on quantity and quality of change	Ferris (1997)
Binary classification	Coded in relationship to whether prompted by peer comment	Mendonca & Johnson (1994)
Multiple coding of each change	Level, type, purpose	Hall (1990)
Hierarchical coding of each change	Faigley & Witte (1981) system Faigley & Witte (1984) system	Connor & Asenavage (1994) Phinney & Khouri (1993)

L1 and L2? (Hall, 1990); and how does experience with a computer and writing proficiency affect revision (Phinney & Khouri, 1993).

The first issue of concern is what the unit of analysis is used in these studies. What are the researchers coding? How does one distinguish one change from two changes? In Ferris' (1997) study, she coded parts of the essays that the teacher commented on. The unit of analysis varied with what was coded. That is, a writer may have changed only a word or added several sentences, and both would have been coded as one change. In her study and in Mendonca and Johnson's (1994) study, such coding seems appropriate to the research questions. Ferris, in fact, incorporated the amount of change in her scale. At first glance it seems problematic that she was mixing amount of change and quality of change, but she never treated the scores on the scale as ordinal data in her analysis, only categorical.

Faigley and Witte's (1981) hierarchical system, at the highest level, codes surface versus text-based changes, the latter also called *meaning changes*. In addition, they classify whether those changes involve an addition, deletion, substitution, permutation, and so on. In their 1981 study, they use the sentence as their unit of analysis in that if a change involved more than one sentence (e.g., a paragraph added), each sentence would be counted as a change. They reported the changes as a ratio of changes per 1,000 words. It appears that Connor and Asenavage (1994) followed this system, but Phinney and Khouri (1993) reported the length of the change classifying it a graphic, word, phrase, clause, sentence, or multisentence based on a later study by Faigley and Witte (1984). Hall, (1990) too coded the length of the change separately. The idea of a change of any length is misleading and does not distinguish between adding one or five sentences. Coding the length of the change may be problematic as well. What if, for example, two related sentences are added to different parts of a paragraph? Is this to be counted as two sentence-length changes or one multisentential change? Thus, it is not completely clear what is being compared from one draft to the next. Furthermore, given the hierarchical nature of language, how does one distinguish one change from two, particularly if two noncontinguous changes are related or one change dictates the other?

One possible solution is to compare versions according T-units. This system was attempted in Polio and Knibloe (1999). If there was no comparable T-unit in one of the drafts, a change was considered an addition or deletion. We did not consider the length of the change in a T-unit. On one hand, over 80% reliability was achieved, but on the other hand, the system may have been too rigid in that we were comparing T-units that the writer had no intention of being related. It also did not take into account the length of a change within a T-unit.

With regard to reliability of these coding systems, Ferris (1997) reported a fairly respectable reliability at 0.82 and Mendoca and Johnson (1994) did not report any. Hall (1990) and Phinney and Khouri (1993) did not report reliability, and Connor and Asenavage (1994) reported almost complete agreement on a portion of the data. Ferris made the point that coders in her study had difficulty agreeing on a minimal versus a substantive change. In Polio and Knibloe (1999), we could not agree on a micro- versus macrochange. The latter according to Faigley and Witte (1981) change a summary of the text. It was only by eliminating this distinction that we were able to achieve more than 80% agreement. Distinguishing between a surface and meaning change is problematic as well. Faigley and Witte (1981) said that a surface change is one that does not bring new information to the text. We took this literally and thus coded the addition of an intensifier as a meaning change. We rationalized this by arguing that the writer was probably paying attention to and concerned with the meaning of the text, not simply the grammar. It is not clear if this was the correct decision, but we achieved reliability, and we made our decisions explicit. One recommendation here is that studies include excerpts of coded essays and examples of the coding categories.

IMPLICATIONS FOR EMPIRICAL RESEARCH ON L2 WRITING

This chapter identified the range of choices that researchers of L2 writing have to make when analyzing L2 writers' texts and the various issues that they need to be concerned with. This chapter ends by extending these issues to L2 writing research in general.

Reporting

Researchers should be more explicit when reporting methodology. According to the *Publication Manual of the American Psychological Association*, enough information needs to be reported so that another researcher can replicate the study (see Polio & Gass, 1997 for further discussion). This would include printing any rating scales used, carefully defining terms (i.e., What is an error? What is a meaning change?), and providing readers with examples of these to supplement the definitions. Even more helpful is when a study provides an example of a fully coded text, such as the one presented in Schneider and Connor (1990).

Full reporting of methodology is important to all types of L2 writing research. Research on teacher or student attitudes using questionnaires should include the questionnaires in the appendix. Qualitative research using interviews to get at student or teacher beliefs, for example, should include the interview questions. Research on the writing process often analyzes think-aloud protocols or stimulated recall interviews. Samples of these and the coding schemes used should be fully described with a definition of terms and examples just as for analyses of L2 writers' texts. For examples of such studies see Bosher (1998) or Sasaki (1999).

Reliability

As noted earlier, reliability is an important, yet neglected, issue in measuring features of L2 writers' texts. Polio (1997) reported that more than one half of the studies examining accuracy did not report reliability, and Wolf-Quintero et al. (1998) reported that the one half of the studies that used holistic ratings did not report reliability. This is a problem because poor reliability can mask significant relation and hence nonsignificant findings should be very cautiously reported. One case in point is Truscott's (1996) argument against error correction in which he cited studies (e.g., Robb et al., 1986[6]; Semke, 1984) that report nonsignificant findings but do not report reliability.

Research on aspects of writing other than the text also needs to be concerned with reliability. Most research on the writing process that codes stimulated recall interviews or think-aloud protocols do not report reliability of the coding schemes, an exception being Sasaki (1999). Survey research needs to be concerned with reliability as well. Confusing formats can cause inconsistent responses, as can giving L2 writers surveys in their L2, possibly causing them to misinterpret questions.

Validity

To better understand the issue of validity in studying L2 writers' texts, we first need to consider why the text is being studied. Looking at the various research questions asked when studying texts, excluding studies such as Allison (1995) that simply describe a particular feature, we see that researchers are usually ultimately concerned with quality of a text or with development, writers' change over time.[7] The problem is that quality and language development can be obscured. Consider the following example: If a group of students is taught a new technique for editing and it is found that after one class, the experimental group's papers have fewer errors than a control group, we can say then that the technique has improved the quality of their essays, realizing that accuracy is only one contributor to the quality of a text (Sweedler-Brown, 1993).

Development is, however, is more complex. It would be difficult to argue that the hypothetical experimental group's language has developed after one class. Several studies, one of my own (Polio et al., 1998) included, examined the effect of some intervention over a period of time, not just a day or week. Are these studies concerned with quality or development? That is, are they arguing that such interventions will improve the quality of an essay, perhaps because the writer has learned some new skill, such as editing, or are they also saying that the writer's language has developed due to the intervention? I would argue that we cannot interpret fewer errors as an indication of development.[8]

And so what is needed are studies with a goal to validate measures of development and quality. These would include studies such as Wolfe-Quintero's (1998) study of development using a group difference's approach,[9] as well as Laufer and Nation's (1995) study of vocabulary development measures and Ishikawa's (1995) study of accuracy and complexity measures. Engber's (1995) study attempted to find a lexical measure that correlated best with quality. That measure may not, however, be measuring a learner's acquisition or development.

With regard to other types of research, particularly qualitative research, the idea of validity is somewhat nebulous. On one hand, some argue that validity (and reliablity and generalizability) cannot be discussed in the traditional sense in qualitative research. (For a discussion, see Janesick, 1994, who suggested moving beyond the "trinity of psychometrica," p. 217.) On the other hand, triangulation, used in qualitative research to check findings through different instruments or from different participants' perspectives, has been referred to by some as checking validity (e.g., Fraenkel & Wallen, 1996).

I hope that this chapter has provided a useful taxonomy for those wanting to examine L2 writers' texts. More importantly, I hope that I have raised some issues that researchers and readers of L2 writing studies need to be concerned with. Simply taking the results of empirical research at face value, without thinking about the methods used to get those results, can actually move the field backward, a field that has made much progress.

ACKNOWLEDGMENTS

This research was produced with partial support from a U.S. Department of Education Grant (CFDA 84.229 and P229A60012-96). The contents do not necessarily represent the policies of the Department of Education, and endorsement by the federal government should not be assumed.

ENDNOTES

1. The studies included here are mostly from major journals as opposed to unpublished dissertations and conference presentations. Whereas I hope that the taxonomy is fairly comprehensive, it is not my intention to provide an exhaustive list of references of research on written L2 texts, only representative examples.

2. Additional examples of empirical research are provided in tables throughout this chapter Although space prohibits a discussion of all these studies, the references are provided as a resource for those who want further examples.

3. Polio (1997) achieved more than 0.99 interrater reliability on number of T-units in a group of high-intermediate ESL essays.

4. In fact, Wolfe-Quintero et al. (1998) argued that words per T-unit is not measuring complexity but rather fluency, and they cited a study of spoken language (Ortega, 1995) that supports this claim.

5. These are elaborated on in Quellmalz (1985).

6. Robb, Ross, and Shortreed (1986) reported an average reliability of several measures but none on the accuracy measures alone.

7. As discussed earlier, some studies that measure accuracy and complexity are actually getting at the writing process in that their research question is concerned with neither quality nor development but rather task demands. Kobayashi and Rinnert (1992) looked at differences in writers' accuracy on two tasks: a translation and a direct writing. Zhang (1987) looked at how the cognitive complexity of a prompt affected accuracy. These studies are not concerned with development, or with quality; rather, they are concerned with the attentional resources that the writer is allocating to various things that one has to do when one writes. In fact, L2 writing research has only touched on these issues. Researchers in L2 acquisition have been investigating the various components of task demands and their influence on production. Skehan (1998) reviewed much of this research that is potentially useful to examining the effect of writing task demands on L2 writers' texts.

8. Fewer errors could certainly co-occur with development, but if we look to early research from L2 acquisition, we see that, as first argued by Schacter and Celce-Murcia (1977), problem structures can simply be avoided, and this could account for a decrease in errors Alternatively, if a writer is skilled at avoiding problematic structures, the quality of his or her writing could improve, but there has not necessarily been language development. Furthermore, an increase in error could be indicative of some kind of restructuring that will in turn lead to development.

9. See Cumming (1996) for a thorough discussion of the various ways to validate measures.

REFERENCES

Allison, D. (1995). Assertions and alternatives: Helping ESL undergraduates extend their choice in academic writing. *Journal of Second Language Writing, 4,* 1–16.

American Psychological Association. (1994). *Publication manual of the American Psychological Association* (4th ed.). Washington, DC: American Psychological Association.

Bardovi-Harlig, K., (1992). A second look at T-unit analysis: Reconsidering the sentence. *TESOL Quarterly, 26,* 390–395.

Bardovi-Harlig, K., & Bofman, T. (1989). Attainment of syntactic and morphological accuracy by advanced language learners. *Studies in Second Language Acquisition, 11,* 17–34.

Bartelt, H. (1992). Rhetorical transfer in Apachean English. In S. Gass & L. Selinker (Eds.), *Language transfer in language learning* (pp. 101–108). Amsterdam: Benjamins.

Bosher, S. (1998). The composing process of three Southeast Asian writers at the post-secondary level: An exploratory study. *Journal of Second Language Writing, 7,* 205–242.

Braine, G. (1996). ESL students in first-year writing courses: ESL versus mainstream classes. *Journal of Second Language Writing, 5,* 91–107.

Carlisle, R. (1989). The writing of Anglo and Hispanic elementary school students in bilingual, submersion, and regular programs. *Studies in Second Language Acquisition, 11,* 257–280.

Casanave, C. (1994). Language development in students' journals. *Journal of Second Language Writing, 3,* 179–201.

Chastain, K. (1990). Characteristics of graded and ungraded compositions. *Modern Language Journal, 74,* 10–14.

Conner, U., & Asenavage, K. (1994). Peer response groups in ESL writing classes: How much impact on revision? *Journal of Second Language Writing, 3,* 257–276.

Coombs, V. (1986). Syntax and communicative strategies in intermediate German composition. *The Modern Language Journal, 70,* 114–124.

Cooper, T. C. (1981). Sentence combining: An experiment in teaching writing. *Modern Language Journal, 65,* 158–165.

Cumming, A. (1996). Introduction: The concept of validation in language testing. In A. Cumming & R. Berwick (Eds.), *Validation in language testing* (p. 1–14). Clevedon, UK: Multilingual Matters.

Devine, J., Railey, K., & Boshoff, P. (1993). The implications of cognitive models in L1 and L2 writing. *Journal of Second Language Writing, 2,* 203–225.

Engber, C. (1995). The relationship of lexical proficiency to the quality of ESL compositions. *Journal of Second Language Writing, 4,* 139–155.

Faigley, L., & Witte, S. (1981). Analyzing revision. *College Composition and Communication, 32,* 400–414.

Faigley, L., & Witte, S. (1984). Measuring the effects of revisions on text structure. In R. Beach & L. S. Bridwell (Eds.), *New directions in composition research* (pp. 95–108). New York: Guildford Press.

Ferris, D. (1997). The influence of teacher commentary on student revision. *TESOL Quarterly, 31,* 315–352.

Fischer, R. (1984). Testing written communicative competence in French. *The Modern Language Journal, 68,* 13–20.

Foster, P., & Skehan, P. (1996). The influence of planning and task type on second language performance. *Studies in Second Language Acquisition, 18,* 299–323.

Fraenkel, J., & Wallen, N. (1996). *How to design and evaluate educational research.* New York: McGraw Hill.

Frantzen, D. (1995). The effects of grammar supplementation on written accuracy in an intermediate Spanish content course. *Modern Language Journal, 79,* 329–344.

Friedlander, A. (1990). Composing in English: Effects of a first language on writing in English as Second Language. In B. Kroll (Ed.), *Second language writing: Research insight for the classroom* (pp. 109–125). Cambridge: Cambridge University Press.

Hall, C. (1990). Managing the complexity of revising across languages. *TESOL Quarterly, 24,* 43–60.

Hamp-Lyons, L., & Henning, G. (1991). Communicative writing profiles: An investigation of the transferability of a multiple-trait scoring instrument across ESL writing assessment contexts. *Language Learning, 41,* 337–373.

Hamp-Lyons, L., & Mathias, S. P. (1994). Examining expert judgments of task difficulty on essay tests. *Journal of Second Language Writing, 3,* 49–68.

Harley, B., & King, M. (1989). Verb lexis in the written compositions of young L2 learners. *Studies in Second Language Acquisition, 11,* 415–439.

Hedgcock, J., & Lefkowitz, N. (1992). Collaborative oral/aural revision in foreign language writing instruction. *Journal of Second Language Writing, 3,* 255–276.

Henry, K. (1996). Early L2 writing development: A study of autobiographical essays by university-level students of Russian. *The Modern Language Journal, 80,* 309–326.

Hoey, M. (1991). *Patterns of lexis in text.* New York: Oxford University Press.

Homburg, T. (1984). Holistic evaluation of ESL compositions: Can it be validated objectively? *TESOL Quarterly, 18,* 87–107.

Hyland, K., & Milton, J. (1997). Qualification and certainty in L1 and L2 students' writing. *Journal of Second Language Writing, 6,* 183–205.

Intaraprawat, P., & Steffensen, M. S. (1995). The use of metadiscourse in good and poor ESL essays. *Journal of Second Language Writing, 4,* 253–272.

Ishikawa, S. (1995). Objective measurement of low-proficiency EFL narrative writing. *Journal of Second Language Writing, 4,* 51–69.

Jacobs, H., Zinkgraf, S., Wormuth, D. Hartfiel, V., & Hughey, J. (1981). *Testing ESL composition: A practical approach.* Rowley, MA: Newbury House.

Janesick, V. (1994). The dance of qualitative research design: Metaphor, methodolatry, and meaning. In N. Denzin, & Y. Lincoln (Eds.), *Handbook of qualitative research* (pp. 199–208). Thousand Oaks, CA: Sage.

Kameen, P. (1979). Syntactic skill and ESL writing quality. In C. Yorio, K. Perkins, & J. Schachter (Eds.), *On TESOL '79: The learner in focus* (pp. 343–364). Washington, DC: TESOL.

Kaplan, R. (1966). Cultural thought patterns in inter-cultural education. *Language Learning, 16,* 1–20.

Kepner, C. (1991). An experiment in the relationship of types of written feedback to the development of second-language writing skills. *Modern Language Journal, 75,* 305–313.

Kern, R. G., & Schultz, J. M. (1992). The effects of composition instruction on intermediate level French students' writing performance: Some preliminary findings. *The Modern Language Journal, 76,* 1–13.

Kintsch, W., & Keenan, J. (1973). Reading rate and retention as a function of the number of propositions in the base structure of sentences. *Cognitive Psychology, 5,* 257–274.

Kobayashi, H., & Rinnert, C. (1992). Effects of first language on second language writing: Translation vs. direct composition. *Language Learning, 42,* 183–215.

Kubota, R. (1998). An investigation of L1-L2 transfer in writing among Japanese university students: Implications for contrastive rhetoric. *Journal of Second Language Writing, 7,* 43–68.

Laufer, B. (1991). The development of L2 lexis in the expression of the advanced learner. *Modern Language Journal, 75,* 440–448.

Laufer, B., & Nation, P. (1995). Vocabulary size and use: Lexical richness in L2 written production. *Applied Linguistics, 16,* 307–322.

Lennon, P. (1990). Investigating fluency in EFL: A quantitative approach. *Language Learning, 40,* 387–417.

Madden, C., & Myers, C. (1998, March). *Investigating genre as instruction in an EAP context.* Paper presented at the American Association of Applied Linguistics, Seattle, WA.

Mauranen, A. (1993). Contrastive ESP rhetoric: Metatext in Finnish-English economics texts. *English for Specific Purposes, 12,* 3–22.

McClure, E. (1991). A comparison of lexical strategies in L1 and L2 written English narratives. *Pragmatics and Language Learning, 2,* 141–154.

Mendonca, C., & Johnson, K. (1994). Peer review negotiations: Revision activities in ESL writing instruction. *TESOL Quarterly, 28,* 745–769.

Ortega, L. (1995). *Planning and second language oral performance.* Unpublished thesis, University of Hawaii, Manoa.

Pennington, M., & So, S. (1993). Comparing writing process and product across two languages: a study of 6 Singaporean University student writers. *Journal of Second Language Writing, 2,* 41–63.

Phinney, M., & Khouri, S. (1993). Computers, revision, and ESL writers: The role of experience. *Journal of Second Language Writing, 2,* 257–277.

Pienemann, M., Johnston, M., & Brindley, G. (1988). Constructing an acquisition-based procedure for second language assessment. *Studies in Second Language Acquisition, 10,* 217–244.

Polio, C. (1997). Measures of linguistic accuracy in second language writing research. *Language Learning, 47,* 101–143.

Polio, C., Fleck, C., & Leder, N. (1998). "If I only had more time:" ESL learners' changes in linguistic accuracy on essay revisions. *Journal of Second Language Writing, 7,* 43–68.

Polio, C., & Gass, S. (1997). Replication and reporting: A commentary. *Studies in Second Language Acquisition, 19,* 499–508.

Polio, C., & Knibloe, D. (1999). The relationship between sentence-level revision and changes in linguistic accuracy. Paper presented at the TESOL convention, New York City.

Quellmalz, E. (1985). Needed: Better methods for testing higher-order thinking skills. *Educational Leadership, 43,* 29–35.

Reid, J. (1992). A computer text analysis of four cohesion devices in English discourse by native and nonnative writers. *Journal of Second Language Writing,* 79–107.

Reynolds, D. (1995). Repetition in nonnative speaker writing: More than quantity. *Studies in Second Language Acquisition, 17,* 185–210.

Robb T., Ross, S., & Shortreed, I. (1986). Salience of feedback on error and its effect on EFL writing quality. *TESOL Quarterly, 20,* 83–95.

Sasaki, M. (1999). *Empirical model of L2 writing process.* Manuscript submitted for publication.

Schachter, J., & Celce-Murcia, M. (1977). Some reservations concerning error analysis. *TESOL Quarterly, 11,* 441–451.

Schleppegrell, M. (1996). Conjunction in spoken English and ESL writing. *Applied Linguistics, 17,* 271–285.

Schmidt, R. (1992). Psychological mechanisms underlying second language fluency. *Studies in Second Language Acquisition, 11,* 129–158.

Schneider, M., & Connor, U. (1990). Analyzing topical structure in ESL essays: Not all topics are equal. *Studies in Second Language Acquisition, 12,* 411–427.

Semke, H. (1984). Effects of the red pen. *Foreign Language Annals, 17,* 195–202.

Shaw, P., & Liu, E. (1998). What develops in the development of second-language writing? *Applied Linguistics, 19,* 225–254.

Skehan, P. (1998). *A cognitive approach to language learning.* Oxford: Oxford University Press.

Snowdon, D., Kemper, S., Mortimer, J., Greiner, L., Wekstein, D., & Markesbery, W. (1996). Linguistic ability in early life and cognitive function and Alzheimer's disease in late life. *Journal of the American Medical Association, 275,* 528–532.

Sweedler-Brown, C. (1993). ESL essay evaluation: The influence of sentence-level and rhetorical features. *Journal of Second Language Writing, 2,* 3–17.

Tarone, E., Downing, B., Cohen, A., Gillette, S., Murie, R., & Dailey, B. (1993). The writing of Southeast Asian-American students in secondary school and university. *Journal of Second Language Writing, 2,* 149–172.

Tsang, W. K. (1996). Comparing the effects of reading and writing on writing performance. *Applied Linguistics, 17,* 210–233.

Truscott, J. (1996). The case against grammar correction in L2 writing classes. *Language Learning, 46,* 327–369.

Valdes, G., Haro, P., & Echevarriarza, M. (1992). The development of writing abilities in a foreign language: contributions toward a general theory of L2 writing. *The Modern Language Journal, 76,* 333–352.

Wesche, M. B. (1987). Second language performance testing: the Ontario Test of ESL as an example. *Language Testing, 37,* 28–47.

Wolfe-Quintero. K. (1998, March). Relative clause hierarchies and second language writing. Paper presented at American Association of Applied Linguistics. Seattle.

Wolfe-Quintero, K., Inagaki, S., & Kim, H. Y. (1998). *Second language development in writing: Measures of fluency, accuracy, and complexity* (Tech. Rep. No. 17). Honolulu, HI: National Foreign Language Resource Center.

Zhang, S. (1987). Cognitive complexity and written production in English as a second language. *Language Learning, 37,* 469–481.

8

Fourth Generation Writing Assessment

Liz Hamp-Lyons
The Hong Kong Polytechnic University

This chapter begins with brief history of the first three "generations" of writing assessment and then describes the key qualities I believe will characterize the fourth generation in writing assessment. I express the view that this fourth generation will be both humanistic and technological, drawing on advances in computer applications and an understanding of writing assessment as a complex of processes in which multiple authors and readers are involved and revealed. Further, I believe the fourth generation in writing assessment, in common with a movement building in assessment generally, will acknowledge that all assessment practices are political, will accept a shared responsibility for the impact of these practices, and will be reactive to and proactive about their political uses and abuses.

Although the general principles laid out are relevant to many educational contexts, I will in this elaboration pays special attention to the assessment of second language writing, especially the evaluation of written work in English for Academic Purposes (EAP) contexts (i.e., in universities and other tertiary institutions, whether in courses for English majors or in "service" provision for non-English majors, and whether for the undergraduate or the postgraduate context).

A BRIEF HISTORY

The first three generations in writing assessment can be described, crudely, as: direct testing (i.e., essay tests); multiple-choice testing; and portfolio-based

117

assessment. It is not normally acknowledged that direct assessment of writing is the first rather than the second generation in writing assessment: Conventionally, people think of essay testing as being a reaction against and result of multiple-choice, "objective" testing. But, in fact, essay testing has been around for thousands of years, at least from the Chou period in China (1111–771 B.C.). In the Sung period, the wider availability of education placed pressures on the traditional system for selecting officials. A key response to these pressures was *kung*, the idea of impartiality (Lee, 1985), perhaps the earliest precursor of what has become known as reliability. Impartiality in the examination process was ensured through a rigorous, indeed traumatic, sequence of increasingly demanding exams in which candidates and examiners were locked away together, candidates' scripts were recopied by scribes to ensure anonymity, and more than one examiner marked each script. However, in practice these ideals were marred by bribery, cheating, and sometimes extreme measures such as tunneling below exam cubicles to bring in books from outside (Cleverley, 1985).

In Britain and Europe, university education, open only to a tiny (male) elite, had always consisted primarily of tutor–student dialogue and seminar-style debate and enquiry, but as British colonial power grew, the need was for larger numbers of literate, reasonably educated men to run the colonial administrations around the world. The colonies themselves also needed local people with rudimentary literacy to work under their colonial masters, and the highly systematized and rigorous Chinese examination system influenced the British colonial powers, so that the oral examination gave way to written examinations in the colonies, and more gradually, in most British universities. As written exams were administered to larger and larger numbers of candidates, the burgeoning "science" of statistics was increasingly applied to the problem of objectively measuring, or obtaining a "true judgement" of, written work (e.g., Edgeworth, 1888; who claimed to have found ways of establishing the "true worth" of a pupil's ability).

Lunsford (1986) described the introduction of written exams in U.S. universities, tracing them to Harvard University's 1873–1874 introduction of a written composition as an entrance examination, replacing the traditional oral examination. This led seemingly inevitably to calls for increased standardization, and work focussed on ways of achieving that standardization. Hillegas (1912) proposed a 1,000-point scale to assess writing that also proposed the separation of writing into its form and the content. This content-form split was the lever that pried open the door of so-called "objective" tests for application to writing. From this point on, it could be argued that the skills that multiple-choice tests measure (e.g., the ability to recognise conventions of grammar, sentence structure, and mechanics, and the ability to make an appropriate stylistic choice among several options) represent the skills that comprise writing. Form *became* writing, and writing assessment in the United States became the preserve of the statisticians and their supporters (e.g., Huxtable, 1929; Miller, 1926; Odell, 1928; Paterson, 1925; Stalnaker, 1936; Steel & Talman, 1936; Thomas, 1931). With the founding of the Educational Testing Service in 1947, multiple-choice testing became firmly entrenched as part of "the American way."

But multiple-choice tests cannot measure the skills that most writing *teachers* identify as important to effective writing: inventing ideas and arguments; building material into a coherent and effective overall structure to convince, persuade, and teach readers; revising and editing one's own work to more closely approximate conventions of accurate and excellent text and to meet the expectations of a range of audiences. Classroom teachers never forgot this, but bureaucracies frequently did, and as a result, writing instruction, particularly in schools, began to suffer from the narrowing of the curriculum lamented by educational researchers such as Madaus (1988), Messick (1994), and Smith (1991). Educators such as Fader (1986) argued that writing samples were the only meaningful way to look at the worth of a piece of writing and to make a writer's "minimum ability" clear to someone else, whereas Goodlad (1983) exposed American schooling as composed primarily of passive listening to formulaic expositions and completion of quizzes and worksheets involving one-sentence answers at best. Not surprisingly, by the end of the 1970s a small number of universities were reintroducing the use of formal examinations, but this time the exams were specifically of writing ability rather than of content examined *through* writing. As Fader (1986) described, the University of Michigan was in the forefront of this movement.

Meanwhile, another movement was building in Europe and Canada. In the early 1970s Britain's General Certificate of Education (GCE) 'O' level (at age 16 [end of Year 5 of secondary schooling]) introduced *Mode 3 English*, a writing folio, to complement or replace a single-sitting exam. Since then, the folio has grown in popularity until it is now used in Year 5 and Year 7 (university entrance) examinations as a major component of most subjects. The "portfolio," as it became called, was discussed with excitement at conferences in the early 1980s and was famously tried out by Elbow and Belanoff (1986) at the State University of New York at Stonybrook. It turned out to be the right idea at the right time; portfolios were introduced for placement at the University of Michigan (Condon & Hamp-Lyons, 1991), for exemption at Miami University of Ohio (Sommers, 1991), and were proposed (unsuccessfully) for entry at the University of Minnesota (Anson & Brown, 1991). The use of portfolios at all levels of education in the United States has grown so rapidly that Belanoff and Elbow (1997) called it an explosion, and Yancey and Weiser (1997) added teacher portfolios and electronic portfolios to the list.

The application of a portfolio-based approach in *second language* writing instruction and assessment has been advocated by me (Hamp-Lyons, 1994) and others (Murphy, 1994), but I (Hamp-Lyons, 1996) also expressed concerns and cautions about their use. It remains the case that there is far too little research on the practice and consequences of portfolio-based instruction, and particularly assessment, with L2 writers.

THE FOURTH GENERATION

It may seem that we are not fully into the third generation—portfolios—yet, so it is a little early to be looking at the next generation after it! However, there are signs that people in the field of second-language writing are ready to move on and look more holistically at the assessment needs of students and the assessment methods and strategies now available from a more critical perspective. The fourth generation in writing assessment will, naturally enough, share many qualities with other forms of assessment. However, because the fourth generation will have different qualities than the previous three, it will expand, enrich, and change thinking not only about portfolios but also about essay testing and even multiple-choice testing. The development of a powerful and encompassing explanatory and evaluative paradigm for thinking about how we "do" writing assessment will benefit teachers, students, and maybe even bureaucracies by offering more solidly grounded tools of critique for assessment systems and their uses (and abuses).

What then, are the qualities of fourth generation (writing) assessment likely to be?

Technological

Writing assessment, especially in first language contexts, has frequently functioned counter to the prevailing trend in assessment and evaluation: It has avoided technology as being too distant from the people involved, too difficult for people in the humanities to truck with, and inappropriate. Inappropriate because a great argument in favour of direct assessment of writing has been the benefits gained by real language samples being assessed by real people, the construct being claimed to be inaccessible in other ways. Despite the imaginative considerations of the potentials for information technology for writing assessment of compositionists such as Lunsford (1986), it has been and still is most usually claimed that technological intrusions into writing assessment are not only unduly expensive and complex, they are also too distant from the human participants and make text creation (and perhaps text evaluation) too lonely an enterprise.

But in the last few years a number of studies have been carried out to find ways of applying rapid technological breakthroughs, particularly those associated with text linguistics (concordancing, corpus linguistics, and computational linguistics) to improving writing assessments. Reid (1988) used

Writer's Workbench (AT&T) to count certain salient features of test essays, but the possibilities of that programme were very limited. More recent studies and practical projects have applied updated technologies to similar problems. For example, Robert Landauer at the University of Colorado developed "Project Essay Grader," in which a computer matches student work with a bank of human-scored essays and finds the closest match, in order to give the writer a score and point out what content points he or she may have omitted. Landauer and his colleagues argue that this saves teachers time, which they can then spend on working closely with the most needy students. Since the late 1990s we have also seen the beginnings of attempts to apply the on-line technologies of the Internet and the World Wide Web to the assessment of performances, including writing assessments. For example, Jan Hamilton and others at the Hong Kong Polytechnic University have developed a rater training system to be used through the web; raters can match new writing performances with benchmarked scripts, enabling them to gain rating practice at their own pace.

The advantages of modern technologies for assessment are the ability to perform repeated functions without boredom or variation, adaptability (within preprogrammed pathways), flexibility (testing can be carried out at any time, for a range of purposes, and on any number of candidates), and the ability to make decisions without being judgmental (in the sense of being biased) or confrontational. In writing assessment we have lagged behind other disciplines in making use of these capabilities, but have at last arrived at that point. A project I am leading is developing a "context-led" assessment for business, through which human-resource management personnel can move through pathways to select appropriate tasks, topics, genres, and criteria for making their own judgements of applicants' written samples and (building on Hamilton's work) access rater training matched to the context they are working in. Technologically-fronted assessments such as these have many advantages, but they also have disadvantages. The greatest disadvantage is that they occur without human interaction. Interaction, contact, the sense of the writer as person—and of rater as person—is one of the most precious features of direct assessment for many composition theorists, both L1 and L2. As I argue in the following, if the voices of test-takers are unheard, or at most are indirectly inferred from their texts, assessment is diminished and will not become what I see as the future, the fourth generation, of writing assessment.

Humanistic

It was during the Sung period that the concept of impartiality was first questioned as far as it related to social justice. The government found that impartiality could not address the need for social, regional, and moral justice.

Although it could (or at least, could aggressively attempt to) create equal possibilities for all candidates, it could not create equal opportunities for all members of the society (Lee, 1985). Shen Kou (1028–1067) believed this was because it "concentrated only on laying down detailed regulations . . . [and] therefore did not know what the 'great fairness' (*ta-kung*) in the world is" and ignored the fundamentals of governing a state (quoted in Lee, 1985, p. 205). This tension between fairness and social justice was never resolved by the Chinese examination system. The move toward humanistic values in fourth generation writing assessment is impelled by the same motive, the search for a "great fairness".

What is meant by saying that the fourth generation will be humanistic is that it will be far more conscious of and responsive to the human needs of stakeholders. The notion of stakeholders is one that has come to prominence in educational assessment in the 1990s and that will be a major influence on thinking about assessments in the future. Stakeholders are test takers, test designers, raters of tests, and score users. They can also be generalised to much larger groups of people and institutions that can be said to have some kind of stake in any assessment (Hamp-Lyons, 1998b, 1999; Rea-Dickens, 1997).

We can evidence concern for stakeholders by being conscious of the knowledge and the kinds and levels of skills demanded of each kind of stakeholder in order for them to interact appropriately with the test. We can evidence concern for stakeholders by making sure that each stakeholder group is properly supported in the acquisition of the appropriate skills. We can do this is a range of ways. Deconstructing the processes that test takers and test raters go through in order to judge more fully whether tests are tapping required or expected knowledge, skills, and behaviors is becoming increasingly popular. Evaluation studies of high-stakes tests and testing programmes and agencies, which enable us to learn more about the consequences for some stakeholder groups of the actions and decisions of other stakeholder groups, are also becoming more prominent in educational measurement research and are overdue in the TESOL field (Alderson & Hamp-Lyons, 1996; Hamp-Lyons, 1998a). We can look at the attitudes of different stakeholder groups to specific tests and consider what those attitudes mean for the educational, social, and political use—and possibly, abuse—of test scores. For example, studies of the consequences for test takers of test raters' judgement processes, or of the uses that groups of score users make of test results (such as the ways in which college admissions officers use/misuse TOEFL or IELTS scores) must form an essential part of a humanistic assessment theory and practice. In second-language writing assessment such studies have been too long delayed (but see Hamp-Lyons, 1997b; Haswell, 1998), although the questions are often asked and rhetorical claims often made.

Thinking about stakeholders in such an encompassing fashion implies a far broader reach of influence for any assessment than has been usually accepted. The boundary between the humanistic characteristic of assessment and its political quality becomes blurred.

Political

All assessments are political, and writing assessments are no exception. But politics is an inexact science at best and by definition involves competing interests and irreconcilable differences in fundamental beliefs and values. Throughout the history of China, education has been highly politicized and assessments have had powerful consequences for politics. Sung emperors and Chairman Mao shared a view of education as inherently political, and as a powerful tool of social engineering, by shaping educational access (and the kinds of education to be accessed). In the modern China this is still the case, and Chinese university students are very aware of this, as more than 2 million of them each year sit for the College English Test.

At the microlevel (the classroom, the school, the school district), there is an increasing weight of evidence to suggest that tests and other forms of assessment impact the curriculum, the teaching materials, and the teaching methods teachers use. When the curriculum is affected due to the influence of assessments, this is known as "curricular alignment" (Koretz, Stecher, Klein & McCaffrey, 1994; Linn, 1983; Simmons & Resnick, 1993; Smith, 1991). Curricular alignment is closely related to the more familiar concept in L2 education of washback (Alderson & Hamp-Lyons, 1996; Alderson & Wall, 1996; Wall, 1998). In Hong Kong, school-leaving examinations have been consciously redesigned to create positive washback (Andrews & Fullilove, 1994); for instance, a speaking component was introduced to the Hong Kong Certificate of Elementary Education's (HKCEE) English examination to make sure that speaking was taught in the schools. Although the speaking test is not very reliable, its use is justified by its washback effect (King, 1994). At a macrolevel, it is also argued that the kinds of assessment available; the roles of different stakeholders in them; the uses they are put to in society; and the attitudes of society toward examination processes, results, and status have direct and indirect consequences for the value given to education throughout a society (Hamp-Lyons, 1998c). This type of influence of testing on society is known as impact (Wall, 1997).

In fourth generation writing assessment, we will be very aware of the political forces for and against the methods we use for test development, delivery, and reporting. We will have no choice but to stand up and be counted and to take on the responsibility for the consequences of the tests we develop and that we use in own classrooms, or that we condone for use on our students. This political role for us all as consumers of tests and their effects will often be painful, but it is one we can no longer ignore (Hamp-Lyons, 1998b, in press; Shohamy, 1997, 1993).

Ethical

Although the ethical dimension of fourth generation writing assessment may seem to follow logically from the humanistic and political dimensions, we must realise that it also follows from the technological dimension. It is all too easy in high-tech contexts to create a distance for ourselves from learners and test takers: Here is the tension between technology and humanism. When distance is created, it becomes easier to forget that tests are about people and that people as individuals are affected by tests and the outcomes of tests. Sometimes we are told that a particular test is not intended for decision making about individuals, and the implication is often that there is therefore no impact on individuals. But the experience of taking a test rarely passes without a tremor by test takers; it is little consolation to them (even if they believe it) that the results will not affect them. For many people, taking a test of any kind is an occasion of considerable anxiety.

Too little research has been done on the effects of tests on test takers: Cohen's (1984) ground-breaking study has been far too infrequently replicated. Hamp-Lyons and Lynch (1998) found in their survey of papers presented at the Language Testing Research Colloquium over the years from 1979 to 1992 that there had been a tiny minority of studies that allowed students'/test takers' voices to be heard.

When we speak of ethics in assessment, we speak of fairness: the language tester has no more inherent right to decide what is fair for other people than anyone else does. But the language tester does have the responsibility to use all means available to make any language test she or he is involved in as fair as possible (Hamp-Lyons, 1997a). Because people's needs may conflict, and each group will find it fair that *their* needs take precedence, "ethics," for the language tester, involves decisions about whose voices are to be heard, whose needs are to be met, and how a society determines what is best for the largest number when fairnesses are in conflict. Some of the questions we must ask ourselves are: How do we ensure test takers' rights? How do we ensure that decisions made are meaningful? Whose judgements count when decisions are made? How do we decide among competing approaches (e.g., to reliability, validity, practicality, and fairness)? Above all, we must ask: How do we monitor our own conduct, when in most contexts no one else is doing it? The International Association for Language Testing has made a start on these issues and has prepared a set of ethical codes for the profession (ILTA, 1999). But the effort has been delayed too long and must be replicated by all our professional associations because all teachers, not only those who *call* themselves assessment specialists, are involved in assessment and testing decisions. As our technical skills expand, as our definition of a test is refined, as our political consciousness of the power of tests is heightened, we raise our expectations of ourselves. We expect more excellent tests, and the definition of excellence is broadened to include consequences as well as development and delivery.

A BEGINNING

What then, is the fourth generation in writing assessment? It is deeply conflicted; it is dark and light; it is peril and promise. However, as we begin to face the conflicts and find increasingly effective ways to resolve them, we shall find that it is a more intelligent generation than any that have gone before it. Whether that will be good or bad, better or worse, will be up to us. All of us.

ACKNOWLEDGMENTS

Parts of this work were made possible within a Central Allocation grant from the Hong Kong Polytechnic University.

REFERENCES

Alderson, J. C., & Hamp-Lyons, L. (1996). TOEFL preparation courses: A study of washback. *Language Testing, 13,* 280–297.

Alderson, J. C., & Wall, D. (1996). Does washback exist? *Applied Linguistics, 14,* 115–129.

Andrews, S., & Fullilove, J. (1994). Assessing spoken English in the public examinations: Why and how? In J. Boyle & P. Falvey (Eds.), *English language testing in Hong Kong* (pp. 57–86). Hong Kong: Chinese University Press.

Anson, C., & Brown, R. L. (1991). Large-scale portfolio assessment: Ideological sensitivity and institutional change. In P. Belanoff & P. Elbow (Eds.), *Portfolios: Process and product* (pp. 248–269). Portsmouth, NH: Boynton/Cook.

Belanoff, P. & Elbow, P. (1997). Reflections on an explosion: Portfolios in the 90's and beyond. In K. Yancey & I. Weiser (Eds.), *Situating portfolios: Four Perspectives* (pp. 21–33). Logan: Utah State University Press.

Cleverley, J. (1985). *The schooling of China.* London: George Allen & Unwin.

Cohen, A. (1984). On taking tests: what the students report. *Language Testing, 1,* 70–81.

Condon, W., & Hamp-Lyons, L. (1991). Introducing a portfolio-based writing assessment: practice through problems. In P. Belanoff & P. Elbow (Eds.), *Portfolios: Process and product* (pp. 231–247). Portsmouth, NH: Boynton/Cook.

Edgeworth, F. Y. (1888). The statistics of examinations. *Journal of the Royal Statistical Society, 51,* 599–635.

Elbow, P., & Belanoff, P. (1986). Portfolios as a substitute for proficiency examinations. *College Composition and Communication, 37,* 336–339.

Fader, D. (1986). Writing samples and virtues. In K. L. Greenberg, H. S. Weiner, & R. A. Donovan (Eds.), *Writing assessment: Issues and strategies* (pp. 79–92). White Plains, NY: Longman.

Goodlad, J. I. (1983). *A place called school: Prospects for the future.* New York: McGraw-Hill.

Hamp-Lyons, L. (1994). Interweaving assessment and instruction in college ESL writing courses. *College ESL: A Journal of Theory and Practice in TESL, 4,* 43–55.

Hamp-Lyons, L. (1996). The challenges of second language writing assessment. In E. White, W. Lutz, & S. Kamusikiri (Eds.), *Assessment of writing: Policies, politics, practices,* (pp. 226–240). New York: Modern Language Association.

Hamp-Lyons, L. (1997a). Ethics and language testing. In C. Clapham (Ed.) *The encyclopedia of language and education (Vol. 7): Language testing and assessment.* Dordrecht, Netherlands: Kluwer.

Hamp-Lyons, L. (1997b). Exploring the bias in essay tests. In J. Butler, J. Guerra, & C. Severino (Eds.), *Writing in multicultural settings* (pp. 51–55). New York: Modern Language Association.

Hamp-Lyons, L. (1998a). Ethical test preparation practice: The case of the TOEFL. *TESOL Quarterly, 32,* 329–337.

Hamp-Lyons, L. (1998b). Washback, impact and validity. *Language Testing, 14,* 295–303.

Hamp-Lyons, L. (1999). Fairnesses in language testing. In A. Kunnan (Ed.), *Fairness and validation in language assessment* (pp. 99–104). Cambridge: Cambridge University Press.

Hamp-Lyons, L. (in press). Ethics, fairness(es), and developments in language testing. In C. Elder, A. Brown, K. Hill, T. Lumley, & N. Iwashita (Eds.), *Experimenting with uncertainty: Language testing essays in honour of Alan Davies.* New York: Cambridge University Press.

Hamp-Lyons, L., & Lynch, B. (1998). Perspectives on validity: A historical analysis of language testing conference abstracts. In A. Kunnan (Ed.), *Validation in language assessment research* (pp. 253–277). Mahwah, NJ: Lawrence Erlbaum Associates.

Haswell, R. (1998). Searching for Kiyoko: Bettering mandatory ESL writing placement. *Journal of Second Language Writing, 7,* 133–174.

Hillegas, M. B. (1912). A scale for the measurement of quality in English composition by young people. *Teacher's College Record, 13,* 331–384.

Huxtable, Z. (1929). Criteria for judging thought content in written English. *Journal of Educational Research, 19,* 188–195.

ILTA (International Language Testing Association). (1999). *Code of Conduct.* Available from ILTA Secretariat, English Language Centre, University of Hong Kong.

King, R. (1994). Historical survey of language testing in Hong Kong. In J. Boyle & P. Falvey (Eds.), *English language testing in Hong Kong* (pp. 3–29). Hong Kong: The Chinese University Press.

Koretz, D., Stecher, B., Klein, S., & McCaffrey, D. (1994). *The evolution of a portfolio program: The impact and quality of the Vermont program in its second year (1992–1993)* (CSE Tech. Rep. No. 385). Los Angeles: University of California, Centre for Research on Evaluation, Standards, and Student Testing.

Lee, T. H. C. (1985). *Government education and examinations in Sung China.* Hong Kong: The Chinese University Press.

Linn, R. L. (1983). Testing and instruction: Links and distinctions. *Journal of Educational Measurement, 20,* 179–189.

Lunsford, A. A. (1986). The past—and future—of writing assessment. In K. L. Greenberg, H. S. Weiner, & R. A. Donovan (Eds.), Writing *assessment: Issues and strategies* (pp. 1–12). White Plains, NY: Longman.

Madaus, G. F. (1988). The influence of testing on the curriculum: From compliant servant to dictatorial master. In L. Travers (Ed.), *Critical Issues in Curriculum: 87th NSSE Yearbook,* (Part 1, pp. 83–121). Chicago: National Society for the Study of Education/University of Chicago Press.

Messick, S. (1994). The interplay of evidence and consequences in the validation of performance assessments. *Educational Researcher, 23*(1), 13–24.

Miller, G. F. (1926). *Objective tests in high school subjects.* Norman: Oklahoma School District.

Murphy, S. (1994). Writing portfolios in K–12 schools: Implications for linguistically diverse students. In L. Black, D. A. Daiker, J. Sommers, & G. Stygall (Eds.), *New directions in portfolio assessment* (pp. 140–156). Portsmouth NH: Boynton/Cook Heinemann.

Odell, C. W. (1928). *Traditional examinations and new-type tests.* Englewood Cliffs, NJ: Prentice-Hall.

Paterson, D. (1925). Do new and old type examinations measure different mental functions? *School and Society, 24*, 246–248.

Rea-Dickens, P. (1997). So, why do we need relationships with stakeholders in language testing? A view from the UK. *Language Testing, 14*, 304–314.

Reid, J. (1988). *Quantitative differences in English prose written by Arabic, Chinese, Spanish, and English students.* Unpublished dissertation, Colorado State University, Fort Collins.

Shohamy, E. (1993, June 1–19). *The power of tests: The impact of language tests on teaching and learning.* National Foreign Language Center Occasional Papers.

Shohamy, E. (1997). Testing methods, testing consequences: Are they ethical? Are they fair? *Language Testing 14*, 340–349.

Simmons, W. & Resnick, L. (1993). Assessment as a catalyst of school reform. *Educational Leadership, 50*(5), 11–15.

Smith, M. L. (1991). Put to the test: The effects of external testing on teachers. *Educational Researcher, 20*, 8–11.

Sommers, J. (1991). Bringing practice in line with theory: Using portfolio grading in the composition classroom. In K. L. Greenberg, H. S. Weiner, & R. A. Donovan (Eds.), *Writing assessment: Issues and strategies* (pp. 153–164). White Plains, NY: Longman.

Stalnaker, J. M. (1936). The measurement of the ability to write. In W. S. Gray (Ed.), *Tests and measurement in higher education* (pp. 203–215). Chicago: University of Chicago.

Steel, J. H., & Talman, J. (1936). *The marking of composition.* London: Nisbet.

Thomas, C. S. (1931). *Examining the examinations in English: Report to the College Examinations Board.* Cambridge, MA: Harvard University Press.

Wall, D. (1997). Impact and washback in language testing. In C. Clapham (Ed.), *The Kluwer encyclopedia of language in education: Vol. 7. Testing and assessment.* Dordrecht: Kluwer.

Yancey, K. & Weiser, I. (Eds.). *Situating portfolios: Four perspectives.* Logan: Utah State University Press.

9

Instructional Strategies for Making ESL Students Integral to the University[1]

Trudy Smoke
Hunter College, CUNY

On January 25, 1999, the Board of Trustees of the City University of New York (CUNY) passed a resolution stating "that all remedial course instruction shall be phased-out of all baccalaureate degree programs at CUNY senior colleges" (see appendix for complete text of the policy). At CUNY, students are defined as remedial by their failing any of the Freshman Skills Assessment Tests (FSATs), which include the CUNY Mathematics Assessment Test (MAT), Reading Assessment Test (RAT), and Writing Assessment Test (WAT).[2] Students take these FSATs after admission to CUNY and prior to placement in courses. The exams of those students who fail the WAT are reread, and students are placed in English as a Second Language (ESL) or non-ESL remedial-writing classes. In order to exit remediation, at the end of their courses, students must retake any exams they failed and must pass them in order to continue in CUNY. This resolution, denying the entrance of remedial students to CUNY senior colleges, will go down in history as a major step in ending open admissions in public colleges and could, perhaps unintentionally, eliminate or downsize the numbers of ESL students in CUNY.

What has happened in New York and, similarly, what has happened with affirmative action, bilingual education, and remediation in California, and with the recent imposition of new testing regulations in Massachusetts, Texas, and Florida are all part of a conservative political trend, partially an anti-immigration trend and partially an antientitlement trend, which will eventually have an impact on all of our programs and consequently on our students' access to college if in no other way than to make ESL and developmental education highly politicized endeavors.

To show just how politicized, during one of the Trustees' meetings prior to the final vote, a trustee stood up and said that he refused to vote for the passage of any resolution that would adversely affect ESL students in CUNY. Soon after that meeting, the following statement was added to the original resolution, "This resolution does not apply to ESL students who received a secondary education abroad and who otherwise are not in need of remediation." The term *ESL students* was later interpreted to include any students who had spent one or more semesters in a high school abroad in a non-English-speaking country and who were otherwise nonremedial, meaning that the students had passed the MAT.

We need to question the definition and the impact of the resolution on ESL students. Why should students who received a secondary education abroad be admitted to CUNY senior colleges when ESL immigrant students who graduated from New York City high schools are denied admission? Is it because English as a Foreign Language (EFL), nonimmigrant, students pay double tuition? Are the ESL students graduating from New York City high schools deemed to be too similar to the remedial native speakers of English? Why is ESL considered remedial at all? Why are any students who attended poorly funded high schools in New York being rejected? Is a Puerto Rican high school considered to be abroad? Why should a student who does not pass the MAT because he or she cannot understand the directions and questions in English not be permitted to take ESL classes in CUNY senior colleges? Why, when the research done by the CUNY Chancellor's Office shows the effectiveness of ESL programs, are ESL classes being taken out of the colleges? Why is there a suggestion that these courses should be privatized and outsourced to external noncredit institutes? What rights do individuals have to get an education? Why in our highly technical society are students being denied higher education, and why is it occurring at the same time that cuts are being made in welfare and precollegiate education budgets? How do students gain power in such a situation? These are just some of the questions we need to think about.

Despite the fact that the resolution did not go into effect until Spring 2000, soon after the resolution passed the demographics of CUNY colleges were altered. A survey conducted by Julia Carroll (1999) of Queensborough Community College revealed that the number of *ESL students*, defined as those placed in ESL classes, had declined dramatically. According to Carroll, in the fall of 1994, there were approximately 15,499 ESL students enrolled in CUNY undergraduate courses. By Fall 1998, that number had precipitously declined to 8,571 students (pp. 14-15). Carroll pointed out, however, that the senior colleges had suffered the greatest losses in students, while some of the community colleges had actually increased their undergraduate ESL student enrollment (p. 15).[3] Baruch, Brooklyn, Hunter, and Queens Colleges, the four senior colleges specified in the Board resolution as admitting only those students who had passed all three Freshman Skills Assessment Tests as of Spring 2000 suffered the greatest losses.[4]

To the extent that ESL was saved in CUNY, it was saved both through the concerted effort of ESL and non-ESL faculty, politicians, and students and because of the various strategies that were in place for integrating ESL into the college and for making ESL students integral to the college and thereby not easily expendable. Although the strategies described here are specific to CUNY, they correspond to what Cummins (1990) described as a necessary theoretical framework for educational progress for language-minority students. According to him, such educational progress is influenced "by the extent to which individual educators become advocates for the promotion of students' linguistic talents, actively encourage community participation in developing students' academic and cultural resources, and implement pedagogical approaches that succeed in liberating students from instructional dependence" (p. 64).

Building on Cummins' (1990) framework, in my focus on instruction, I would like to describe four specific academic and political strategies that have strengthened support throughout the college and community, strategies that have helped convince colleagues, friends, and students to advocate on behalf of ESL programs and support services. I recently edited a book for Lawrence Erlbaum Associates, *Adult ESL: Politics, Pedagogy, and Participation in Classroom and Community Programs*, that describes in detail some of the strategies that are mentioned as well as others and that tells how ESL faculty across the country have worked to maintain their programs and access to higher education for their ESL students despite an unsupportive, even hostile, political environment.

LINKING ESL CLASSES WITH DISCIPLINE-SPECIFIC COURSES

Since 1990 I have been working with faculty members in my college linking my ESL writing courses to a variety of discipline-area courses. Content-based instruction has been found to be pedagogically effective by many ESL instructors (Benesch, 1988; Brinton, Snow, & Wesche, 1989; Crandall, 1993; Haas, Hernández, & Smoke, 1991; Smoke & Haas, 1995; Snow & Brinton, 1988); additionally, I have found it has the political function of building advocacy for ESL students and programs. To begin with, how we choose the courses with which to link our ESL courses depends on the setting and the faculty involved. In some colleges, the links are made by the administration and in others, faculty decide to work together, often forging collaborative relationships. What we teach in the ESL writing course is determined by the teachers involved; instructors may act in a service capacity enhancing what is taught in the discipline-specific course or may present additional, but related, perspectives on the particular subject or theme. In describing the link between her intermediate ESL writing course and an introductory psychology course, a biweekly lecture with more than 400 students, Sarah Benesch (1998) wrote that rather than become a recitation teacher for the psychology class, she chose to focus on a specific topic. Aware that any topic she chose would create some resistance on the part of some students, Benesch decided to focus on anorexia, a topic more closely associated with women. She felt this inclusion was important because the psychology professor had presented only male psychologists except for Anna Freud and had only mentioned her in connection with her father and Erik Erikson. Benesch wrote, "Given the lack of attention to women's issues and women psychologists and the superficial treatment of topics in the survey course, I wanted students to thoroughly examine one area connecting women, psychology and social issues" (p. 105). In her writing class, students explored this issue in some depth. (See Terry Santos', chap. 12, this volume, for a further discussion of this model.) Once, when Benesch was unable to attend class, the psychology teacher met with Benesch's class, and for the first and only time, he saw the students at close range, and they saw him out of the lecture hall and were able to ask questions.

I linked my ESL classes at various times with a large lecture class of more than 100 students and with small lecture classes of between 15 and 25 students. The large lecture class, "Conquered Peoples in the Americas," offered through the Black and Puerto Rican Studies Department and taught by José Hernández:

> describes the consequences of nineteenth-century United States' expansion and compares the Puerto Rican experience to that of Native Americans, Chicanos, and Pacific Island peoples, specifically the Filipinos and Native Hawaiians. It expresses the common situation among these groups who lost control over their homelands, describes their cultures, and provides a detailed study of their colonization. (Haas et al., 1991, p. 114)

Students read, wrote about, made presentations on, and did research relating to the themes of the course. I also linked my ESL writing classes with a course in the history of the "United States" from the Western discovery until the middle 1800s (see Smoke & Haas, 1995) and linked my intermediate ESL writing class with the Classics Department's "Greek and Latin Roots of English" and my upper level ESL writing class with "Classical Mythology." These links were effective because the joint assignments helped students to see connections between the courses and the writing and reading they did, as well as helping them in their acquisition of English and understanding of course material and in vocabulary development. Students in these linked classes tended to do better in both courses than students in the unlinked classes.

Beyond the pedagogical reasons for the linking model in the cases I described—Benesch's Psychology link and my links with Black and Puerto Rican Studies and the History courses—the students were introduced to political content that encouraged them to critically examine our society. As Lisa Delpit (1990) wrote, "If you are not already a participant in the culture of power, being told explicitly the rules of that culture makes acquiring power easier" (p. 87). Students were informed about their rights, and they were offered tools intended to help them become participants in the college and in their communities; a few from my classes have gone on to take a more active role in college government and in student clubs. Some of my former ESL students who support public higher education for a broad spectrum of students testified at the Board of Trustees' meetings and met with reporters to discuss the Trustees' antiremediation resolution.

Faculty involved in the linked classes also often became advocates for ESL and developmental programs. Professor Hernández and I recently discussed how the linking experience we had had several years before had transformed his teaching. He is now teaching his course to a block program of entering freshman, and many in his class have not passed one of the Freshman Skills Tests. His goal is to make sure that all students do sufficient reading and writing so that they will be ready to take and pass both the reading and writing skills tests. He holds himself responsible to make sure that no student in his class gets dismissed from our college. Professor Hernández is exemplary in his dedication to students and to helping them become more politically aware. He is also a strong force on committees throughout the college and a consistent advocate of ESL and remedial programs.

COLLABORATING WITH TEACHERS ACROSS DISCIPLINES IN THE COLLEGE

Not only discipline-specific faculty, but also ESL faculty gain much by being involved in interdisciplinary projects. Teachers in these projects may begin to perceive their students' strengths in other disciplines and learn to interact outside the narrow range of their own department. At Hunter College, we have a block program for entering students in which a group of students is blocked in the same courses, such as ESL Writing, Reading, the Greek and Latin Roots of English, Conquered Peoples in the Americas, and a math course. Other blocks have been developed around such themes as New York City, Teacher Education, and Health Science. Teachers in these blocks meet several times during the semester to discuss students, courses, and writing and reading requirements, and together they develop strategies for working with their students. Most faculty agree that the blocks should not be continued beyond the first year of college because they can lead to high school-like behavior, but they also feel that one of the chief advantages of the blocks is its participatory effect on faculty who work together on assignments. Moreover, as Marguerite Ann Snow and Lia Kamhi-Stein (1996) suggested in the description of their cross-discipline project at California State University, working together collaboratively with native speakers and ESL students extends to all faculty the responsibility "for improving the academic literacy skills of language minority students" (p. iv). These collaborations also make it possible for adjunct or part-time faculty, who often are maginalized, to work with and get to know faculty, both part time and full time, across the disciplines, as well as for L2 teachers to work with L1 writing teachers.

Teachers in the blocks sometimes develop joint writing assignments and joint responses to these assignments. In linking our ESL writing and history classes one of the methods that Professor McCauley and I worked out was that she would be the reader of the first draft, and I would read the second draft of one of the three jointly required papers. I was the first reader, and she was the second on the next paper. We did not always agree about what we valued in students' papers: How the paper was organized, how the ideas were supported, and how important correct grammar and word usage should be. However, we spent many hours discussing these issues. Together, we dealt with a problem that is interdisciplinary and complex, responding to writing. We did not solve the problem, but a genuine dialogue grew out of it; we learned to work together and to have respect for each other's way of handling the problem.

OBTAINING GRANTS FOR COLLABORATIVE PROJECTS

Another area on which faculty can collaborate across disciplines is on obtaining grants. Grants bring money and prestige to colleges. They also can be used as seed money for innovative programs and to fund effective teaching models. As an example, Tamara Green, the chair of the Classics Department at Hunter (Personal Communication, 1994), asked me to work with her as the codirector of her Fund for the Improvement of Postsecondary Education (FIPSE) grant to link intermediate ESL writing classes with her course, "The Greek and Latin Roots of English." This grant was remarkably successful in the 3 years of FIPSE funding when we had many sections of intermediate ESL writing.

During our first semester working together, we altered our individual courses somewhat, and we each added a linguistics component to what we taught, working with students describing and comparing the structure of

English and the structure of their native languages. We asked students to write a research paper, which had never been done before at that level of language proficiency and because of the focus of our classes, it was natural that their research papers would involve a description of their first language or a comparison of it with English. Looking at discrete linguistic features such as the positioning of adjectives, the use of the interrogative, and the use of tense, the students wrote papers about Russian, Spanish, Mandarin, Japanese, Korean, Hindi, Urdu, Ukrainian, and Haitian Creole among others. We recognized that students were the experts in their own languages and had much to offer in class.

Professor Green and I frequently attended each other's classes, and when we returned the research papers, we put students in groups of four and had each member of the group (we had carefully set it up so that each member spoke a different language) share her or his paper and teach the other members of the group some feature of her or his language. Professor Green and I went from group to group meeting with the students and learning from them. At the end of the class, a student from each language represented wrote the message "Happiness and Good Luck" in her or his language on the board and then read it aloud. ESL students had regained the right to their own languages, and this experience also provided them the opportunity to teach others something of their languages. The fact that the students' bilingualism had been recognized and valued matters because of the dominance and hegemony of English in the college, country, and much of the world. Professor Green also advocated on behalf of ESL students in the many committees she chairs and participates in throughout the college.

Recognizing students' abilities and enabling them to share these with each other empowers students "to assume greater control over setting their own learning goals and to collaborate actively with each other in achieving these goals" (Cummins, 1990, p. 60). One effective program that does this and that also brings together ESL and native-English speakers was started at the University of Rhode Island (URI) and also funded by FIPSE. Richard Blakely, the creator of the project, began to observe that more ESL students entering URI were immigrants with limited exposure to academic English and that teachers were unaware of how to work with these students. His program, the "English Language Fellows Program" (ELF), involves native-English speakers in tutoring ESL students in courses both students happen to be taking together. ELF is "content based in that the language learning [takes] place while focusing on other academic subjects—geology, literature, economics, and so on" (Blakely, 1998, p. 240).

The Fellows were native speakers of English who were trained and initially paid $6.00 an hour to work with ESL students in their classes. Fellows spent an average of 5 hours a week, "including time spent preparing, reading their classmates' papers, and so on, for which they were also paid" (p. 265).

As might be expected, the Fellows did better in their courses than they thought they would have done had they not put in the extra work associated with the tutoring. The faculty teaching the courses were satisfied that ESL students were performing better in their classes, and the teachers felt that they could concentrate more on the content of their classes. As one faculty member put it, "The ELF program has worked wonderfully to eliminate the disadvantages experienced by nonnative speakers and allow them to maximize both learning and grades" (Blakely, 1998, p. 262). The contacts made between the project director and the various faculty members created a positive dialogue about ESL students in the college. In a true reciprocal interaction, ESL and EFL students also frequently tutored the native speakers in their foreign-language classes, again drawing on the strengths of the ESL students as in the link with the Classics' class mentioned earlier.

The problem with relying on outside funding to support projects as valuable as these is that funding runs dry and circumstances change. The linking between the Classics Department and the English Department has continued beyond the FIPSE grant, but this semester we have only two linked sections because the number of ESL students is so reduced at Hunter. The ELF project continues but the structure has changed somewhat since Richard Blakely is no longer at the University of Rhode Island. What these experiences tell us is that although making the effort to obtain funds to get projects off the ground is valuable, it may be even more critical to get your colleges involved in the projects so that they will continue to support them once the grants run out. These two grants instituted a successful teaching model and a successful tutoring model that simultaneously made colleagues aware of the strengths of ESL students and also valued ESL students' native languages. They were conscious attempts to help the ESL students gain power and become more active participants in their colleges.

DEVELOPING WRITING ASSIGNMENTS THAT HELP STUDENTS TO GAIN POLITICAL POWER

Although there are many ways to assist students in gaining linguistic and social power, helping ESL students gain the tools to think critically has motivated students in my classes to participate and ultimately to succeed in the college. I am using *critical thinking* in the sense of what Shor (1992) defined as a "critical-democratic pedagogy [which] situates curriculum in issues and language from everyday life. Generative themes make up the primary subject matter; they grow out of student culture and express problematic conditions in daily life that are useful for generating critical discussion" (p. 55). Some caution needs to be exercised about such an approach, for as Leki (1992) wrote, "the ominous reverse side of the writing teacher's job of helping to initiate writing students into the discourse community is the attempt to indoctrinate them into a particular worldview, and for ESL students most notably, to colonize them" (p. 126). This is a serious charge and one we must be aware of as we construct our assignments. Using engaging and provocative material may turn off some ESL students, but the other side of this is that it may get students to use English as a tool of reflection and action.

To illustrate how this might work, many teachers use short stories, novels, poems, and nonfiction articles as the focus of their class discussions and writing assignments as my class did, but last semester in light of all the CUNY problems, my writing class focused on the theme of higher education and the lives of students. We read an essay about the difficulties a paraplegic man had faced in trying to navigate through a world made for the able bodied (Dardick, 1992), which led my class to discuss the Americans with Disabilities Act (ADA) of 1990. Most of my students knew little about the provisions of the ADA itself, but one of them, Kota, an EFL student from Japan said that the act had been a motivating factor in his coming to the United States. Kota is a sculptor with an interest in architecture, and he had been very curious to find out what the United States had done to make life more accessible for people with disabilities. He told the class how limited the resources for the disabled were in Japan. Several students from other parts of the world echoed his words. They began a research project to find out how accessible our college was for people with a variety of disabilities. As it turned out, Kota's cousin came from Japan to visit. This cousin uses a wheelchair, and his visit to the college revealed some limitations that Kota wrote about and shared with the class. After praising the electronic doors to buildings, the ramps, and elevator accessibility to all floors, he criticized the crowded space and said that the limited number of elevators that stopped at all floors made it difficult for someone in a wheelchair to get to classes on time. The classroom doors were heavy and hard to hold open while also navigating a wheelchair into a classroom. He also explained that although each bathroom had one wheelchair-accessible toilet, often the toilet door was made of cloth and did not provide privacy.

Moreover, the flush mechanism was difficult to manipulate in the tight quarters of the bathroom. The bathroom sinks were hard to reach from a wheelchair and the faucets almost impossible to turn on or even get one's hands under for someone with weak hands or with limited reach. His paper was an eye-opener for many students in the class. He then sent it to the college newspaper, but it was not printed. Instead of just doing writing for writing's sake, this project involved a student in looking critically at his community and perhaps becoming proactive in making changes. Some students said that after hearing his paper, they had become more cognizant of the needs of the disabled and had tried to be more patient in our crowded hallways and had even held the doors open for students in wheelchairs. This is another example of an assignment that gave a student an opportunity to generate knowledge and teach the class something he had researched and about which he had become an authority.

Teaching ESL writing classes during a time of downsizing and cutbacks has the peculiar advantage of giving students a natural subject to investigate, a subject about which their writing may even have a positive impact. Much of the research that other students in this class did was about issues related to higher education, such as remediation, affirmative action, or bilingual education. Almost daily, articles were written in the various newspapers for students to read and write about. The different coverage of the CUNY situation in *The New York Times*, the *Daily News*, and the *New York Post* gave them a good lesson in sensationalistic writing, in how journalists voice opinions by choice of words and phrases. And then, when I was quoted out of context in a *Times* article, I could share with students my full testimony before the Board of Trustees and what had been printed to illustrate how reportage is slanted to make a point. This literacy experience made the situation more immediate to them and encouraged them to think about issues directly relating to their education, to write about real issues, and to discover evidence and learn to quote and paraphrase it to support their opinions. Many of them, on their own, wrote letters in support of public higher education and specifically in support of ESL education to state legislators, the Mayor, the Governor, and, in one case, to the President. These letters, while not from the voting public, do carry some weight and made students feel that their writing could have an impact and deal with a real and pressing subject. At a time when the CUNY degree was routinely being degraded in the media, taking action gave the students some power over their own education. Additionally, students got responses from the various elected officials to whom they wrote; some brought these to class and seemed convinced that their opinions counted and perhaps even had an influence on the legislators.

Moreover, once they feel confident to speak in public situations, ESL students may decide to participate in college committees, on college senates, and in public debates. No more powerful moments occurred than when former ESL and developmental students, especially those who are now successful professionals, stood before the Board of Trustees and told their stories about how ESL and developmental programs had helped them to succeed in college.

We make decisions in every class we teach about how we present our society, our language, the students' languages and cultures, and the sociopolitical world in which we live. As Carol Severino (1998) wrote, "The ascendance and dominance of English, contributing to the proliferation of ESL or English as a Foreign Language (EFL) programs both in the United

States and abroad, are obviously political, thus causing the situation of any ESL student in any classroom inside or outside a college to be politically charged" (p. 187). Our instructional choices take place in this politically charged atmosphere, and we need to be aware of just how political these choices are. As our experience at CUNY may indicate, we are in a changing political climate in this country. Beliefs that we have had about educating the many are called into question, and programs for these students that we have fought to create and expand are being defunded and downsized for political reasons. Rather than feel defeated by these attacks, we should use this opportunity to work to make ESL students integral to higher education. Instruction does not only happen in the classroom. It happens every time we collaborate with colleagues, participate in projects, serve on committees, and are active in our communities.

APPENDIX

The policy printed below was adopted at the CUNY Board of Trustees January 25, 1999 meeting and approved by the New York State Regents on November 22, 1999:

RESOLVED, That all remedial course instruction shall be phased-out of all baccalaureate degree programs at the CUNY senior colleges as of the following dates: January 2000, for Baruch, Brooklyn, Queens, and Hunter Colleges; September 2000, for Lehman, John Jay, City, The College of Staten Island, and New York City Technical; and September 2001, for York and Medgar Evers Colleges. Following a college's discontinuation of remediation, no student who has not passed all three Freshman Skills Assessment Tests, and any other admissions criteria which may exist, shall be allowed to enroll and/or transfer into that college's baccalaureate degree programs. Students seeking admission to CUNY senior college baccalaureate degree programs who are in need of remediation shall be able to obtain such remediation services at a CUNY community college, at a senior college only during its summer sessions, or elsewhere as may be made available. This resolution does not apply to ESL students who received a secondary education abroad and who otherwise are not in need of remediation; and be it further

RESOLVED, That this Resolution supersedes Calendar Item No. 10 adopted by the Board of Trustees on May 26, 1998.

EXPLANATION: On May 26, 1998, the Board of Trustees adopted Calendar Item No. 10 (the "1998 Remediation Resolution"), which was substantively identical to the present resolution (other than with respect to the various dates). In June 1998, plaintiffs in the case of Crain v. Reynolds filed a motion for a preliminary injunction, seeking to prevent the University from implementing the 1998 Remediation Resolution, on the ground that the May 26,

1998 Board Meeting was held in violation of the State's Open Meetings Law. State Supreme Court Justice Elliott Wilk issued a decision, granting plaintiffs' motion for a preliminary injunction. Justice Wilk barred the University from taking any steps to eliminate or reduce the availability of remedial education at the senior colleges, except to the extent possible before the adoption of the 1998 Remediation Resolution. The University has appealed Justice Wilk's decision to the Appellate Division, First Department.

Justice Wilk's decision found that the Board Room at the University's Central Office is too small to convene its public meetings. The Board believes this ruling will present an unworkable obstacle to the orderly operation of University business, is uncalled for under the letter and spirit of the Open Meetings Law, and will be reversed on appeal. However, given that the Board wishes to move forward to implement this important academic policy without further undue delay, it has arranged to hold this one particular Board meeting in a special and accessible location, away from the Board headquarters, in order to preclude any claim that the size of the meeting room violates the Open Meetings Law. The Board expects and intends to return to its regular Board Room for future meetings.

ENDNOTES

1. When I was asked to focus on instruction, immersed as I am in the developments in public higher education in New York City these days, I realized that my chapter would have to be situated in the local context of my university at this historic moment in time However, I believe that the suggestions I make, strategies to make English as a Second Language/English as a Foreign Language (ESL/EFL) education integral to the college, of course altered to fit individual settings and needs, will make it easier to maintain programs that serve the needs of our second language students across a variety of settings.

2. Freshmen Skills Assessment Tests (FSATs) - Students take three skills tests on admission to CUNY. The RAT is a 45-minute multiple-choice reading test; the WAT is a 50-minute essay exam; the MAT is a 150-minute multiple-choice math test. Scores on the RAT and MAT are computer generated; the WAT is read holistically by CUNY-certified readers. On the basis of their scores on these exams, students are placed in remedial or nonremedial, ESL or non-ESL classes.

3. From Fall 1997 to Fall 1998, the ESL population at Queensborough Community College had increased by about 200 students. At Borough of Manhattan Community College, the population had increased from 1,349 students in the fall of 1997 to 1,532 students in 1998. Kingsborough Community College increased its numbers by nine students and LaGuardia Community College increased by 60 students (Carroll, 1999, p. 15).

4. The number of undergraduate ESL students enrolled at Baruch in the fall of 1997 was 442, and by the fall of 1998, the number had dropped to only 256 students. At Hunter, the [ESL] student population fell from 400 students in the fall of 1997 to 211 students in the fall of 1998. The ESL population at Brooklyn also changed dramatically, moving from 596 students in fall of 1997 to 328 students in fall of 1998. Queens College suffered less of a loss, moving from 246 students to 219 students (Carroll, 1999, p. 15).

REFERENCES

Benesch, S. (1988). *Ending remediation: Linking ESL and content in higher education.* Washington, DC: TESOL.

Benesch, S. (1998). Anorexia: A feminist EAP curriculum. In T. Smoke (Ed.), *Adult ESL: Politics, pedagogy, and participation in classroom and community programs* (pp. 101–114). Mahwah, NJ: Lawrence Erlbaum Associates.

Blakely, R. (1998). An orphan at the table: The English language fellows program. In T. Smoke (Ed.), *Adult ESL: Politics, pedagogy, and participation in classroom and community programs* (pp. 239–266). Mahwah, NJ: Lawrence Erlbaum Associates.

Brinton, D., Snow, M., & Wesche, M. (1989). *Content-based second language instruction.* Boston: Heinle & Heinle.

Carroll, J. (1999, Spring), Where are all the students? Changes in enrollment at CUNY. *Idiom, 29*(1), 1, 14–16.

Crandall, J. (1993). Content-centered learning in the United States. *Annual Review of Applied Linguistics, 13,* 111–126.

Cummins, J. (1990). Empowering minority students: A framework for intervention. In N. M. Hidalgo, C. L. McDowell, & E. V. Siddle (Eds.), *Facing racism in education* (pp. 50–68). Cambridge, MA: Harvard Educational Review.

Dardick, G. (1992). Moving toward independence. In T. Smoke (Ed.), *A writer's worlds: Explorations through reading* (2nd ed.); (pp. 311–315). New York: St. Martin's Press.

Delpit. L. (1990). The silenced dialogue: Power and pedagogy in educating other people's children. In N. M. Hidalgo, C. L. McDowell, & E. V. Siddle (Eds.), *Facing racism in education* (pp. 84–102). Cambridge, MA: Harvard Educational Review.

Haas, T., Hernández, J., & Smoke, T. (1991). A collaborative model for empowering nontraditional students. In S. Benesch (Ed.), *ESL in America: Myths and possibilities* (pp. 112–129). Portsmouth, NH: Heinemann.

Leki, I. (1992). *Understanding ESL writers: A guide for teachers.* Portsmouth, NH: Heinemann.

Severino, C. (1998). The political implications of responses to second language writing. In T. Smoke (Ed.), *Adult ESL: Politics, pedagogy, and participation in classroom and community programs* (pp. 185–206). Mahwah, NJ: Lawrence Erlbaum Associates.

Shor, I. (1992). *Empowering education: Critical teaching for social change.* Chicago: University of Chicago Press.

Smoke, T., & Haas, T. (1995). Ideas in practice: Linking classes to develop students' academic voices. *Journal of Development Education, 19,* 28–32.

Snow, M., & Brinton, D. (1988). *The adjunct model of language instruction: Integrating language and content at the university* (OERI Contract No. 400-85-1010). Los Angeles: Center for Language Education and Research, UCLA. Washington, DC: Office of Educational Research and Improvement (ERIC Document Reproduction Service No. 298-764).

Snow, M., & Kamhi-Stein, L. D. (Eds.). (1996). *Teaching academic literacy skills: Strategies for content faculty.* Los Angeles: California State University, Los Angeles and the Fund for the Improvement of Postsecondary Education

10

Advanced EAP Writing and Curriculum Design: What Do We Need to Know?

Joy Reid
University of Wyoming

The field of composition is relatively new; the specialized area of English as a Second Language (ESL) composition is younger still, not yet a quarter-century old (Santos, 1992). Research has increased substantially since 1990, particularly concerning such issues as assessment, pedagogical practices, and the differences between first language (L1) and second language (L2) composition   students and teaching (Atkinson & Ramanathan, 1995; Ferris & Hedgcock, 1998; Grabe & Kaplan, 1996, 1997; Hamp-Lyons, 1991; Leki & Carson, 1994, 1997; Reid, 1995; Silva, 1993, 1997). English for Academic Purposes (EAP) researchers have only begun to determine the needs of ESL writers in college and university settings (Braine, 1989, 1996; Canesco & Byrd, 1989; Horowitz, 1986a, 1986b; Shuck, 1995). This chapter focuses on the implications of such research, on the development of additional multiple-needs analyses to identify the writing demands of the college and university, and on issues that must be investigated if curricular integration is to be accomplished.

CURRICULUM DESIGN AND NEEDS ANALYSIS

Curriculum design—a plan that guides the processes of teaching and learning—is an old topic, with processes and products well-documented in Teaching English as a Second Language (TESL) textbooks (Dubin & Olshtain, 1986; Genesee, 1994; Nunan, 1989; Reid, 1995; Van Lier, 1996). This chapter narrows the definition to a dynamic overall plan for a writing

143

program that is based on the needs of the students, the principles that underlie both the theories and practices of learning and teaching, and essential external expectations and constraints.

Because EAP students must be prepared to respond successfully to college and university writing assignments, an advanced EAP writing course cannot exist in a vacuum. Instead, it should be thoughtfully designed to integrate immediate student needs with the hierarchy of institutional values, disciplinary goals, and professorial expectations. Effective curriculum comprises the results of multiple-needs analyses that "describe existing elements of the target situation to provide the basis for curriculum development" (Benesch, 1996, p. 723).

In truth, such needs analysis have been more a part of English for Specific Purposes (ESP), adult ESL, and workplace ESL than of EAP (Hammond, Wickert, Burns, Joyce, & Miller 1992; Johns, 1997; Prior, 1995a; Robinson, 1991). For example, workplace ESL curriculum designers work on site, considering corporate goals, evaluating departmental objectives, describing the job task and language demands of the ESL workers, and developing curriculum to meet those demands. In postsecondary composition programs, EAP curriculum designers can use the same processes of collecting, describing, and assessing authentic information, then integrating the results into course objectives that will structure classroom pedagogy.

However, although the processes of needs analysis are similar from institution to institution, the *products*—the interpretation of the results and the resulting curriculum design—are not necessarily transportable. After all, writing requirements and standards in one institution may not reflect those in another, and educational values may differ significantly. Moreover, no writing program can meet every goal of the institution, every departmental demand, every writing program objective, and every student's needs. *Human constraints*—time, energy, and resources—play a part in the priority setting and implementation of curriculum.

One caveat: Teaching EAP writing is a service, the objectives of which are not only to make college- and university-course instructors' lives easier, or to provide departments with high-quality writers, or just to accomplish institutional goals, or solely to fulfill program requirements, but especially to serve ESL students—to prepare them to become successful, confident, efficient, effective academic writers.

INSTITUTIONAL VALUES, EXPECTATIONS, AND CONSTRAINTS

Although ESL composition teachers may only rarely venture into their college or university other than the intensive English program or the writing program, either physically or reflectively, and may never have examined the values of their institutions beyond their programs, curriculum designers must. To develop pedagogical frameworks that will adequately prepare EAP· students for their postsecondary careers, they must formulate and administer well-designed needs analyses, then interpret and consider the results in order to understand institutional values, and finally design curriculum that links the EAP course(s) to college and university objectives.

Such institutional goals are culturally based. Some cultures have as their overriding value the preparation of active, involved citizens; other cultures value the preparation of needed workers who can further the progress of the country; still others may value cooperation and harmony and prepare their students for those community behaviors above all others. Educational values involve such concepts as the nature and purpose of learning, ideas about the roles of the learner and the teacher, about effective and ineffective study methods, about the nature of curriculum and syllabus design, and about teaching and learning techniques (Althen, 1994; Brick, 1991; Fu, 1995; Townsend & Fu, 1998).

Because many of these values are assumed by members of the educational community, values are often easier to discern in other cultures. ESL composition teachers learn (and experience), for example, that many Asian students matriculate successfully from institutional systems that value their ability to accurately recall the knowledge presented to them—the mastery of a body of knowledge. Instructors in China are "knowers" who are responsible for the transmission and the conservation of knowledge (Ballard & Clanchy, 1991). In contrast, observing classrooms in the United States and analyzing the grading procedures in those classrooms reveal the focus on active and visible participation of U.S. students in those classes (Brislin, 1993; Byrd, 1986). The impulsive responses and questions, students challenging each other and even their instructors, are valued in participation grades. Creativity, competition, individualism, and the extension of knowledge—with the student, not the instructor, responsible for learning—are among U.S. educational values. Incidentally, we might hypothesize that in China, there are students who would be valued in U.S. classrooms as good students, but because their classroom behaviors are not valued in China, we do not see those students in our writing programs.

Both quantitative and qualitative approaches are necessary in an investigation of values. Curriculum designers will analyze official documents, test data, and empirical data from well-designed surveys as well as ethnographic information gathered through interviews and from observations of attitudes and behaviors. To a limited extent, they can begin to discover the values of an educational system by perusing the mission statement of the institution ("University undergraduates will . . . have facility in using language"). They might also analyze information about alumni honored by the institution, their qualities and achievements, and their position as role models in their communities. The college and university bulletin will contain more specific goals, including, for example, descriptions of required composition courses and writing-intensive courses: "The goals of the University Studies Program," which include first-year composition, one midlevel writing or writing intensive course, and one upper division writing or writing intensive course "are to provide a general education which will help students develop skills in written and oral communication" (*University of Wyoming General Bulletin*, 1998–1999, p. 50). Course descriptions in the bulletin may provide additional information about writing assignments and requirements:

> *Research in Psychological Methods*: Requires written and oral reports.
>
> *Broadcast Writing*: Intensive practice in gathering and writing broadcast news.
>
> *Health Care of the Older Adult*: Students are expected to synthesize knowledge gained from a series of focused interviews with an older adult.
>
> *Cytotechnique*: Requires special research project.
>
> *Experimental Foods*: Students develop ability to use and interpret recent research findings, as well as skills in planning, conducting, and reporting food experiments.
>
> *Range Utilization and Grazing Management*: Acquaints students with most commonly used grazing management systems and improves students' writing in a technical subject.
>
> *Problems in Finance*: Written report required.

Within the college and university, curriculum designers should investigate in-house gate-keeping processes: SAT, ACT, and TOEFL admission cut-off scores, including the Test of Written English (TWE), required first-year placement exams in writing, and "rising junior" and/or exit writing examinations. In addition to the design and types of writing topics, the selected assessment tools (and personnel) for the evaluation procedures of those exams will reveal a substantial amount of information about the institution's goals for written literacy. Which linguistic, rhetorical, and contextual skills are valued? Which are not highly valued? How will those values impact curriculum design for the writing program? (One scoring guide for a direct test of writing for a university first-year placement examination is in the Appendix.)

Another effective approach is to examine the standardized tests in the culture; as beliefs change, so will the barrier examinations that separate the successful from the unsuccessful students. Recently, for example, the SAT, ACT, LSAT and GMAT have, in addition to the multiple-choice single-answer questions, included test questions (or sections) to determine critical-thinking skills and problem-solving abilities, as well as direct tests of writing skills, in which students must perform individually, select topics and ideas, and present those ideas in persuasive ways. These written products are evaluated according to scoring guidelines; analyzing those guidelines can provide valuable insights in both institutional and broader educational values in society.

As curriculum designers examine artifacts that demonstrate institutional goals, they become aware of what Van Lier (1996) called the "tests, generalized hierarchies for success, ladders of achievement, profiles of outcomes and lists of competencies, do-as-you're told measurements of professional adequacy, and in general the bureaucratic accountability" (p. 10) that they must consider as they develop writing program frameworks.

COLLEGE/UNIVERSITY COURSE DEMANDS

What do we know about the writing assigned in courses across the college and university curriculum? If the institution requires writing-intensive courses, what do the writing tasks comprise? What writing assignments are required of undergraduates in general education courses? What assignments are required in major field courses, especially those with heavy ESL enrollments (e.g., business, engineering, physical and biological sciences)?

Two areas of composition research have provided some information about the types of writing assignments and the expectations of instructors in discipline-specific courses in colleges and universities. In L1 research, the writing-across-the-curriculum (WAC) movement has focused on helping instructors outside of English departments design, assign, and assess writing in their fields. Research has included investigation of typical writing assignments, and assessment criteria used to evaluate the assignments (Bernhardt, 1985; Herrington & Moran, 1992; Kirscht, Levine, & Reiff, 1994; LeCourt, 1996; McLeod, 1995; Peterson, 1992; Soven, 1992). In L2 teaching and research, ESP researchers have been especially interested in examining the linguistic and rhetorical purposes and audiences in such fields as business, engineering, and science (Bhatia, 1993; Braine, 1995; Halliday & Martin, 1993; Hanania & Akhtar, 1985; Hyland, 1996, 2000; Miles, 1997; Salager-Meyer, 1994). In their efforts to link form, function, and social context in discipline-specific areas of study, ESP and EAP researchers have examined the types of writing representative of academic literacy, from short-answers to in-class examination questions to research papers, and from laboratory reports to book reviews (Allison, Cooley, Lewkowicz, & Nunan, 1999; Braine, 1989; Dong, 1998; Frodesen, 1995; Gosden, 1996; Harklau, 1999; Horowitz, 1986a, 1986b; Paltridge, 1997).

In addition, L1 and L2 composition teachers and researchers have examined the topic types of assignments in disciplines across the curriculum by gathering actual assignments from departments and instructors, interviewing instructors, collecting assignments, and surveying students (Bennett, 1996; Fox, 1996; Prior, 1995a, 1995b). For example, Horowitz (1986b) queried faculty members concerning the amount and types of writing assignments; he also collected and analyzed in-class examinations that required writing (Horowitz, 1986a). Canesco and Byrd (1989) analyzed the syllabi and the topic types of writing assignments for 48 graduate business courses; Carson and her colleagues (1992) examined the literacy requirements of an undergraduate history course. Many of the studies indicate that little writing, formal or informal, is actually required in college and university undergraduate courses although more institutional focus on essential communication skills may be slowly influencing departmental academic goals.

Although the data are preliminary, some even anecdotal (and so the issues involved deserve further research), they seem intuitively accurate. Following are some of the general factors found in WAC assignments. Excerpts from authentic examples of typical out-of-class assignments are also listed.

* In-class writing assignments are almost solely short-answer tasks and essays.
* Nearly all writing topics to be completed in or outside of class are assigned; some allow choice of topic within limited scope, and some allow narrowing.
* All topics grow out of class material.
* Most extended tasks require work external to the class.
* The most common out-of-class assignments are the
  * *the library research paper*
    * *U.S. History:* For your final paper, you will write a 5–10 page essay answering the following: What is American Democracy? Is it an adequate vehicle for achieving the "good life"?
  * *the report with interpretation*
    * *Marketing:* Write a short report (3 pages maximum) that identifies a real, current example of product positioning.
  * *the summary, with or without analysis*
    * *Macroeconomics:* You are assigned to select a member country of the United Nations and to create a macroeconomic summary of events that have occurred in the last decade. Imagine that you are a correspondent for the *Wall Street Journal* or for CNN, and that you have to write for the business community.
  * *the plan/proposal*
    * *Pest Management:* The term paper should be written as what USAID terms a PPD (Preproject document) which is used to justify

the need to create and implement a project. The paper should design a pest management scheme at two management levels (high input and low input) for a cropping system of your choice in the ecological zone of your choice.

○ *the book review/critique*

◻ *Introduction to Political Science:* Write a five-page review of a book concerning elections in America. About two thirds of the review should summarize the contents of the book. The concluding third should relate the book to some of the themes about American elections that we have discussed in class.

In more large-scale research, the Educational Testing Service has undertaken several analyses to determine the needs of native English speaking (NES) and ESL students in colleges and universities and to discover the writing tasks and skills used across the curriculum. These investigations surveyed representative U.S. universities and colleges, collected assignments, and interviewed students and instructors. In an earlier study, Bridgeman and Carlson (1983) surveyed faculty in seven disciplines at 34 institutions to determine what topic types they used as writing assignments; the results were diverse, suggesting that science and technology faculty required descriptive tasks (of apparatus or procedures) as well as summary and analysis, whereas social sciences and humanities faculty more often chose the broadly defined argument. Ginther and Grant (1996) reviewed the literature concerning the academic needs, in particular the reading and writing needs, of college and university students in the United States. Hamp-Lyons and Kroll (1996) examined writing "as an act that takes place within a context, accomplishes a particular purpose, and is appropriately shaped for its intended audience" (p. iv) in order to determine the "universe of writing skills . . . needed to succeed in an academic context" (p. 8). Their study focused on assessment of college and university writing skills and included examination writing tasks, text types, settings (reasons and situations or scenarios for writing), and performance expectations. Finally, Hale and his associates (1997) surveyed academic writing purposes by collecting writing assignments, interviewing instructors and students, and then categorizing the writing required at eight major research universities.

Among the conclusions of these ETS research reports are the following:

• English departments are anomalous in assignments and evaluation practices.

• In-class writing (i.e., responses to short-answer examination questions) is the most common occurrence of college and university writing.

• The major function of in-class writing is to provide an opportunity for students to display knowledge. This demonstration of acquired knowledge is more important than the ability to express and develop original ideas in terms of student grades and academic success.

* Evidence overwhelmingly suggests that graduates and undergraduates have different needs in the nature of their writing requirements. That is, differences existed between undergraduate and graduate courses' writing tasks, types, and audience expectations. Specifically, extended exposition and development are more characteristic of graduate-level courses.

In addition, the Hale et al. (1997) study, which focused on a classification and description of writing requirements in colleges and universities, concluded that some disciplinary differences exist in writing tasks. For example, short writing tasks were more common in physical and mathematical science and engineering, and short tasks (of less than a page) were more common at the undergraduate level. Of the types of writing taught across the curriculum, virtually no personal narratives were found although some types of nonpersonal narrative were used as a form of evidence. Further, no literary analysis was found outside of English courses, but there were frequent assignments of summaries and/or reviews of sources within fields, for instance, to "critique five articles not previously assigned on the reading list," in an agricultural economics course. Similarly, no poetic or personal descriptions were assigned (again, outside of English departments), but much sensory description was assigned, as, for example, background information about laboratory experiments and scenario setting in case studies.

Hale et al. (1997) also found that the most common characteristics of assignments in all disciplines required expository (explaining) skills that were frequently supported by cause–effect; less often, they were supported by comparison–contrast, classification, and analysis. Assignments also required problem-solving skills: analysis, synthesis, and persuasion. Following is a typical example in an undergraduate course; explanations are added in brackets:

> *Environmental Issues:* In an 8 to 10 page paper, *analyze* one environmental issue. *Explain* the issue; describe the *cause*(s) and the *effect*(s) of the issue; *compare* [and *synthesize*] the differing beliefs (those ideas concerning the issue, whether true or false), the values (the guides that reflect the importance of the beliefs), and/or solutions (the various strategies used to resolve the issue) that exist. Present your position about the issue; give evidence that supports [*persuades* the audience of] the value of your position.

Often the required persuasion skills comprised the use of persuasive language, mediating hedges (Hyland, 1999), and appropriate authoritative evidence rather than the more formal, debate-based, confrontational argument task. That is, the expected persuasive style consisted of material presented in a more affiliative manner rather than in the strictly conventional, argument and counterargument format taught in many ESL and EFL textbooks.

The results of this preliminary but persuasive research indicate that writing-program curriculum designers should examine the practical implications in their own institutions by discovering whether or not similar patterns occur, collecting actual assignments to explore the purpose(s) and audience expectations of short and long writing tasks, and designing curricula that include the study of appropriate presentations of demonstrating knowledge.

DESIGNING THE WRITING PROGRAM CURRICULUM: NONLITERARY DISCOURSE GENRES

Both WAC and ESP research stimulated the current interest in nonliterary academic *genres* in L1 and L2 contexts. NES and ESL composition researchers define genre as the linguistic, rhetorical, and communicative (i.e., social) conventions in the discourses of various academic disciplines (Bazerman, 1994; Biber, 1988; Biber, Conrad, & Reppen, 1994, 1998; Coe, 1994; Allison et al., 1999; Hinkel, 1999; Hyland, 1998, in press; Miller, 1994; Thetela, 1997). Fundamental to this research is the concept of discourse community: Writing competence requires comprehension of and the abilities to produce writing that adheres to the conventions of a discourse particular to a disciplinary community of readers (Berkenkotter & Huckin, 1993, 1995; Dudley-Evans, 1994, 1997; Fahnestock, 1993). In a discipline such as chemistry or geology, or in a social context such as a term paper in a psychology class or a case study in a management course, there are substantial differences in how knowledge and ideas are communicated in writing.

Initial work in genre studies, based on Halliday's (Halliday & Hasan, 1989) functional approach to language, began in Australia (see Christie, 1992; Hyon, 1996); results are currently used in writing curricula throughout the Australian NES school system. In postsecondary settings, English L2 genre studies have been most widely investigated in ESP and English for Science and Technology (EST) contexts (Flowerdew, 1993; Hanania & Akhtar, 1985; Johns, 1997; Love, 1993; Riazi, 1997; Salager-Meyer, 1994). Swales (1990) described nonliterary genre specifically as writing in which there are constraints in writing conventions in "content, positioning, and form" (p. 52). More recently, EAP teachers and researchers have found that although their students may understand fully the content that must be communicated in writing, they may not understand how that information should be presented, argued, and supported (Casanave & Hubbard, 1992; Currie, 1993; Dong, 1998; Johns, 1995; Ramanathan & Kaplan, 1996; Thompson & Ye, 1991).

Results of genre research, in addition to the WAC, ESP, and EAP investigations, provide a basis for EAP writing program curriculum design. Perhaps the most important results of L2 genre research confirm Farris' (1993) statement that we must abandon the "politically and economically convenient myth of a common unified academic discourse that the faculty believes can be taught" (p. 1). As teachers and researchers learn more about these academic genres, and as they discover the subskills common to most writing assignments across the curriculum, they must design curriculum that, as Meyer (1996) noted, explicitly offers students "not only the grammatical and discourse building blocks, but also, more importantly, the skills needed to learn and use those building blocks in community-appropriate interactions in order to build a genre" (p. 41).

Genre and Curriculum Design

Curriculum designers begin by examining institutional and departmental demands and expectations through multiple empirical and ethnographic needs analyses, then, as ESL writing specialists, they consider the development of a writing program philosophy that incorporates the (dynamic) principles that underlie both the theories and practices of L2 learning and teaching, students' needs, program teachers' educational and experiential backgrounds, and institutional and program constraints (time, energy, and resources).

In other words, those designing writing program curricula will focus on determining the roles of various rhetorical, contextual, and linguistic tasks and skills across the broad spectrum of disciplinary genres and designing a writing program that will give students the opportunity to learn and practice the skills and types of writing indicated by previous research. More specific questions might include:

- How can the curriculum provide appropriate aims and helpful structures that will support student learning?
- What sequences of learning experiences will most benefit L2 writing students in their college and university writing experiences?
- Which writing skills are transferable (i.e., follow the students into their college and university careers)?
- How can ESL student writers develop linguistic, rhetorical, contextual, and content competence in those skills and strategies most effectively and efficiently?
- What writing skills are more or less cognitively complex? How to structure the necessary sequencing and spiraling that will provide students with adequate scaffolding to master those skills?

The resulting program philosophy will cut across the "oppositions and rigid distinctions among theory, research, and practice" (Van Lier, 1996, p. 28). The curriculum will empower EAP writing students by preparing them adequately in skills, self-confidence, and abilities to fulfill institutional expectations. The students will learn how to learn, and they will become aware of necessary resources and opportunities.

Resistance to Curricular Change

Some composition teachers are quite judgmental about the demonstration types of writing described earlier, calling them "stupid little reports" or "mouthing someone else's words instead of thinking for themselves," and determining that they are therefore not worth teaching. In contrast, exposing ESL students to the functions and forms of the writing requirements and assignments they are almost certain to encounter in their future courses is essential to EAP instruction. Indeed, for L2 students, the need is critical because they often have little or no acquaintance with such functions and forms by which writers fulfill the linguistic and rhetorical expectations of the academic audience. Further, available research indicates that *showing knowledge* (i.e., demonstrating to an instructor that one has learned what has been taught) is a substantial part of college and university writing for at least most undergraduates; knowing the writing conventions for displaying knowledge is therefore necessary for students' success in courses (Carson et al., 1992). Being deprived of the opportunities to learn about these functions and forms will, quite simply, further marginalize ESL writers.

Other composition teachers may find the development of writing program goals based on institutional and disciplinary demands extremely constraining in their course planning, and they may believe that the explicitness of genre instruction will be inhibiting for students. Yet both L1 and L2 composition research indicates that today's NES and ESL college and university students lack experience in recognizing and analyzing the expectations of disciplinary readers. Even if they read various genres, these students do not have the background experience to identify the conventions. Therefore, without explicit instruction in the function and form of writing tasks across the curriculum, students can fail to gain access to the power of literacy (Cope & Kalantzis, 1993). Indeed, explicit modeling, guided practice, and discussions about language can make overt and transparent the hidden curriculum of schooling, especially for students from cultures that employ different writing conventions (Berkenkotter & Huckin, 1995).

EAP researchers have specifically advocated the explicit teaching of the writing conventions of cross-curricular writing text types. As Hamp-Lyons and Kroll (1997) stated, "each writer needs both guidance on what is important about [a] writing task and what qualities will be valued" (p. 22) by those who assess the writing. Explicit training in the rhetorics and contexts, the audiences and purposes of disciplinary genres, is even more essential for ESL writers than it is for middle-class NES students who have had only limited access to what Gee (1990) called *discourse literacies*: the more formal institutionalized modes of talking, acting, believing, and valuing. Further, advanced EAP writers, both undergraduate and graduate students, find the more direct teaching of functions and forms relatively easy to understand and to acquire, thereby leaving them less burdened by how to present material, with more time and energy to focus on the material itself, and more confident about fulfilling the assignment. They also see the relevance and pragmatism of the course; in fact, in my classes they often ask, "Why didn't someone just teach us this before?"

CONCLUSION

The first purpose in this chapter was to show that writing program curriculum design is not for the inexperienced, the faint of heart, or the out-of-touch. Second, the necessity of multiple-needs analyses in curriculum design—before, during, and ongoing—seems clear, as does the fact that the results of analyses in one institution cannot be easily or accurately transferred to others. Third, identifying ESL student needs in future college and university writing must be the overall goal of curriculum designers; recent nonliterary genre studies provide the best information for meeting those needs.

Finally, because the L2 writing area is still so new, teachers and researchers should be aware of the substantial amount of future research needed. First, we need continued development of needs analysis processes and interpretation of results. Next, ongoing genre study is needed to better determine what students actually have to write in different disciplines and what writing subskills are evident. Teachers and researchers must continue to gather writing assignments in and across postsecondary institutions and to analyze those assignments; discourse analysis research, including the linguistic, rhetorical, and contextual conventions of discipline-specific writing, can provide significant information about genre teaching. Interviewing instructors about their reasons for designing writing task(s), their specific task expectations, and the importance of the writing task(s) on students' success in the course will also prove fruitful in developing criteria for teaching. Interviewing students about what they thought the audience expectations were and what they did to fulfill those expectations will provide valuable information for curriculum modification.

In short, knowledge is empowering, for researchers, for teachers, and for students. The complexity of writing typically expected in academic settings requires that teachers and curriculum designers explore theories of writing and literacy development, that they determine the demands and expectations ESL writers will encounter, and that they offer students the parameters and pragmatics of fulfilling assignments that will allow them to participate fully in academic literacies.

Appendix
Scoring Guide: First-Year English Placement Examination
Colorado State University
Summer, 1998, "Birth Order in America"

9–8 The upper range responses satisfy the following criteria:

  a. Summary—The summary should identify and distinguish between Sulloway's birth order thesis and Devlin's disagreement with Sulloway. It should note some of the reasons why Devlin disagrees with Sulloway (e.g., unscientific, illogical, subjective, and/or not very useful).

  b. Focus of agreement or disagreement—Agreement or disagreement may be complete or partial, but the writer must establish, explain, and maintain the focus of agreement or disagreement with Devlin's argument.

  c. Support for agreement and/or disagreement—Support should provide an analysis of Devlin's argument or relevant and concrete examples from the writer's experience or general knowledge.

  d. Style and coherence—These papers demonstrate clear style, overall organization, consecutiveness of thought, and often a strong voice. They contain few errors in usage, grammar, or mechanics.

7 This score should be used for papers that fulfill the basic requirements for the 9–8 score but have less development, support, or analysis.

6–5 Middle-range papers omit or are deficient in one of the four criteria:

  a. Summary—Summary absent, inaccurate, incomplete, or inadequate.

  b. Focus of agreement or disagreement—What the writer is agreeing or disagreeing with is not clear, is not well maintained, or is not related to Devlin's main argument.

  c. Support—Writer only asserts or counterasserts; writer's examples are highly generalized or not distinguishable from examples given in the article; the writer's analysis of Devlin's argument may be specious, irrelevant, inaccurate, or thin.

   d. Style and coherence—These papers are loosely organized or contain noticeable errors in usage, grammar, or mechanics.

4 This score should be used for papers that fulfill the basic requirement for the 6–5 score but are slightly weaker. Digressive essays that are otherwise satisfactory typically receive a 4.

3 Lower range papers are deficient in *two* or more of the criteria—typically, they have no summary and no support. Often these papers are preachy, clichéd, or platitudinous, OR they have serious organization/coherence problems.

2 Papers with serious, repeated errors in usage, grammar or mechanics OR papers with significant focus or coherence problems that seriously disrupt communication must be given a 2.

1 This score should be given to papers that have overwhelming problems.

Note, an essay written in fluent, stylistic prose may be scored one point higher than the guide would normally permit. Please give 1s, 2s, 8s, 9s, LD, ESL, and unresponsive papers to the table leader.

Used with permission.

REFERENCES

Allison, D., Cooley, L., Lewkowicz, J., & Nunan, D. (1999). Dissertation writing in action: The development of a disseration writing support program for ESL graduate research students. *English for Specific Purposes, 17*(2), 199–217.

Althen, G. (Ed.). (1994). Culture differences on campus. In G. Althen (Ed.) *Learning across cultures* (pp. 57–72). Washington DC: NAFSA:AIE.

Atkinson, D., & V. Ramanathan. (1995). Cultures of writing: An ethnographic comparison of L1 and L2 university writing/language programs. *TESOL Quarterly, 29*, 539–566.

Ballard, B., & Clanchy, J. (1991). Assessment by misconception: Cultural influences and intellectual traditions. In L. Hamp-Lyons (Ed.), *Assessing second language writing in academic contexts* (pp. 19–36). Norwood, NJ: Ablex.

Bazerman, C. (1994). Systems of genres and the enactment of social intentions. In A. Freedman & P. Medway (Eds.), *Genre and the new rhetoric* (pp. 79–101). London: Taylor & Francis.

Bennett, S. T. (1996). A survey of the teaching of composition at forty-six high profile university and college intensive English programs. *Dissertation Abstracts International, 57*(12), 5033A.

Benesch, S. (1996). Needs analysis and curriculum development in EAP: An example of a critical approach. *TESOL Quarterly, 30*, 723–738.

Berkenkotter, C., & Huckin, T. (1993). Rethinking genre from a sociocognitive perspective. *Written Communication, 4*, 475–509.

Berkenkotter, C., & Huckin, T. (1995). *Genre knowledge in disciplinary communication: Cognition/culture/power.* Hillsdale, NJ: Lawrence Erlbaum Associates.

Bernhardt, S. A. (1985). Writing across the curriculum at one university: A survey of faculty members and students. *ADE Bulletin, 82,* 55–59.

Bhatia, V. K. (1993). *Analysing genre: Language use in professional settings.* London: Longman.

Biber, D. (1988). *Variation Across Speech and Writing.* New York: Cambridge University Press.

Biber, D., Conrad, S., & Reppen, R. (1994). Corpus-based approaches to issues in applied linguistics. *Applied Linguistics, 15*(2), 169–189.

Biber, D., Conrad, S., & Reppen, R. (1998). *Corpus linguistics: Investigating language structure and use.* Cambridge, UK: Cambridge University Press.

Braine, G. (1989). Writing in science and technology: An analysis of assignments from ten undergraduate courses. *English for Specific Purposes, 8,* 3–15.

Braine, G. (1995). Writing in the natural sciences and engineering. In D. Belcher & G. Braine (Eds.), *Academic writing in a second language: Essays on research and pedagogy* (pp. 113–134). Norwood, NJ; Ablex.

Braine, G. (1996). ESL students in first-year writing courses: ESL versus mainstream classes. *Journal of Second Language Writing, 5,* 91–107.

Brick, J. (1991). *China: A handbook in intercultural communication.* Macquarie University, Sydney: National Centre for English Language Teaching and Research.

Bridgeman, B., & Carlson, S. (1983). *Survey of academic writing tasks required of graduate and undergraduate foreign students.* (TOEFL Research Report No. 15; ETS Research Report No. 83-18). Princeton NJ: Educational Testing Service.

Brislin, R. (1993). *Understanding culture's influence on behavior.* Fort Worth: Harcourt Brace.

Byrd, P. (1986). *Teaching across cultures in the university ESL program.* Washington, DC: NAFSA.

Canesco, G., & Byrd, P. (1989). Writing required in graduate courses in business administration. *TESOL Quarterly, 23,* 305–316.

Carson, J., Chase, H. D., Gibson, S. U., & Hargrove, M. F. (1992). Literacy demands of the undergraduate curriculum. *Reading Research and Instruction, 31,* 25–50.

Casanave, C. P., & Hubbard, P. (1992). The writing assignments and writing problems of doctoral students: Faculty perceptions, pedagogical issues, and needed research. *English for Specific Purposes, 11,* 33–49.

Christie, F. (1992). Literacy in Australia. *Annual Review of Applied Linguistics, 12,* 142–155.

Coe, R. (1994). "An arousing and fulfillment of desires": The rhetoric of genre in the process era—and beyond. In A. Freedman & P. Medway (Eds.), *Genre and the new rhetoric* (pp. 181–190). London: Taylor & Francis.

Cope, B., & Kalantzis, M. (Eds.). (1993). *The powers of literacy: A genre approach to teaching writing.* New York: The Falmer Press.

Currie, P. (1993). Entering a disciplinary community: Conceptual activities required to write for one introductory university course. *Journal of Second Language Writing, 7*(2), 101–117.

Dong, Y. R. (1998). Non-native graduate students' thesis/dissertation writing in science: Self-reports by students and their advisors from two U.S. institutions. *English for Specific Purposes, 17*(4), 369–390.

Dubin, F., & Olshtain, E. (1986). *Course Design: Developing programs and materials for language learning.* Cambridge, UK: Cambridge University Press.

Dudley-Evans, T. (1994). Variations in the discourse patterns favoured by different disciplines and their pedagogical implications. In J. Flowerdew (Ed.), *Academic listening: Research perspectives* (pp. 146–158). Cambridge, UK: Cambridge University Press.

Dudley-Evans, T. (1997). Genre: How far can we, should we, go? *World Englishes, 16*(13), 351–358.

Fahnestock, J. (1993). Genre and rhetorical craft. *Research in the Teaching of English, 27,* 265–271.

Farris, C. (1993). *Disciplining the disciplines: The paradox of writing across the curriculum claims*. (ERIC Document Reproduction Service No. ED 358 468).

Ferris, D., & Hedgcock, J. S. (1998). *Teaching ESL composition: Purpose, process, and practice*. Mahwah, NJ: Lawrence Erlbaum Associates.

Flowerdew, J. (1993). An educational, or process, approach to the teaching of professional genres. *ELT Journal, 47*, 305–316.

Fox, H. (1996). *"And never the twain shall meet:" International students writing for a U.S. university audience*. (ERIC Document Reproduction Service No. ED 300 540).

Frodesen, J. (1995). Negotiating the syllabus: A learner-centered, interactive approach to ESL graduate writing course design. In D. Belcher & G. Braine (Eds.), *Academic writing in a second language: Essays on research and pedagogy* (pp. 313–350). Norwood, NJ: Ablex.

Fu, D. (1995). *"My trouble is my English:" Asian students and the American dream*. Portsmouth, NH: Heinemann.

Gee, J. P. (1990). *Social linguistics and literacies: Ideology in discourses*. New York: The Falmer Press.

Genesee, F. (Ed.). (1994). *Educating second language children: The whole child, the whole curriculum, the whole community*. Cambridge, UK: Cambridge University Press.

Ginther, A., & Grant, L. (1996, September). *A review of the academic needs of native English-speaking college students in the United States*. (TOEFL Monograph Series, MS-1). Princeton NJ: Educational Testing Service.

Gosden, H. (1996). Verbal reports of Japanese novices' research writing practices in English. *Journal of Second Language Writing, 5*(2), 109–128.

Grabe, W., & Kaplan, R. B. (1996). *Theory and practice of writing*. New York: Longman.

Grabe, W., & Kaplan, R. B. (1997). The writing course. In K. Bardovi-Harlig & B. Hartford (Eds.), *Beyond methods: Components of second language teacher education* (pp. 172–197). New York: McGraw-Hill.

Hale, G., Taylor, C., Bridgeman, B., Carson, J., Kroll, B., & Kantor, R. (1997). *A study of writing tasks assigned in academic degree programs*. (TOEFL Research Report 54). Princeton, NJ: Educational Testing Service.

Halliday, M. A. K., & Hasan, R. (1989). *Language, context, and text: Aspects of language and meaning*. London: Edward Arnold.

Halliday, M. A. K., & Martin, J. R. (1993). *Writing science: Literacy and discursive power*. Pittsburgh, PA: University of Pittsburgh Press.

Hammond, J., Wickert, R., Burns, A., Joyce, H., & Miller, A. (1992). *The pedagogical relations between adult ESL and adult literacy*. Canberra: Commonwealth of Australia.

Hamp-Lyons, L. (Ed.). (1991). *Assessing second language writing in academic contexts*. Norwood, NJ: Ablex.

Hamp-Lyons, L., & Kroll, B. (1996). Issues in ESL writing assessment: An overview. *College ESL, 6*, 52–72.

Hamp-Lyons, L., & Kroll, B. (March, 1997). *TOEFL 2000—writing: Composition, community, and assessment*. TOEFL Monographic Series MS-5. Princeton, NJ: Educational Testing Service.

Hanania, E. A. S., & Akhtar, K. (1985). Verb form and rhetorical function in science writing: A study of MS theses in biology, chemistry, and physics. *English for Specific Purposes, 7*, 113–121.

Harklau, L. (1999). Representing culture in the ESL writing classroom. In E. Hinkel (Ed.), *Culture in second language learning* (pp. 10–130). Cambridge, UK: Cambridge University Press.

Herrington, A., & Moran, C. (Eds.). (1992). *Writing, teaching, and learning in the disciplines*. New York: Modern Language Association.

Hinkel, E. (1999). Objectivity and credibility in L1 and L2 academic writing. In E. Hinkel (Ed.), *Culture in second language learning* (pp. 90–108). Cambridge, UK: Cambridge University Press.

Horowitz, D. (1986a). Essay examination prompts and the teaching of academic writing. *English for Specific Purposes, 5,* 107–120.

Horowitz, D. (1986b). What professors actually require: Academic tasks for the ESL classroom. *TESOL Quarterly, 20,* 445–482.

Hyland, K. (1996). Nurturing hedges in the ESP curriculum. *System, 24*(4), 477–490.

Hyland, K. (1998). *Hedging in scientific research articles.* Amsterdam: Benjamins.

Hyland, K. (1999). Academic attribution: Citation and the construction of disciplinary knowledge. *Applied Linguisitics, 20*(3), 341–367.

Hyland, K. (2000). Disciplinary discourses: Writer stance in research articles. In C. Candlin & K. Hyland (Eds.), *Writing: Texts, processes and practices.* London: Longman.

Hyon, S. (1996). Genre in three traditions: Implications for ESL. *TESOL Quarterly, 30,* 693–722.

Johns, A. (1995). Teaching classroom and authentic genres: Initiating students into academic cultures and discourses. In D. Belcher and G. Braine (Eds.), *Academic writing in a second language* (pp. 277–291). Norwood, NJ: Ablex.

Johns, A. (1997). *Text, role, and context: Developing academic literacies.* Cambridge, UK: Cambridge University Press.

Kirscht, J., Levine, R., & Reiff, J. (1994). Evolving paradigms: WAC and the rhetoric of inquiry. *College Composition and Communication, 45,* 369–380.

LeCourt, D. (1996). WAC as critical pedagogy: The third stage? *Journal of Advanced Composition, 16*(3), 389–404.

Leki, I., & Carson, J. (1994). Students' perceptions of EAP writing instruction and writing needs across the disciplines. *TESOL Quarterly, 28,* 81–101.

Leki, I., & Carson, J. (1997). "Completely different worlds:" EAP and the writing experiences of ESL students in university courses. *TESOL Quarterly, 31,* 39–69.

Love, A. (1993). Lexico-grammatical features of geology textbooks: Process and product revisited. *English for Specific Purposes, 12,* 197–218.

McLeod, S. (1995). The foreigner: WAC directors as agents of change. Janangelo & K. Hansen (Eds.), *Resituating writing* (pp. 108–116). Portsmouth, NH: Boynton.

Meyer, L. (1996). The contribution of genre theory to theme-based EAP: Navigating foreign fiords. *TESL Canada Journal, 13*(2), 33–44.

Miles, L. (1997). Globalizing professional writing curricula: Positioning students and re-positioning textbooks. *Technical Communication Quarterly, 6*(2), 179–200.

Miller, C. R. (1994). Rhetorical community: The cultural basis of genre. In A. Freedman & P. Medway (Eds.), *Genre and the new rhetoric* (pp. 67–78). London: Taylor & Francis.

Nunan, D. (1989). *Understanding language classrooms.* Upper Saddle River, NJ: Prentice-Hall.

Paltridge, B. (1997). Thesis and dissertation writing: Preparing ESL students for research. *English for Specific Purposes, 16*(1), 61–70.

Peterson, L. H. (1992). Writing across the curriculum and/in the freshman English program. In S. McLeod, & M. Soven, (Eds.), *Writing across the curriculum: A guide to developing programs* (pp. 58–70). Newbury Park, CA: Sage.

Prior, P. (1995a). Redefining the task: An ethnographic examination of writing and response in graduate seminars. In D. Belcher & G. Braine (Eds.), *Academic writing in a second language: Essays on research and pedagogy* (pp. 47–82). Norwood, NJ: Ablex.

Prior, P. (1995b). Tracing authoritative and internally persuasive discourses: A case study of response, revision, and disciplinary enculturation. *Research in the Teaching of English, 29,* 288–325.

Ramanathan, V., & Kaplan, R. B. (1996). Audience and voice in current L1 composition texts: Some implications for ESL student writers. *Journal of Second Language Writing 5*(1), 21–24.

Reid, J. (1995). *Teaching ESL writing.* Upper Saddle River, NJ: Prentice Hall-Regents.

Riazi, A. (1997). Acquiring disciplinary literacy: A social-cognitive analysis of text production and learning among Iranian graduate students of education. *Journal of Second Language Writing, 6*(2), 105–137.

Robinson, P. (1991). *ESP today: A practitioner's guide.* London: Prentice Hall International.

Salager-Meyer, F. (1994). Hedges and textual communicative function in medical English written discourse. *English for Specific Purposes, 13,* 149–170.

Santos, T. (1992). Ideology in composition: L1 and ESL. *Journal of Second Language Writing, 1,* 1–15.

Shuck, G. (1995). Preparing for university writing courses: A survey of students' perceptions. *Journal of Intensive English Studies, 9,* 38–49.

Silva, T. (1993). Toward an understanding of the distinct nature of L2 writing: Directions in ESL. In B. Kroll (Ed.), *Second language writing: Research insights for the classroom* (pp. 11–23). New York: Cambridge University Press.

Silva, T. (1997). Differences in ESL and native-English-speaker writing: The research and its implications. In C. Severino, J. Guerra, & J. Butler (Eds.), *Writing in multicultural settings* (pp. 209–219). New York: MLA.

Soven, M. (Ed.). (1992). *Writing across the curriculum: A guide to developing programs.* Newbury Park, CA: Sage.

Swales, J. M. (1990). *Genre analysis.* Cambridge, UK: Cambridge University Press.

Thetela, P. (1997). Evaluated entities and parameters of value in academic research articles. *English for Specific Purposes, 16,* 101–118.

Thompson, G., & Ye, Y. (1991). Evaluation of the reporting verbs used in academic papers. *Applied Linguistics, 12,* 365–382.

Townsend, J., & Fu, D. (1998). Quiet students across cultures and contexts. *English Education, 31*(1), 4–19.

University of Wyoming General Bulletin (1999–2000) Laramie, WY.

Van Lier, L. (1996). *Interaction in the language curriculum: Awareness, autonomy, and authenticity.* New York: Longman.

11

Critical Pragmatism: A Politics of L2 Composition

Sarah Benesch
The College of Staten Island, The City University of New York

"Recognition of the politics of pedagogy" is an emerging tradition in the field of second language (L2) writing, according to Raimes (1991). An increase in publications addressing the social context of English language teaching (ELT) and L2 composition supports that claim, including a special issue of *TESOL Quarterly* on language and identity in 1996, a special issue of *TESOL Quarterly* on critical approaches in 1999, and a forthcoming issue of *TESOL Journal* on language policies and learners' rights. Various chapters in this volume offer further evidence of growing interest in the politics of L2 writing: Belcher (Chap. 5, this volume) calls for consideration of feminist theory in L2 writing theory; Grabe (Chap. 4, this volume) includes social-context influences in his discussion of L2 writing theory; Cumming (Chap. 15, this volume) acknowledges the politics of evaluation in underscoring the genesis of standards (*whose*) as well as the content (*what*); Hamp-Lyons (Chap. 8, this volume) declares unequivocally, "All assessment procedures are political"; and Smoke (Chap. 9, this volume) explores the political context of L2 composition instruction at publicly funded U.S. universities.

Greater attention to the politics of L2 composition, however, has been met by opposition to its emergence (Allison, 1994; Atkinson, 1997; Ramanathan & Kaplan, 1996; Santos, 1992, Chap. 12, this volume). A central assumption of the opposition is that L2 writing theory and practice should be driven by the pragmatic mission of preparing students for target situations and not by political concerns, such as power relations and social inequities. Although the pragmatic choice to ignore political issues is as ideological as acknowledging politics, it is presented variously as a concern about cognitive overload

161

or about cultural imposition. The cognitive argument is that a level of proficiency in L2 must be attained before students can begin to question the status quo and that composition teachers should therefore concentrate on target-situation demands (see Santos, Chap. 12, this volume). The cultural argument is that critical thinking is uniquely Western and that ESL composition teachers should therefore avoid imposing this type of thinking on their nonnative speaking (NNS) students (Atkinson, 1997; Ramanathan & Kaplan, 1996). These authors, however, do not argue that academic discourse is culturally determined and should also, therefore, be avoided. Rather, they choose to sanction certain types of thinking and writing over others, a political choice.

Elsewhere I (Benesch, 1993) argued that pragmatism is an ideological stance, not a neutral one as its proponents claim. There is a vast literature demonstrating that educational decisions are political. For example, seating arrangements, selection of textbooks and syllabus topics, and evaluation of students are all areas of debate and choice (Shor & Freire, 1987). The choices are mediated by power relations in an institution and in the society and on decision-makers' relation to the status quo: Do they uphold it or question and perhaps change the way things are?

The goal of this chapter is to show that L2 composition does not have to choose between pragmatism and critical teaching. Target-situation demands and students' right to challenge them can be simultaneously addressed through what Pennycook (1997; quoting Cherryholmes, 1988) called "critical pragmatism" (p. 255). This is not a compromise position but rather a way to broaden the discussion of students' needs to consider not only *what is* but also *what might be*. To demonstrate how critical pragmatism might work in L2 composition, both the theoretical underpinnings and practical possibilities are discussed. First, I discuss how critical research addresses important issues overlooked by a strictly pragmatic stance. Next, I outline the assumptions and goals of critical research and pedagogy, including ways critical theory interrogates itself. Then I briefly discuss current opposition to politics in ELT, L2 composition, and English for Academic Purposes (EAP), and I end with an example of critical pragmatism from my own teaching.

THE CRITICAL CHALLENGE TO PRAGMATISM

Traditional L2 composition research assumes that students' relationships to their native language and to English are unproblematic, that learners can simply add an additional language to their linguistic repertoire with positive results. This "ideology of pragmatism" (Benesch, 1993) is the one Santos

(1992) referred to in her comparison of first language (L1) and L2 composition:

> The influence of EFL in TESOL may also help account for the fact that the question of students' "rights" to their own language in writing has not been the source of controversy that it has in L1 composition. It is simply a given in ESL/EFL writing that students have their native languages, and "right" has nothing to do with it. The point is to help them become more proficient writers in English. (p. 10)

Although it may be true that L2 composition has traditionally rested on the notions that NNS students' relationship to L1 is uncomplicated by questions about language rights and that the role of the ESL teacher is to simply add English to students' repertoires, these assumptions are now being challenged in critical research and pedagogy. The aim is to capture the complexity of L2 learning in a variety of contexts by students of various social backgrounds, problematizing monolithic portraits of NNS students and questioning the myth of the neutrality of English.

For example, the research of Canagarajah (1993) called to question the ease of adding spoken and written English to a stable native language foundation in an EFL context. Canagarajah described the complex relationship between varieties of Sri Lankan English, analyzing the impact of differing class and educational backgrounds on L2 acquisition and use. His subjects were native speakers of Tamil from rural Sri Lanka whose use of English was ridiculed both by more educated middle-class Sri Lankans and by their peers. These students' encounters with English were far from conflict free, both inside and outside their communities: "English then provided unfavorable subject positions to such students, making them feel disadvantaged, helpless, inferior, and uneducated. Students also felt that the use of English for interactions would be interpreted by their peers as an attempt to discard their local rural identity and pass off as an anglicized bourgeois or even a foreigner" (p. 616). Yet, despite the cultural conflicts English presented for Canagarajah's subjects, the potential socioeconomic advantages of English proficiency sustained their interest in studying the language. However, they developed ways to study that were compatible with their ambivalence by choosing which types of instruction to accept and reject. On the one hand, they participated in more formal lessons in grammar and academic genres. These activities prepared them for tests while allowing them to keep a cultural distance. On the other hand, they balked at communicative activities in which cultural content was more explicit, such as communicative activities in the U.S. English textbook whose alien values, such as consumerism, they did not want to adopt. Through interviews, questionnaires, and analyses of students' comments and drawings in their textbooks, Canagarajah was able to discover ways his subjects protected themselves from English while learning it for economic purposes. One implication of this critical ethnography is the importance of "unravel[ing] the ambiguous strands of students' behavior" (p. 624) to arrive at a more complex understanding of L2 acquisition.

By taking into account his subjects' positionality (class, ethnicity, gender, race) and agency (their active embrace and rejection of various facets of learning), Canagarajah (1993) gave a complicated picture of learning English. Far from easily accepting and integrating L2 into their linguistic repertoire, his subjects struggled with both wanting and resisting English. Critical research that allows this ambivalence to emerge raises questions about linguistic rights and power relations, in both EFL and ESL settings. It also implies that pragmatically teaching the demands of the target situation is an inadequate response to the complexities of L2 learning. More nuanced and critical approaches to research and teaching are required. The assumptions of such approaches are outlined next.

ASSUMPTIONS OF CRITICAL RESEARCH
AND PEDAGOGY

Six tenets of critical research, according to Peirce (1995a) are: (a) acknowledging the researcher's subjectivity; (b) aiming for social and educational change; (c) investigating the relationship between individuals' everyday lives and the social structures affecting them; (d) studying ways individuals make sense of their experience; (e) taking into account social hierarchies and the inequities of gender, race, class, ethnicity, and sexual orientation; and (f) taking into account the historical context, that is, the relation between present and past conditions and events.

Auerbach (1991) and Freire (1994) offered the following features of critical pedagogy: situated in the conditions of students' lives; dialogic; questions the status quo; promotes democracy and equality; examines *limit-situations*, (a Freirean term referring to personal and social obstacles), experiments with *untested feasibility* (facing limit-situations by moving toward a solution, not knowing what critical reflection and actions will produce); studies power relations and; acknowledges the inseparability of teaching and politics.

One way these assumptions and goals are enacted is by interrogating such terms as *native speaker, native language, academic discourse* and even *English* whose meanings are often taken for granted in the L2 literature although they are contested, as Nayar (1997) showed. This type of interrogation allows critical theory to problematize not just traditional research but also itself, with critical researchers questioning the meaning, for example, of *critical* and *power* (see Ellsworth, 1989; Gore, 1992).

Weiler's (1991) questioning of Freire's (1970) totalizing use of such terms as oppression and liberation offers an example of critical theory's self-scrutiny. Weiler, a supporter of Freirean pedagogy's basic precepts, pointed out that by presenting oppression as monolithic, Freire omits its contradictory forms, such as a worker who is oppressed by his boss at work oppressing his wife at home. Informed by feminist theory, Weiler refined critical theory by including the overlapping positions of being oppressed and oppressing, inside and outside the classroom, making room for a more complicated understanding of power relations.

Vandrick (1995) showed how this type of refinement can be applied to the study of privileged L2 university students in the U.S. whose elite status can be an area of struggle with their middle-class teachers. Vandrick further complicated these students' identity by examining their overlapping positions as *privileged insiders*, by virtue of their elevated social class, and *oppressed outsiders*, by virtue of their foreign student status. Vandrick argued that these complications should inform research and teaching, just as the working-class status of many immigrant students in U.S. institutions should be taken into account.

The types of modifications made by Weiler (1991), Vandrick (1995), and others demonstrate that critical theory is vibrant and receptive to critique and reform. However, as shown in the following, the opposition to critical theory in L2 composition and EAP overlooks these refinements, presenting it as an orthodoxy with a narrow political agenda, a tool for indoctrinating students and dominating professional discussions.

OPPOSITION TO POLITICS IN ELT, L2 COMPOSITION, AND EAP

A letter to the editor in the June/July 1998, *TESOL Matters* (*TM*) opposed the publication of an article by James Crawford, in a prior issue, critical of the Unz proposal to end bilingual education in California public schools (Wall, 1998). Wall, an EFL teacher in Mexico, argued that the *TM* editor was getting "mixed up in politics" (p. 27) by allowing Crawford's article to appear. That is, rather than giving his opinion of the Unz proposal or the Crawford article, Wall called for the suppression of a probilingual article in a journal devoted to English language teaching. He did this without recognizing that his request was political and that no one participating in the exchange, Crawford, the editor, the author of the letter, or authors of subsequent letters, was a neutral party. They were all, inevitably, mixed up in politics.

Like Wall (1998), opponents of critical L2 composition claim neutrality for their choice to take a pragmatic position and accuse those who are not strictly pragmatic of imposing a social agenda on students (see Santos,

Chap. 12, this volume). For example, Ramanathan and Kaplan (1996) opposed the teaching of critical thinking in L2 composition classes in U.S. universities on the grounds that it is a uniquely Western cultural practice that "impos[es] on all students one way of ordering and making sense of the world" (p. 230). In place of critical thinking, they offer "ways specific academic disciplines organize information" (p. 242), that is, writing across the curriculum, claiming this type of instruction is "freer of cultural constraints," (p. 242) than teaching critical thinking.

However, this either–or scenario (critical thinking vs. writing in the disciplines) perpetuates the myth that some types of discourse are freer of cultural contamination than others and do not, therefore, impose on students; it also omits debates in the L1 and L2 composition communities about what skills, genres, and methods best prepare students for the demands of academic content courses. For example, Johns (1997) demonstrated that even among faculty in the same department, there are significant differences in course demands and practices, making it almost impossible for EAP teachers whose courses are not linked to particular academic content courses to prepare their students for future courses. One way to help students, according to Johns, is to encourage them to question faculty about course assignments, not simply surrender to their sometimes confusing or poorly articulated demands. That is, she has called for highly contextualized writing across the curriculum, or EAP, along with critical thinking about linked academic classes. As shown in the next section of this chapter, when NNS students' active and critical engagement is encouraged in an EAP class, the content class can be enhanced (Benesch, 1999).

Another objection to critical research and pedagogy in the L2 literature has been that discussions of politics and ideology could overwhelm the field, shutting out other theories and approaches. This view is reflected in Allison's (1994) response to an article I (Benesch, 1993) published in the *TESOL Quarterly* entitled "ESL, ideology and the politics of pragmatism." In his response, Allison labeled my discourse *ideologist* and warned readers that it has a colonizing effect. That is, according to Allison, so-called ideologist discourse is imperialistic; it tries to dominate and hold all other orientations and viewpoints hostage. Allison even expresses reluctance to respond to my article because he believes that in doing so he is forced to adopt a discourse he finds objectionable: "As a pragmatically-inclined EAP practitioner, I choose to resist what I see as a current bid on the part of ideologist discourse to invade EAP discourse. I cannot therefore ignore that bid, nor can I afford to debate extensively on ideologist terrain as such participation already entails acceptance of a metaideological agenda" (Allison, 1994, p. 618).

Although I disagree with Allison (1994), Ramanathan and Kaplan (1996), and Santos (Chap. 12, this volume) that critical theorists are interested in colonizing other viewpoints or imposing a single way of thinking on students, I believe their concerns are a reaction to an increase in the number of articles in L2 publications taking a critical stance. They may fear that L2 composition and EAP will be dominated by discussions of politics and ideology, interfering with the pragmatic mission of teaching L2 and preparing students for the target situation.

To respond to that concern, the next section shows that the pragmatic goal of preparing students for the demands of academic courses in EAP can be balanced with the critical goals of situating the pedagogy in the students' social context and encouraging them to question the status quo.

AN EXAMPLE OF CRITICAL PRAGMATISM IN EAP

The example offered in this section is intended to illustrate both a limit-situation and untested feasibility, experimenting with ways to face an undemocratic or unfavorable situation rather than surrendering to its obstacles. The course was a paired EAP writing and introduction to anthropology. The 19 students in the EAP class attended the anthropology class with about the same number of native-speaking students who were not enrolled in any linked class. My EAP class was heterogeneous, having 6 international students and 13 permanent residents who had received some part of their high school education in New York City public schools.

When the anthropology teacher, Professor Gold,[1] and I decided to link our classes, she warned me that she was not well-organized. Once the course began I understood the implications of her disorganized style: The readings, lectures, and assignments were interesting to those who understood them, but they were often hard to follow. Lectures posed the greatest challenge, moving from one topic to the next with no signaling, summing up, or introductions to new topics. And due dates for assignments were often ambiguous. Therefore the students had to understand the material while navigating the chaos of the class. This was the limit-situation. However, although the EAP students were frustrated by the lectures, they respected Gold and generously attributed her lecturing style to the complexity of anthropology. One said, "She has so much to say she sometimes forgets the point." And another said, "Anthropology is so many fields: history, sociology, philosophy. You have to know so much that it's hard to explain everything."

In a traditional EAP arrangement, my job would have been to make the material comprehensible to the students by adapting the materials. I would have recorded the lectures and transcribed and rewritten them to make Professor Gold's points clearer and less obfuscated by the many tangents she took. Instead, whereas some of the activities revolved around making sense of the course material, others focused on how to change conditions in the anthropology class so that the students could participate more fully.

In the EAP class we developed various strategies to meet the limit-situation of the anthropology class: making the lectures more comprehensible and the assignments more clearly defined. Two of the strategies were: taking good enough notes so that when Gold got off track, the students were able to refer to their notes and let her know what she had been talking about, and writing questions to Gold about the assignments so that she could give the students a set of clear guidelines to follow.

But another strategy, that initially seemed simply pragmatic, mobilized the EAP class to begin acting as a community, to collectively get what they needed from the anthropology class and teacher. This strategy arose when one student asked the others about the due date of one of their anthropology assignments during an EAP class meeting. Francesca, a confident Italian student said, "Oh, I asked her. She said it's due on . . ." and gave the date. Patrick, a Haitian student, said about Francesca's answer: "She went for herself. She should go for the whole class," meaning that all the students could have benefited from the information Francesca had gotten for herself. Then Edward asked, "Why don't you ask her at the beginning of class instead of the end?" His question was intended to suggest that the information would be available to all the students if Francesca or another student queried Gold in front of them all before the lecture began rather than after the class had ended.

This exchange led to a class discussion about how the students might help each other rather than just working for themselves. Given the difficult conditions in the anthropology class, if the EAP students behaved as a community they might all do better, including the permanent residents whose disrupted lives and educational backgrounds had put them at a disadvantage compared to other students. We worked it out that those who felt most comfortable asking about assignments in class would do so and those who asked privately would share the information with the other students as soon as possible.

The growing strength of the community was revealed at another crucial moment in the semester. After spring break and only 20 days before the end of the term, Gold surprised the students with an unscheduled assignment: They were required to visit to the American Museum of Natural History in Manhattan and write a two-page paper on one of the human-evolution exhibits. This was in addition to completing their final research paper, writing a soap opera based in their own culture, and beginning a second textbook, on human evolution. After Gold told the students about the museum visit and the paper, they asked detailed questions to shape the assignment more clearly. But it was only when they arrived in my class that they began to express their frustration at this unexpected task. Eleni, a Greek woman protested: "We have 20 days left to do all this work. Why didn't she make the museum assignment when we had 10 days off for spring break? So far only two assignments have been due. Two assignments in three months. Now in the last month of class, she gives us these new assignments [the visit and the paper about it], not on the syllabus." Their indignation at having to pay for Gold's impulsive decision was clear.

Here's where untested feasibility came in. To address their concerns, I asked the students to detail the list of assignments that were due and I wrote them on the board. Next I asked how they wanted to deal with the problem and Eleni suggested they ask her to eliminate the museum visit saying, "We have no time; we're in class everyday." She also said that she had thought about making this suggestion during the anthropology class but had decided it wouldn't be effective for only one person to speak up.

I suggested forming a delegation and four students—Eleni, Francesca, Jorge, and Jusuf—immediately volunteered. I asked Georges, a Haitian student to join them, knowing that he had cultivated a relationship with Gold by asking her for help with his papers. "How will you present yourselves?" I asked. Eleni said that they would ask her to drop the museum visit and paper. Georges, on the other hand, objected more to the soap opera paper, "I didn't think we had to do the soap opera because according to the syllabus, it was due on March 30." (It was then late April). After further discussion with the whole class, the delegation met after class, formulated their requests, and went to Gold's office to talk them over. The upshot of the delegation's visit, announced at the beginning of the next anthropology class meeting, was that Gold dropped the soap opera assignment but kept the museum visit, saying that it would help them understand the text on human evolution and the final research paper. The students were very pleased about the elimination of the soap opera paper and set aside their fears about traveling to Manhattan from Staten Island. Gold remarked to me privately that she had been pleased to hear from the students.

This example shows how critical pragmatism in EAP differs from a strictly pragmatic approach. The EAP students organized themselves so that they could get more from the lectures and more time and help with the assignments. The pedagogy did not indoctrinate the students to a single way of viewing the world, as opponents of critical thinking and teaching have charged. Nor did it proceed with an a priori notion of what should be achieved. Rather it addressed content courses objectives while attending to students' concerns about inequities in that class. Although it may appear that the last part of the example is simply about reducing the workload in the anthropology class, it is ultimately about giving students control and voice in a situation whose demands were, at times, unreasonable and arbitrary. The EAP class gave students tools to work together to turn complaints about unfavorable conditions into actions. And throughout the semester, they were using academic English and fulfilling the anthropology assignments.[2]

One objection to the example might be that engaging nonnative students in questioning and changing unfavorable conditions in a university lecture course is more politics than language teaching. The response of critical pedagogy is that teaching and politics are inseparable. The experiment in critical EAP I described aimed to question the status quo: Why are things the way they are? What might be done to improve conditions? Critical pedagogy assumes that if students are given opportunities to question in classrooms, they are more likely to speak up when their rights and others' are ignored in the larger society.

CONCLUSION

This chapter is concluded by addressing a concern some people have raised with me privately about what would happen if the fields of L2 composition and EAP became more overtly politicized. Would there be battles over competing theories, leading to a loss of collegiality? My response is twofold. First, a fear of adversity should not be allowed to impede reconsideration of L2 composition theory in light of postmodern assumptions. Second, disagreements over theories can be discussed congenially if those who hold varying positions agree to maintain mutual respect. The discussions need not be adversarial; politics can be acknowledged and challenged through open and cordial intellectual exchanges.[3]

However, even if ideological differences are discussed respectfully, some colleagues will be alienated by consideration of politics, linguistic rights, power, and dissent. They will claim, as Wall (1998) did in his letter to *TM*, that politics should be avoided, but their discomfort should not be allowed to silence discussion of politics of L2 composition. Nor should it short circuit attempts to refine L2 composition theory through the healthy exchange of ideas and debates about diverse positions.

ENDNOTES

1. This name and those of the students, mentioned in the following, are pseudonyms.

2. For other examples of critical research and pedagogy in L2 settings, see Auerbach et al. (1996), Benesch (1999), Janks and Ivanič (1992), Morgan (1992), Moriarty (1998), Peirce (1995b), and Schenke (1991).

3. This type of exchange occurred at the Symposium on Second Language Writing at Purdue University in September 1998 when Terry Santos and I presented papers whose ideological positions on the place of politics in L2 composition differed. We presented our disagreements with mutual respect while not avoiding opposition.

REFERENCES

Allison, D. (1994). Comments on Sarah Benesch's "ESL, ideology, and the politics of pragmatism." *TESOL Quarterly, 28*, 618–623.

Atkinson, D. (1997). A critical approach to critical thinking in TESOL. *TESOL Quarterly, 31*, 71–94.

Auerbach, E. (1991). Rosa's challenge: Connecting classroom and community contexts. In S. Benesch (Ed.), *ESL in America: Myths and possibilities* (pp. 96–111). Portsmouth NH: Boynton/Cook Heinemann.

Auerbach, E., Barahona, B., Midy, J., Vaquerano, F., Zambrano, A., & Arnaud, J. (1996). *Adult ESL/literacy from the community to the community: A guidebook for participatory literacy training*. Mahwah NJ: Lawrence Erlbaum Associates.

Benesch, S. (1993). ESL, ideology and the politics of pragmatism. *TESOL Quarterly, 27*, 705–717.

Benesch, S. (1999). Rights analysis: Studying power relations in an academic setting. *English for Specific Purposes, 18*, 313–327.

Canagarajah, S. (1993). Critical ethnography of a Sri Lankan classroom: Ambiguities in student opposition to reproduction through ESOL. *TESOL Quarterly, 27*, 601–626.

Cherryholmes, C. (1988). *Power and criticism: Poststructural investigations in education*. New York: Teacher's College Press.

Ellsworth, E. (1989). Why doesn't this feel empowering? Working through repressive myths of critical pedagogy. *Harvard Educational Review, 59*, 297–324.

Freire, P. (1970). *Pedagogy of the oppressed*. New York: Continuum.

Freire, P. (1994). *Pedagogy of hope: Reliving pedagogy of the oppressed*. New York: Continuum.

Gore, J. (1992). What we can do for you! What *can* "we" do for "you"? Struggling over empowerment in critical and feminist pedagogy. In C. Luke & J. Gore (Eds.), *Feminisms and critical pedagogy* (pp. 54–73). New York: Routledge.

Janks, H., & Ivanič, R. (1992). Critical language awareness and emancipatory discourse. In N. Fairclough (Ed.), *Critical language awareness* (pp. 305–331). Essex, UK: Longman Group.

Johns, A. M. (1997). *Text, role, and context: Developing academic literacies*. Cambridge UK: Cambridge University Press.

Morgan, B. (1992). Teaching the Gulf War in an ESL classroom. *TESOL Journal, 2*, 13–17.

Moriarty, P. (1998). Learning to be legal: Unintended meanings for adult schools. In T. Smoke (Ed.), *Adult ESL: Politics, pedagogy, and participation in classroom and community programs* (pp. 17–39). Mahwah NJ: Lawrence Erlbaum Associates.

Nayar, P. B. (1997). ESL/EFL dichotomy today: Language politics or pragmatics? *TESOL Quarterly, 27*, 9–37

Peirce, B. N. (1995a). The theory of methodology in qualitative research. *TESOL Quarterly, 29*, 569–576.

Peirce, B. N. (1995b). Social identity, investment, and language learning. *TESOL Quarterly, 29*, 9–31.

Pennycook, A. (1997). Vulgar pragmatism, critical pragmatism, and EAP. *English for Specific Purposes, 16*, 253–267.

Raimes, A. (1991). Out of the woods: Emerging traditions in the teaching of writing. *TESOL Quarterly, 25*, 407–430.

Ramanathan, V., & Kaplan, R. (1996). Some problematic "channels" in the teaching of critical thinking in current L1 composition textbooks: Implications for L2 student-writers. *Issues in Applied Linguistics, 7*, 225–249.

Santos, T. (1992). Ideology in composition: L1 and ESL. *Journal of Second Language Writing, 1*, 1–15.

Schenke, A. (1991). The "will to reciprocity" and the work of memory: Fictioning speaking out in silence in ESL and feminist pedagogy. *Resources for Feminist Research, 20*, 47–55.

Shor, I., & Freire, P. (1987). *A pedagogy for liberation: Dialogues on transforming education.* New York: Bergin & Garvey.

Vandrick, S. (1995). Privileged ESL university students. *TESOL Quarterly, 29*, 375–380.

Wall, A. (1998, June/July). Letter to the Editor. *TESOL Matters, 27*.

Weiler, K. (1991). Freire and a feminist pedagogy of difference. *Harvard Educational Review, 61*, 449–474.

12

The Place of Politics in Second Language Writing

Terry Santos
Humboldt State University

In the 1990s, Teaching English to Speakers of Other Languages (TESOL) has seen the emergence of an alternative perspective known as *critical applied linguistics*, which has an explicitly sociopolitical orientation and is an extension of critical theory found predominantly in the humanities and social sciences. Although the focus of this chapter is the role of politics in second language (L2) writing, it is imperative to place that role in the larger context of critical applied linguistics. Therefore, this chapter on politics and L2 writing begins by briefly reviewing the central concerns of critical theory, critical pedagogy, and critical applied linguistics to show how and why they constitute a major reassessment of the goals and practices of mainstream TESOL. I then consider the extension of this critical perspective to L2 writing, specifically, the theoretical positions and pedagogical recommendations of critical theory in relation to L2 writing. I also offer my own critique of critical approaches to L2 writing, and conclude with my view of the future role of the sociopolitical in second language writing.

CRITICAL THEORY

As a branch of critical theory, critical applied linguistics adopts both the postmodernist and poststructuralist positions on Western culture and language and discourse. From postmodernism comes the critique and rejection of the ideals of the modern period in Western civilization spanning the 2 centuries from the Enlightenment of the 18th century to the late stage of capitalism

(Jameson, 1984) of the 20th century. These ideals include, above all, rationalism (in particular, science as the preeminent manifestation of reason), liberalism and the primacy of the individual, objectivity and objective truth, and any overarching account or *metanarrative* (Lyotard, 1979) of history that claims coherence or linear direction (e.g., the march of progress or the drive toward freedom). Postmodernists claim that the radically changed conditions of the present—postindustrialism, postcolonialism, multiculturalism, transnational capitalism, global communication, consumerism, and virtual and hyper-reality—have caused an irreparable rupture with the past that makes the guiding principles of the modern age no longer viable, meaningful, or believable. Modernity has broken apart, and the postmodern world is left to deal with the pieces.

Thus, the postmodern condition is seen as decentered, destabilized, fragmented, indeterminate, incongruent, highlighted by difference, and open to question (*problematization*) and challenge (*contestation*) because there is no ascertainable truth but rather just truth claims about reality. As Rorty (1989) wrote, "reality is discussable... figurative, available only within language" (p. 60). Truth claims and contestation bring us to the centrality of language and discourse, the analysis, or deconstruction, of which has been the focus of poststructuralism. For the purposes of this chapter, the essential concept of poststructuralism is *discourse*, which is the use of language to construct and organize knowledge, meaning, and identity. For poststructuralists, without discursive practices we would have no way of knowing anything or making sense of our environment or ourselves. Knowledge is discourse; society is discourse; identity is discourse, all of which is to say that knowledge and identity are social constructions, not objective or autonomous entities.

> Thus, in contrast to the humanist version of language, which emphasizes the centrality of human rationality in social relations and therefore considers language to be a medium through which rational, conscious subjects convey their meanings back and forth, this [poststructuralist] view suggests that meaning, and ultimately subjectivity, are produced through language. (Pennycook, 1997, p. 258)

Because different groups in society have very different discourses, or social constructions—and because there is no method or justification for determining the truth of one group's discourses over another's, the ones that have been heard more and accepted as the standard in a society have come as a result of domination. Poststructuralists such as Rabinow (1985) see no basis other than power for relations among groups with different discourses in society.

But power relations can be called into question and challenged, which is the domain of critical theory, with its neo-Marxist focus on inequality and social injustice. The aims and methods of critical theory are threefold: (a) To problematize every dominant site in society (e.g., the legal and educational systems) and every subject matter (e.g., literature and language studies) by exposing the unequal power relations operating within them that marginalize and exclude subordinate groups; (b) to contest the power structures of these sites and subjects through challenge and resistance; and (c) to subvert and transform them through actions that will "effect a shift in power from the privileged and the powerful to those groups struggling to gain a measure of control over their lives" (Aronowitz & Giroux, 1991, p. 115).

CRITICAL PEDAGOGY

In education, critical theory turned into practice is known as critical pedagogy or, alternately, pedagogy of possibility, liberatory pedagogy, (after Freire, 1970), empowerment pedagogy, or radical pedagogy (as in *Radical Teacher*, the flagship journal of critical pedagogy in the United States). Shor (in Shor & Graff, 1997), a leading proponent and practitioner of critical pedagogy, described it as:

> a pedagogy that questions the status quo. I also consider it a student-centered pedagogy that has certain values, orientations, or interests, such as being democratic, dialogic, interdisciplinary, activist, and also being what I call 'desocializing.' I understand that human beings are social constructions...[and]...I understand critical pedagogy as one of those social processes for the reconstruction of the social self...I would like critical pedagogy to be understood as a political stance and an activist posture and not as technical wizardry. (pp. 3; 16)

Schools are seen as sites of political struggle, critical educators as "transformative intellectuals" (Aronowitz & Giroux, 1993, p. 45) and the goals of education as individual empowerment and social transformation (Weiler, 1988). Advocates of critical pedagogy also invoke the language of "utopian visions" as a way of "moving beyond the despair into which a critical and ethical view of the world can often lead us" (Pennycook, 1994b, p. 299). Because it is opposed to the standard curriculum and to mainstream classroom practices, critical pedagogy seeks to fashion alternative approaches to both, eschewing on principle any formal set or statement of methods and procedures (technical wizardry) in favor of experimentation and practices tailored to local settings, conditions, and concerns. The common denominators, however, remain the critique of institutional power arrangements and social inequities, the encouragement of social and political activism, and professed faith in a utopian future.

CRITICAL APPLIED LINGUISTICS

In bringing critical theory and pedagogy to bear on TESOL, some critical applied linguists have moved to reposition, or resituate, TESOL in the domain of cultural studies and cultural politics (also the self-identified home of critical theory in literature, composition studies, postcolonial theory, women's studies, and multicultural studies), in which sociocultural and ideological issues are central, whereas the issues traditionally associated with TESOL research and practice (e.g., "technical details of language acquisition, reading and writing, and so forth"; Pennycook, 1996, p. 170) are peripheral. Thus repositioned, critical research in applied linguistics "will almost inevitably stand in opposition to much of what goes on in mainstream research in TESOL... [because it is] answerable to a broader politics of social transformation" (Pennycook, 1994c, p. 691). Likewise, critical English as a Second Language (ESL) pedagogy will problematize sociopolitical power relations and inequality in language teaching and will challenge English language programs, curricula, and teaching approaches for, among other things, reinforcing the hegemony of English internationally (Phillipson, 1992), preparing immigrant students to be passive, second-class citizens in English-speaking countries (Auerbach & Burgess, 1987; Tollefson, 1991), and accepting gatekeeping roles in admission, placement, and exit assessments for ESL students (Benesch, 1993).

With the rise of critical applied linguistics in the 1990s has come the emergence of various subbranches such as *critical ethnography*, "an ideologically sensitive orientation to the study of culture [in relation to] issues of power" (Canagarajah, 1993, p. 605); *critical needs analysis*, which sees needs analysis as "a political and subjective process... [and] assumes that institutions are hierarchical and that those at the bottom are often entitled to more power than they have. It seeks areas where greater equality might be achieved" (Benesch, 1996, p. 736); *critical discourse analysis* (e.g., Fairclough, 1995), which studies discourse in terms of social and ideological relations and examines the ways they reinforce each other; and *critical curriculum development*, which critiques standard curricula for their "underlying assumption... that learners should assimilate into preexisting structures and practices without questioning the power relations inherent in them" and develops alternatives "not to fit learners into the existing order, but to enable them to critically examine it and become active in shaping their own roles in it" (Auerbach, 1995, pp. 14–15).

CRITICAL EAP AND L2 WRITING

Critical applied linguistics has also carried over to L2 writing, usually under the heading of *critical EAP* (English for academic purposes). In passing, it is interesting to note that we do not find references in the literature to *critical second language writing* per se, which is a reminder of the historical difficulty—and lateness—of L2 writing in achieving independent status as an area of specialization in TESOL. This difficulty is most likely attributable to the fact that writing is always confronted with the question of what content it should be connected to; without such a connection, it exists in something of a vacuum, and this is true whether we are talking about writing from a mainstream or a critical perspective. In the case of a critical approach to L2 writing, the connection is to the larger area of EAP.

In 1993, in response to my (Santos, 1992) article arguing that L1 composition sees itself ideologically whereas L2 writing identifies itself pragmatically, with different pedagogical practices stemming from the contrast, Benesch stated that "the kind of sociopolitical analysis carried out by Tollefson, Auerbach, and others has not yet been applied to English for academic purposes" (p. 710) and acknowledged "the self-professed pragmatism" (p. 711) of EAP specialists who are primarily concerned with helping students meet the demands of academic writing they will encounter in the university. However, she rejected the dichotomy between an ideological approach to teaching, with its goal of sociopolitical transformation, and a pragmatic approach, with its goal of socializing students into the academy. For Benesch, as for all critical theorists and critical educators, pragmatism in teaching is as ideological as critical pedagogy, except its ideology is "an accommodationist ideology, an endorsement of traditional academic teaching and of current power relations in academia and in society" (p. 711).

Additional critical analyses of EAP have been put forth to challenge mainstream perspectives and approaches. Canagarajah (1993) characterized the challenge as one of "enabl[ing] students to employ their own local knowledge and counter-discourses to resist ideological domination, forge positive subject positions, and engage in emancipatory interests" (p. 303). He went on to argue that rather than accepting academic discourse on its terms, ESL students should negotiate with the academy to "construct alternate... [or] competing discourses" (p. 304) based on their indigenous languages and ways of knowing. Although recognizing that universities might not appreciate such a challenge, ultimately, Canagarajah claimed, they would benefit as much as students from the greater democratization, pluralization, and intellectual variety that would result.

Like Canagarajah, McKay (1993) questioned the assumption that it is the responsibility of L2 writing teachers to help their students acquire the conventions of academic discourse when that discourse reflects only "a particular orientation toward knowledge" (p. 76) that is socially constructed. Because L2 students bring their own equally valid discourses and knowledge orientations to the university, it is purely a matter of dominant and uncontested power relations that students are expected unilaterally to conform to the university rather than the university adjusting to the students through a process of negotiation.

Whereas Canagarajah and McKay focused on students' languages and discourses of knowledge, Benesch (1995) supported a critical EAP approach that ties course content and materials to sociopolitical issues in the service of social change. In her view, the question of content (i.e., whether it is better to link EAP courses to subject-specific courses or keep them separate as a general academic skills courses) is a nonissue in critical EAP because it does not matter. "Critical ESL... is not particular about where the content comes from... as long as it is studied from a social perspective" (p. 194); the assumption, of course, is that any type of content, not just the obviously sociopolitically charged ones such as capital punishment, homosexuality, or abortion, can be problematized ideologically.

Vandrick (1995) speculated on the application of critical pedagogy to her particular L2 writing population, a group not ordinarily given much attention in the critical literature: privileged, affluent international university students who are perhaps the least likely to be interested in the kind of politics of transformation sought by critical pedagogy. She raised a number of questions about the responsibility, intentions, and outcomes of enacting critical pedagogy in this context ("Can we really make a difference? Are we merely making ourselves feel better? Are we simply salving our consciences and allowing our students to salve their consciences with superficial gestures which then allow all of us to go on without making any of the deep structural changes necessary for a more equitable, just world?" [p. 380]) However, despite, or because of, the potential for classroom discomfort, resistance, and even conflict in such a setting, Vandrick supported a critical approach because "it is essential that these fortunate students be led to question the status quo and even to question their own sense of entitlement" (p. 379).

Pennycook (1997) argued for a critical perspective on EAP on both the theoretical and pedagogical levels. In terms of theory, he is concerned that EAP has a ready-made discourse of pragmatism to draw on that he (after Cherryholmes, 1998) referred to as "vulgar pragmatism, a position that runs the danger of reinforcing norms, beliefs and ideologies that maintain inequitable social and cultural relations... [which] is made particularly available by certain 'discourses of neutrality' which construct EAP as a neutral activity, and therefore allow for a position that a pragmatist stance is an ethically viable one" (Pennycook, 1997, pp. 256–57). Instead, Pennycook advocated a critical EAP approach which, in terms of pedagogical practice, critiques and challenges academic norms and standards rather than accepting them and working to socialize L2 students into them. Agreeing with Canagarajah (1993) and McKay (1993) that students bring their own discourses and knowledge to EAP classes, he saw the need for "developing course content that seeks to critically examine the discourses that construct our and our students' understanding of our worlds. . . . A critical understanding of English and its relationship to discourses of science, technology and education, as well as its role as national and international gatekeeper to these domains therefore becomes an integral part of an EAP curriculum" (Pennycook, 1997, p. 265).

To recapitulate, these are the major theoretical positions and pedagogical recommendations of critical EAP and L2 writing:

Theoretical Positions

1. A pragmatic approach to EAP and L2 writing is as ideological as critical pedagogy; the difference is that the ideology of critical pedagogy is explicit, whereas that of pragmatism is implicit, hidden behind a screen of neutrality (Benesch, 1993). Furthermore, such pragmatism is unethical because it supports existing inequalities in society, whereas critical pedagogy works for social transformation (Pennycook, 1997).

2. In the interests of democratization, pluralization, and intellectual diversity, the indigenous languages that nonnative-speaking students bring to higher education are equal to dominant academic discourses (Canagarajah, 1993); universities should therefore adapt to students' discourses rather than vice versa (McKay, 1993).

Pedagogical Recommendations

1. Whatever the content of EAP and L2 writing courses—it can be anything the teacher deems appropriate—it should be presented from a sociopolitical standpoint (Benesch, 1995). Affluent, privileged students need the experience of critical questioning and confrontation as much as oppressed students in order to be made aware of how their own advantages contribute to the disadvantages of those less fortunate (Vandrick, 1995).

2. EAP and L2 writing courses should challenge and deconstruct academic discourses (of science, technology, and any other subject) rather than encourage students to accept and practice them.

A CRITIQUE OF CRITICAL EAP AND L2 WRITING

One of the benefits of following the positions and arguments of alternative approaches to the mainstream (any mainstream) is the opportunity it affords to clarify one's own perspectives and understandings. Thus, as one who supports the mainstream in applied linguistics and L2 writing, it has been interesting to me to reflect on why the positions of critical applied linguistics, critical pedagogy, and critical EAP and L2 writing remain wholly unrepresentative of my intellectual perspectives, professional experiences, observations of student needs and preferences, and general worldview. Also, as an adherent of centrism and pragmatism (which is, after all, America's greatest contribution to philosophy), critical approaches seem to me extreme—extreme in terms of the mainstream—as well as out of touch with the reality I see of people in schools and universities actually living their lives, at least in the United States and other countries I have lived, worked, and traveled in. To use Pennycook's (1994a) term, *critical discourses* and mine are *incommensurable*, and I understand why he feels that "at times I [Pennycook] am no longer able to communicate with my colleagues in applied linguistics, that at times we are no longer engaged in the same discourse" (p. 115). Even after reading and considering innumerable articles and books on postmodernism, poststructuralism, critical theory, critical pedagogy, critical applied linguistics, and critical EAP and L2 writing, I find myself not only in disagreement with both the theoretical positions and pedagogical recommendations they espouse, but in closer embrace of pragmatism, vulgar or otherwise, as a far more satisfying approach to TESOL, EAP and L2 writing, and, for that matter, everyday life.

Theoretical Issues

A prime example of what I consider extreme in critical theory and pedagogy is the premise that everything is political and ideological. There is no escape from its reach: All action, all discussion, all decision making, all relations, have their basis in, and are a reflection of, sociopolitical ideology. ("The political [involves] all relationships in society" [Pennycook, 1989, p. 590]; "All forms of education are political" [Benesch, 1993, p. 707]; "Every pedagogy is imbricated in ideology" [Berlin, 1988, p. 492]). Even if we think we are being nonideological, we are mistaken, for the very thought of being nonideological is itself ideological. There is no such thing as moving beyond it, only a lack of consciousness of its omnipresence or the unwillingness to accept it. Because knowledge, education, and pedagogy are all inherently ideological, and teachers are always behaving ideologically whether they know and accept it or not, then it is only ethical to make ideology the focus of the classroom instead of denying it and keeping it dishonestly hidden; thus, critical pedagogy takes the moral high ground when it openly "announces its intentions [and] proclaims its goals" (Benesch, 1993, p. 707).

One of the ways I understand the meaning of a word or concept is to know not only what it is but what it is not, what boundaries it delimits as well as encompasses. Thus, for my understanding of sociopolitical ideology,

I want to know what it excludes as well as includes, and to be told that it includes everything is, to me, akin to being told that God is everywhere. To me, a worldview that sees ideology in everything is essentially a form of displaced religious faith couched in secular terms.[1] (The religious aspect of critical theory and pedagogy is also revealed in phrases like *utopian visions* that not priests but "transformative intellectuals" will guide us toward.) How many times have we heard similar arguments made, for example, by those who fight for classroom prayer, the teaching of creationism, and Bible study in the schools? After all, because God is omnipresent and there is no escape from His reach, then it is only ethical and honest to make His teachings the center of the classroom instead of denying them and keeping them hidden. This belief is also monistic in that it reduces all thought and behavior to one source, whether God or ideology. In such a monistic worldview, only a dualistic response is possible: in religion, faith or heresy, leading either to salvation or damnation; in ideology, true or false consciousness, leading either to empowerment or submission to the status quo. Hence we have all-or-nothing statements about education, such as "a way of teaching is never innocent" (Berlin, 1988, p. 492); "there can be no neutrality in education" (Benesch, 1993, p. 706).

From my centrist and pragmatic perspective, the move in critical theory from the undeniable fact that education and human relations have a political dimension to the assertion that education and human relations are nothing but political is as falsely reductive as any other all-encompassing claim about humans (e.g., that all human behavior is genetically determined; that all human decision making is economically based, or self-interested). Such views lead to narrow, impoverished, and inaccurate explanations and understandings of the complexity of humans, who live their lives in a multiplicity of ways that, in my view, are neither ideologically driven nor politically motivated. Neither do I share the premise of critical theorists and educators from which so many of their arguments proceed: that there is no such thing as a neutral position, just a constructed discourse of neutrality that hides its special interests. This theoretical formulation does not correspond to the reality I know, which is that in high-stakes situations we not only hope for but rely on the possibility of neutrality. For example, if I find myself caught in a country where war suddenly breaks out between two regions, and a third region declares its neutrality, my reaction will not be that I might as well stay in one of the warring regions because neutrality is a myth; my reaction will be to go there. Similarly, if I am a defendant in a courtroom and am given a choice between two juries, one consisting of people who openly state they will render a verdict based on their prejudices against, say, atheists, feminists, or minorities, and another consisting of people who say they will do their best to be neutral and suspend judgment until they hear both sides, my response will certainly not be that neutrality is a constructed discourse, and therefore it does not matter which one I choose. The premise that neutrality is impossible seems to be based on the faulty idea that because there may be no such thing as perfect or absolute neutrality, there can be no such thing as approximate or relative neutrality. But neutrality is always relative in terms of conflicting positions, if not polar opposites, and it does seem to me quite possible both to assume and to act on neutral grounds in this relative sense.

My belief in the possibility of neutrality is why I find a false equivalence in the claim that critical pedagogy and traditional teaching are equally ideological but that critical pedagogy is just open and honest whereas traditional teaching denies it by hiding behind a myth of neutrality. This equivalence is misleading because it glosses over the day-and-night difference between critical pedagogy that advocates and attempts to implement overt, in-your-face ideological activism in the classroom, and traditional teaching that does not. To use the linguistic binary, traditional teaching is the unmarked, or neutral, form, whereas critical pedagogy is the marked form. The accurate equivalence would be the right-wing ideological counterpart to left-wing critical pedagogy used just as overtly in the classroom, where both would be marked.

The indictment by critical educators that traditional teaching wears a mask of neutrality is its very beauty, the triumph of the liberal and pragmatic tradition of public education in the United States (as is keeping religious instruction out of public schools). Two great advantages result from this established—but always contested—consensus. First, it prevents classrooms from becoming open political training grounds and students from being used by their teachers for the purpose of political proselytizing, on the left or right (just as it was a similar *dystopian vision* of openly warring, proselytizing religious factions that led to the principle of the separation of church and state and that is still hotly contested to this day). Second, it enables teachers and students to turn their attention to other subjects and other ways of seeing and understanding the world, whether through math or science or poetry or language learning or music (or politics in a political science class). Only those who believe that the political is the most important aspect of people's lives will justify centering their teaching around it, but I have not found that such a belief is shared by the majority of either teachers or students, at least in the United States. In fact, I would argue that for anyone who has ever lived in a society where politics and ideology really are in your face (e.g., classroom lectures and discussion audited for political content, or private-life decisions subjected to political monitoring and judgment), it is nothing short of a tremendous relief to be free of them in order to get on with one's life.

Is a pragmatic approach to EAP and L2 writing ethically unacceptable, as Pennycook (1997) claimed because it maintains inequitable relations in society? But is higher education not itself elitist, which by definition means inequality? It cannot be anything but elitist when only about 26% of the adult population in the United States holds a BA or BS degree—a higher percentage, incidentally, than any other country in the world. Thus, whether we like it or not, by our very positions as EAP and L2 writing specialists at the university level, we are involved in academic inequality not only in the United States but in the world because international students are often the most privileged segments of the population in their societies, where only a very small fraction of the population has the opportunity for higher education or for university attendance in the United States. In effect, upholding inequality is a given of our positions, which most of us accept (if not theoretically, then at least in practice; otherwise, we would find it unconscionable to remain in such an environment when there are other, more democratic educational settings). I assume we accept it because we enjoy teaching at that level, elitist although it may be and because we have reason to believe higher education is a good thing for individuals and their societies. The challenge is to increase the number of those who receive it (and those who are prepared to receive it), which clearly is a political matter, dependent as it is on the allocation of resources at every level of education.

How many specialists in EAP and L2 writing honestly believe it is unethical to try to help L2 students, domestic or international, become as proficient as possible in the conventions of academic discourse? I certainly find nothing ethically disgraceful in helping students accommodate to, or assimilate to, the dominant academic discourses because I regard this as essential for academic success; in fact, I would consider it unethical not to do so, as students' very presence in the university along with their stated wishes in essays and discussions tell me this is what they hope to gain from EAP and L2 writing classes. Pennycook (1997) contrasted the vulgar pragmatism of EAP, with its emphasis on functionality, efficiency, rationality, and acquisition of the norms of academic English, to a critical approach that envisions "English classes... as important sites of change and resistance... [opportunities] to help students develop forms of linguistic, social, and cultural criticism that would be of much greater benefit to them for understanding and questioning how language works both inside and outside educational institutions" (p. 263). As I have never heard students themselves express a desire for this oppositional stance, and as the critical literature is replete with reports of student resistance to the imposition of it (e.g., Knoblauch & Brannon, 1993), it seems rather presumptuous to insist it would be of much greater benefit to them. To them and their academic and personal aspirations, or to critical educators seeking converts to a utopian politics of social transformation?

How realistic, or plausible, is it to argue, as Canagarajah (1993) and McKay (1993) did, that the indigenous languages of L2 writing students are, or can be, equal to the dominant academic discourses of Western universities? The standards and expectations of academic writing in the various disciplines have been built up over a long period of time, and their acquisition—or at least as close an approximation to it as possible—is a distinguishing feature of academic identity that is not likely to change any time soon to admit students' indigenous languages. When, for example, was the last time any of us read an article in *TESOL Quarterly, Journal of Second Language Writing* or any other publication in our field that was written in nonstandard English by a writer who was a speaker of an indigenous language? What would be the probable result if such an article were even submitted? Among the assumptions of higher education are that students will be socialized into the norms of both general academic English and the discourse conventions of their particular fields, and that teachers will help them in this process. Only when students have attained a sufficient level of proficiency in academic discourse will they be in a position to challenge academic standards and approaches to knowledge, should they wish to do so.

Although universities are unlikely to accept students' indigenous languages as equal to academic discourse, I have been impressed by how tolerant most university professors are of both the speaking and writing "accents" of international students (and to some extent American ESL students). If they see that nonnative-speaking students are trying to become proficient in academic discourse, and if the students are able to demonstrate their understanding of the course material in other ways (e.g., lab work, problem solving), professors tend to be as understanding as possible of the fact that the students come from language backgrounds very different from English. In this sense, academic discourse is being changed and linguistically pluralized by the varieties of English that international and American ESL students speak and write in universities. But it is not the same sort of pluralization that Canagarajah (1993) had in mind when he argued for students' "own local knowledge and counter-discourses" in the university as a way of resisting "ideological domination" (p. 303). I doubt that professors would be sympathetic to this idea, just as I doubt that it would occur to nonnative-speaking students to make such a claim. Hierarchies do exist, and most of us have learned to work out our lives within them; this, too, is part of the socialization process in any culture.

Pedagogical Recommendations

Although there is a growing literature on various theoretical aspects of critical EAP and L2 writing, there are few discussions of the specifics of critical classroom practice (e.g., curriculum and course design, materials development, lesson plans, teaching techniques, assignments, etc.). In part, this is because supporters of critical pedagogy tend to reject on principle attempts to "solidify and discipline this vibrant area of educational work" (Penny-cook, 1994c, p. 691) by turning it into a methodology that can be widely reproduced because doing so would run counter to the emphasis on local issues and settings. In addition, textbook-publishing companies are generally reluctant to produce texts and materials that may not appeal to a broad market. And yet another reason for the paucity of critical EAP materials and pedagogical recommendations may be that theory, especially a theory that takes an oppositional stance to the mainstream, can remain pure, whereas classroom practice must deal with the everyday realities of university life, including program requirements, students' needs and desires in the academic mainstream, forms of assessment, and so forth. In other words, critical theory is easier said than critical pedagogy done.

In any case, for whatever reasons, it is hard to find detailed examples in the critical EAP and L2 writing literature of exactly what a critical pedagogy would be like in the implementation, and where such examples exist, the authors deserve thanks. Because Benesch has been one of the few advocates of critical EAP to present and describe specific examples of classroom practice from a critical orientation, here is a discussion one of them in detail. For the paired ESL and psychology course she taught, she divided the classroom activities into three categories: those that followed a noncritical, mainstream approach (e.g., focusing on the course content and multiple-choice exam format to help the ESL students meet the requirements of the course); those that "challenged the requirements, and those which worked outside the requirements to create possibilities for social awareness and action" (Benesch, 1996, p. 733). Examples of challenging the requirements were student-generated questions put to the professor during class, an activity not built into the course syllabus, and a visit by the professor to one of the ESL class meetings, where he spoke informally to the students and fielded questions from them. Examples of going beyond the course and the requirements to try to foster social and political change were research and writing assignments on anorexia, a topic treated superficially in the psychology section that Benesch considered "a good candidate for critical scrutiny, being rich in social implications" (p. 735); and an in-class letter-writing activity to legislators to protest the intentions of the newly elected governor to cut funding for public colleges and universities.

On one hand, much of what Benesch (1996) described in this example would be unexceptionable to any mainstream EAP or L2 writing teacher. To begin with, she retained a mainstream component to the class by doing the standard activities with her students that would help them learn the material in the linked psychology course. She did not state what percentage of her course was taken up by this component, but it seems fair to assume it was the major focus. In addition, asking the students to generate questions to be clarified by the professor, and inviting him to speak to her class both seem like good pedagogical ideas, with nothing notably critical or challenging about them, despite the fact they were not part of the course to begin with.

On the other hand, when we turn to the third category of activities, those designed to create possibilities for social awareness and action, we see assignments that move into more problematic territory. According to Benesch (1996), the topic of anorexia was just one of dozens of topics glossed over by the professor, yet it was the one she chose to require research and writing assignments on because of its social and feminist implications, although some male students (and perhaps even some female students who chose to remain silent) resisted it. Would a choice of topics have not led to a more desirable diversity of course material, especially if brief oral presentations had accompanied the assignment so students could hear about each other's topics? Even more important, a choice would have allowed students to research and write about something that interested them, not Benesch's social agenda. Her requirement of a specific topic assignment was a throwback to a time in academia when professors typically set writing topics because they wanted uniformity and believed they knew best what students should write on. Current approaches to writing have moved away from that in favor of student choice, and it is ironic that it should be a critical, liberatory approach to teaching that brings back teacher-imposed topics for the sake of social and political consciousness raising.

The activity I find most troubling was having students write letters in class to legislators protesting cuts in education. Benesch (1996) stated that it was a suggestion, but the fact that class time was used for the activity indicates it was actually an assignment. Of course, I assume students would have been free not to participate, but I also assume they would have had to initiate this move, putting them in an awkward or embarrassing position that they should not have been in the first place. It would be one thing to spend a few minutes informing them of the letter-writing campaign initiated by the student government and faculty senate and even encouraging them to participate in it if they were so inclined. But it is quite another thing to use the class period to have them actually write the letters. What I find inappropriate and problematic is that it opens the way for activist teachers of any political persuasion to justify using students on behalf of teachers' own political positions. It is seductively easy to believe such actions are in the students' best interests, will help empower them, and are ethically and morally right, but all of us think our social and political views are the right ones; that does not give us the right to make our students act on them just because we are in a position to do so.

It is not as though activist-minded teachers had no other forums for working with students to effect social and political change; it is just that these other forums are outside the classroom. Most campuses have special-interest organizations that students and professors can join; on many campuses administrative approval for student organizations even requires professor sponsorship. This is an ideal setting for teacher activism. Another is evening meetings on or off campus where students and teachers can gather and discuss any topic and engage in any political action they wish to. What makes these settings appropriate for teachers to try to influence students is the fact that attendance at them is voluntary, whereas students are a captive audience in courses and classrooms.

I want to emphasize that I do not mean to single Benesch out for criticism here. In fact, I appreciate her willingness to describe an EAP and L2 writing course from a critical perspective in sufficient detail for us to have a clearer idea of what it involves so we can envision and evaluate it for ourselves. I wish others who share a critical orientation would do the same. It is frustrating to read, for example, that critical pedagogy is as applicable to wealthy, privileged international students as to oppressed minority students, and then to have the author state that "it is not [her] intention to propose specific classroom practices" (Vandrick, 1995, p. 378) and to raise only speculative questions about the relevance of critical pedagogy to this population. Similarly, when Pennycook (1997) wrote that a critical EAP or L2 writing course can challenge the dominant discourses of the academy and still provide students access to them so they can succeed in the university, I want to see the syllabus, materials, and tasks that will accomplish this in the time international students have in our writing classes. I also want to hear the reactions of the students themselves to a critical deconstruction of the discourse of their disciplines. If Belcher (1995) found resistance among ESL students to the completely standard academic act of "responding in an evaluative, analytical way" (p. 134) to texts in their own fields—because they feel inadequate to the task as students or intimidated by the authority they perceive to be lodged in texts—how, I wonder, would they react to a writing course that has them "challenge some of the standard formulations of academic knowledge. . . and discourses" (Pennycook, 1997, pp. 264–265)?

FUTURE DIRECTIONS

Critical theory and pedagogy, with their focus on sociopolitical ideology and socioeconomic inequality, have clearly gained a presence in EAP and L2 writing, but equally clear, they have not had a significant effect on mainstream research or teaching practices, nor have they altered the way intensive English programs (IEP/EAP) are designed and administered. Is this likely to change in the future? Critical applied linguistics will continue to attract a minority of specialists who are inspired by, and committed to, a vision of sociopolitical transformation that seems to transcend vulgar pragmatism. These specialists will continue to produce elaborated theoretical arguments in support of oppositional approaches to mainstream assumptions and concerns but will publish far less in the way of textbooks and materials for classroom teaching. The subbranch of critical EAP and L2 writing will lag behind other areas in critical applied linguistics because of the combination of two forces: the quality, desirability, and prestige in the world of attendance at English-speaking universities; and the norms and standards of academic writing. As long as more students in the world than can be admitted want to study in the United States, Canada, Australia, or Great Britain and as long as the acquisition of academic writing is a requirement of entrance to and acceptance in the disciplines, EAP and L2 writing will be primarily concerned with helping students achieve these goals and will attract specialists who share them. I do not see this changing any time soon.

Because the critical perspective is a marked form, it will probably always be peripheral to the mainstream, inhabiting and representing an alternative and marginalized space. When Shor (Shor & Graff, 1997) characterized critical pedagogy as *desocializing*, he revealed an important reason why in all likelihood it will never appeal to more than a small minority of teachers. Most people are far more interested in remaining socialized than in becoming desocialized, and teachers in particular are surely among the most socialized, acculturated members in any society. Whatever their sociopolitical views—and they tend to be more liberal than their fellow citizens—they have been successful in school, believe in its value and importance, understand what is required to do well in the society, and are not usually radical in their goals for their students. Add to this the student population L2 writing specialists work with, particularly international students who come to English-speaking universities with clear academic goals and aspirations, and it is difficult to imagine many L2 writing teachers opting for a critical approach to academic writing over one that focuses on preparing students as quickly and effectively as possible for their immediate, or imminent, academic needs.

Finally, for the United States, the historical rejection of socialism, the distaste for radical politics (and in the current climate, for any politics), the embrace of pragmatism, the emphasis on individualism and socioeconomic mobility, the principle of the separation of church and state extended to overt politics in the schools—in sum, the weight of U.S. political and cultural tradition—all work against the acceptance of critical theory and the implementation of critical pedagogy on any but a very small scale. The critical perspective goes too much against the grain of too many deeply embedded values—social, political, educational, and linguistic—to win a significant place in TESOL or L2 writing now or in the future.

ENDNOTE

1. The following remarks are intended as part of a critique of sociopolitical ideology and are in no way meant to disparage religious beliefs in general or Christianity in particular.

REFERENCES

Aronowitz, S., & Giroux, H. (1991). *Postmodern education: Politics, culture and social criticism.* Minneapolis, MN: University of Minnesota Press.

Aronowitz, S., & Giroux, H. (1993) *Education still under siege.* Westport, CT: Bergin & Garvey.

Auerbach, E. (1995). The politics of the ESL classroom: Issues of power in pedagogical choices. In J. Tollefson (Ed.), *Power and inequality in language education* (pp. 9–33). New York: Cambridge University Press.

Auerbach, E., & Burgess, D. (1987). The hidden curriculum of survival ESL. In I. Shor (Ed.), *Freire for the classroom: A sourcebook for liberatory teaching* (pp. 150–169). Portsmouth, NH: Heinemann/Boynton/Cook.

Belcher, D. (1995). Writing critically across the curriculum. In D. Belcher & G. Braine (Eds.), *Academic writing in a second language* (pp. 135–154). Norwood, NJ: Ablex.

Benesch, S. (1993). ESL, ideology, and the politics of pragmatism. *TESOL Quarterly, 27,* 705–717.

Benesch, S. (1995). Genres and processes in sociocultural context. *Journal of Second Language Writing, 4,* 191–195.

Benesch, S. (1996). Needs analysis and curriculum development in EAP: An example of a critical approach. *TESOL Quarterly, 30,* 723–738.

Berlin, J. (1988). Rhetoric and ideology in the writing class. *College English, 50,* 477–494.

Canagarajah, A. S. (1993). Comments on Ann Raimes' "Out of the woods: Emerging traditions in the teaching of writing." *TESOL Quarterly, 27,* 301–306.

Cherryholmes, C. (1988). *Power and criticism: Poststructural investigations in education.* New York: Teachers College Press.

Fairclough, N. (Ed.). (1995). *Critical discourse analysis.* London: Longman.

Freire, P. (1970). *Pedagogy of the oppressed.* New York: Seabury.

Jameson, F. (1984). Postmodernism or the cultural logic of late capitalism. *New Left Review, 146,* 53–93.

Knoblauch, C. H., & Brannon, L. (1993). *Critical teaching and the idea of literacy.* Portsmouth, NH: Boynton/Cook/Heinemann.

Lyotard, J. -F. (1979). *The postmodern condition.* Minneapolis: University of Minnesota Press.

McKay, S. (1993). Examining L2 composition ideology: A look at literacy education. *Journal of Second Language Writing, 2,* 65–81.

Pennycook, A. (1989). The concept of method, interested knowledge, and the politics of language teaching. *TESOL Quarterly, 23*(3), 401–420.

Pennycook. A. (1994a). Incommensurable discourses? *Applied Linguistics, 15,* 115–138.

Pennycook, A. (1994b). *The cultural politics of English as an international language.* London: Longman.

Pennycook, A. (1994c). Critical pedagogical approaches to research. *TESOL Quarterly, 28,* 690–693.

Pennycook, A. (1996). TESOL and critical literacies: Modern, post, or neo? *TESOL Quarterly, 30,* 163–171.

Pennycook, A. (1997). Vulgar pragmatism, critical pragmatism, and EAP. *English for Specific Purposes, 19,* 253–269.

Phillipson, R. (1992). *Linguistic imperialism.* New York: Oxford University Press.

Rabinow, P. (Ed.). (1985). *The Foucault reader.* NY: Pantheon.

Rorty, R. (1989). *Contingency, irony, and solidarity.* Cambridge: Cambridge University Press.

Santos, T. (1992). Ideology in composition: L1 and ESL. *Journal of Second Language Writing, 1,* 1–15.

Shor, I., & Graff, G. (1997). A conversation with Gerald Graff and Ira Shor. *Journal of Advanced Composition, 17,* 1–21.

Tollefson, J. (1991). *Planning language, planning inequality.* London: Longman.

Vandrick, S. (1995). Privileged ESL university students. *TESOL Quarterly, 29,* 375–380.

Weiler, K. (1988). *Women teaching for change: Gender, class and power.* South Hadley, MA: Bergin & Garvey.

13

Second Language Writing and Second Language Acquisition

Joan G. Carson
Georgia State University

Considering the intersection of second language acquisition (SLA) and second language (L2) writing is no easy task. SLA theory aims to describe and explain learners' competence. L2 writing focuses on models of teaching and learning and is based on learners' performance. Acquisition theories imply a diachronic perspective; models of teaching and learning writing tend to deal more with synchronic issues. Ellis (1994) suggested that the work of SLA researchers attempts to answer four fundamental questions: (a) What does learner language look like?; (b) How do learners acquire it?; (c) What accounts for differences in achievements?; and (d) What are the effects of formal instruction? Contrast these questions with the four usual concerns of writing theorists: writer, reader, text, and context. Of course, many of the questions of SLA researchers are embedded in this writing topic division, but the foci of the two groups are nonetheless quite different.

Issues related to models of teaching and learning L2 writing are driven primarily by the pragmatic concerns of the classrooms in which it is taught, which explains to a large degree why performance issues are the focus. And this seems to be appropriate, given that writing is an ability that is typically developed in formal instructional settings, and a skill most closely tied to educational practices. Nevertheless, an understanding of the development of L2 writing abilities requires an understanding of SLA in general because L2 competence underlies L2 writing ability in a fundamental way. So, it is interesting that SLA competence and L2 writing performance have remained as distinct as they have. Partly this distinction has been influenced by the fact that, until recently, much of SLA research, following

Chomskyan linguistics, has looked at competence on the morphosyntactic level. Furthermore, the more recent focus on the acquisition of communicative competence in SLA research has not extended to writing. According to Ellis (1994),

> the study of interlanguage pragmatic acts in second language acquisition has focused on the spoken medium and has paid little attention to writing. This is particularly the case with illocutionary acts. In effect, therefore, although we know something about how 'contextualized' acts such [as] requests, apologies, and refusals are acquired, we know little about how learners acquire the ability to perform acts found in decontextualized written language.... [T]he ability to perform speech acts... in face-to-face interaction may be distinct from the ability needed to perform speech acts like definitions in writing. (pp. 187–188)

In other words, we simply do not know if the acquisition of oral speech acts is similar to or different from the acquisition of speech acts in writing. Thus, we have, on the one hand, a model of communicative competence that requires a foundation of linguistic competence and that could reasonably include the discourse and appropriateness issues related to the development of writing abilities. On the other hand, we have theories of SLA that have been little informed by studies of the acquisition of pragmatic competence in writing. And even if we were to be satisfied with models of writing that are based on teaching and learning as distinct from an SLA theoretical perspective, Cumming (1998) claimed that "we are far from seeing models that adequately explain learning to write in a second language or precisely how biliterate writing should be taught" (p. 68). Beyond that, we remain unclear about what the goals of a theory of writing would be for L2 learners. In fact, we would be hard pressed to define what a theory of writing would be. It is like a theory of language? A theory of language acquisition? A theory of learning?

Because we are neither at a point where L2 theory can account for the acquisition of writing abilities, nor at a point where we have adequate models of teaching and learning writing, how can we think about the intersection or interaction of these two strands of inquiry? Even if we eventually find that a general theory of SLA does not encompass the acquisition of writing (i.e., that there are qualitative differences between the two), it is clear that SLA theory is, and will continue to be, relevant to models of how we teach and of how students learn to write in a second language. In other words, issues related to teaching and learning writing in a second language must be thought about from the perspective of SLA, but given the distinctions between SLA theory and L2 writing models, it is not clear that this is currently the case.

One way to examine how SLA theory might inform models of L2 teaching and learning is to examine perspectives on error in writing—a construct that is central to L2 writing models—and to consider it from the perspective of the four basic SLA research questions that Ellis (1994) defined.

WHAT DOES LEARNER LANGUAGE LOOK LIKE?

From SLA theory we are aware that learner language has errors, exhibits developmental patterns, and is variable. As Shaughnessy (1977) pointed out for developmental writers, errors are windows on the acquisition process, and they provide information for teachers on the interlanguage stage of L2 writers. Errors are difficult to define and identify, however. First, it is not always clear whether a learner is producing an error (generated by the learner's competence) or a mistake (generated by the learner's performance). Second, because the learners' intended utterances are not always clear to native speakers, what constitutes the specific error is not always evident. In writing, teachers can sometimes correct an error in a way that changes the meaning that the writer originally intended, and writing teachers need to be sensitive to different interpretations of utterances in line with the learner's developmental stage. This is easier to do with morphosyntactic errors than with rhetorical errors because we know so little about the acquisition of discourse and pragmatic competence in writing. Nevertheless, it seems reasonable that we are likely to find developmental patterns here, as well, and models need to account for both unfolding morphosyntactic proficiency and rhetorical ability rather than assuming standards of syntactic and rhetorical correctness that are unrealistic for developing writers. Actually, as practitioners we become attuned to our students' proficiency and can develop a sense of what an appropriate standard of acceptable writing is at different levels. The point here, however, is that lacking a research base from which to understand stages of pragmatic competence in developing writers, we are not yet in a position to develop models that take this phenomenon into account.

Errors in writing can often result from variability, with the writer producing on one occasion a correct form and on another, an incorrect form. This variability is typical of learner's interlanguage and reflects conflicting hypotheses about the target language at a single point in time. A learner who writes, "You depend on other people and they depend of you" has produced the target language in the first clause but not in the second. However, it is not clear from the text itself which rule is dominant in the writer's interlanguage system. Given an opportunity to edit or monitor her or his work, the writer might recognize the need for a single form and change both clauses to "depend of." (This would not necessarily be true of spoken language that does not always allow for, or require, changes to be made in a particular utterance.)

Variability appears to be at odds with the systematicity that governs inter-language rules but in fact represents progress toward the target language as the writer learns to apply the appropriate rules in more and more contexts—linguistic, situational, and psycholinguistic. Linguistic context refers to the language elements that precede and–or follow the variable in question. For example, a learner might produce subject–verb agreement in some sentences (I like this book) but not in linguistically more complex ones (I don't likes this book).

Situational context refers to many factors including speech styles, social factors (e.g., age, gender, class, ethnicity), and stylistic factors (e.g., topic). Friedlander's (1990) research on the influence of topic is relevant here. The results of his study suggest that experiences committed to memory in one language and written about in another are more difficult to write about than experiences committed to memory and written about in the same language. Thus, the potential for error may be greater when the situational context (topic) is that of the L2 writer's first language (L1) experience. Asking the learner to write about experiences from the L2 may then reduce the frequency or type of error.

Psycholinguistic context refers to the cognitive processing constraints imposed by the task being undertaken. Writers must balance the demands of language production with the cognitive demands inherent in the production of a particular text. When the topic is complex or abstract or performed under time constraints, language learners must focus not only on the difficulty of what they are trying to say but also on the language needed to express their ideas. When attention is divided in this way, the writer often attends primarily to the content of the utterance rather than to its form, resulting in language that is less native-like than would be the case if the learner were writing about more familiar, more concrete topics.

Each of these factors can result in variability—the differential application of interlanguage rules. Models of teaching and learning that stress the process of writing need to take in account the way in which a system of variable rules may lead writers to produce less correct drafts than might otherwise be the case as they struggle to apply emergent interlanguage rules in new linguistic, situational, and psycholinguistic contexts.

HOW DO LEARNERS ACQUIRE A SECOND LANGUAGE?

Understanding the process of SLA requires an understanding of both social and cognitive factors, and insights from SLA research can inform issues related to error in writing. Social factors play a major but indirect role in SLA, insofar as acquisition is mediated by learner attitudes. Attitudes toward the acquisition of the target language are related to learner attitudes toward target language speakers, the target language culture, the social value of learning the target language, the particular uses that target language might serve, and the learners' perceptions of themselves as members of their own culture. In Schumann's (1977) Acculturation Model, successful SLA depends on the learner's perceived social and psychological distance from the target language group. When distance is maintained, pidginization is said to be the likely result with the learner's language ability remaining functionally limited.

Learner attitudes are directly related to learner motivation, central to studies of SLA, and the distinction between instrumental and integrative motivation, originally proposed by Gardner and Lambert (1972) may be relevant here. Learners with instrumental motivation are interested in developing the target language for particular purposes such as writing a dissertation. Learners with integrative motivation want to become like target language speakers. Different motivations are likely to result in different goals for L2 writers and thus to different levels of achievement. L2 writers who are focused on producing dissertations in English may not be motivated to write expressivist prose, which they perceive as not particularly relevant to their needs. Resulting errors in essay assignments might be due to a lack of attention or monitoring, or of the writers' failure to acquire aspects of a rhetorical form that they perceive as irrelevant to their ultimate work. Learners' attitudes, motivation, and goals have significant explanatory value for the development of context-specific writing skills, and a teaching and learning model must consider the ways in which these social factors affect a writer's performance.

Transfer from the writer's first language is an important cognitive factor in the interpretation of writing error and has been acknowledged from both a syntactic and a rhetorical perspective. Although L1 transfer is no longer seen as being the sole predictor of writing error at the morphosyntactic level, it is clear that a writer's first language plays a complex and important role in SLA. More recently, the idea of L1 transfer in writing has expanded to consider the transfer of culturally specific rhetorical forms (see Leki, 1991, for an overview of contrastive rhetoric studies). It is interesting that contrastive analysis has fallen into disfavor as a strong predictor of syntactic error but that contrastive rhetoric has managed to maintain a strong reputation as a predictor of rhetorical error in writing. However, the phenomenon of transfer in SLA research has proven to be much more complex than was originally thought, involving not only facilitation and interference, but also avoidance and overgeneralization. Furthermore, transfer is constrained by a number of factors including language level, social factors, markedness, prototypicality, language distance and psychotypology, and developmental factors (Ellis, 1994). Rhetorical error is no doubt related to the findings of researchers in contrastive rhetoric, but explanations of rhetorical error as related to transfer are probably not as simple as most current models of teaching and learning writing assume.

In addition to hypotheses generated by learners on the basis of their L1, learners also use input from the target language to adjust their developing interlanguage system. SLA theorists believe that interactive input focused on communicating comprehensible messages of importance to both parties in a communicative event is what helps learners progress in their L1. Models of teaching and learning writing need to take into account the role that input and interaction play in the writing process. Are writers receiving sufficient L2 input such that they will be able to develop new hypotheses about syntactic and rhetorical forms more nearly like the L2? Lack of input is likely to result in persistent errors if writers have little exposure to the look and feel of target language written texts.

Cognitive factors also include the role of consciousness in SLA. Although writing teachers understand that errors result from both conscious and unconscious processes, Bialystok's (1978) claims for the interaction of conscious and unconscious knowledge are relevant here. According to Bialystok, explicit knowledge arises when there is a focus on the language code and the acquisition of explicit knowledge is facilitated by formal practice. Implicit knowledge is developed through exposure to communicative language use that is facilitated by functional practice. This perspective may account for the fact that techniques such as explicit grammar teaching have been shown to be ineffective in improving writing proficiency. Functional practice, resulting in implicit knowledge, highlights the importance of audience and purpose and suggests why a focus on these aspects of the writing process is more likely to lead to the development of writing ability.

WHAT ACCOUNTS FOR THE DIFFERENCES IN LEARNERS' ACHIEVEMENTS?

The fact that L2 learners rarely achieve native-speaker proficiency is well-recognized in L2 theories. Larsen-Freeman and Long (1991) included the following factors in their survey of the research on learner differences: (a) age; (b) sociopsychological factors, including motivation and attitude; (c) personality, including self-esteem, extroversion, anxiety, risk-taking, sensitivity to rejection, empathy, inhibition, and tolerance of ambiguity; (d) cognitive style, including field dependence–independence, category width, reflexivity–impulsivity, aural–visual, and analytic–gestalt; (e) hemisphere specialization; (f) learning strategies; and (g) other factors such as memory and gender. It is far from clear either that these differences affect L2 learning or that the degree to which learner differences play a role in SLA is significant. Nevertheless, the implications for error in writing are considerable. For example, learners who are not risk takers and who are sensitive to rejection might be cautious writers who make few errors. However, these same learners may limit the progress they make as writers if they are unwilling to chance the errors that might result from trying out new forms or from applying already learned forms in new functional contexts. Learner attitudes having to do with beliefs about language learning might also affect their writing. Learners who believe that learning a language is primarily an oral–aural activity might have little motivation to attend to written tasks with the result being errors in writing that might not occur in speech. The debilitating effects of anxiety might also result in a higher frequency of error. Clearly, individual differences have the potential for explaining variability in error production, uneven progress in the L2, or even lack of progress.

Learning strategies have also been investigated by second language researchers trying to account for differences in learners' achievements. O'Malley and Chamot's (1990) typology includes metacognitive, cognitive, and social–affective strategies, but not all learners employ the full range of strategies. The studies summarized by Ellis (1994) indicate five major characteristics of good language learners: (1) a concern for form, (2) a concern for communication, (3) an active approach to the task, (4) an awareness of the learning process, and (5) the ability to use strategies flexibly depending on the task. Although the evidence for a significant correlation between strategy use and successful language learning are still tentative, attempts to explain and treat error in writing need to take into account the full range of learner strategies and their effective use.

WHAT ARE THE EFFECTS OF FORMAL INSTRUCTION?

Because the development of writing abilities typically takes place in formal instructional settings, it is difficult, if not impossible, to talk about the effects—or lack of effects—of formal instruction, given the lack of alternatives. Still, what SLA researchers have found in their studies on the effects of formal instruction may be applicable to the development of writing ability. Surprisingly, there has been no convincing evidence offered for method superiority, and several explanations have been offered for this finding. First, lessons of any type often result in relatively little progress in language acquisition. Second, individual learners benefit from different types of instruction. Finally, language classes tend to offer similar opportunities for learning irrespective of method, highlighting the importance of providing writing opportunities for L2 learners.

Do learners learn what they are taught? The answer to this question may lie in Pienemann's (1984) Teachability Hypothesis, which argues that learners will learn what they are taught only if they are developmentally ready. This possibility calls into question the role of error correction, particularly given the fact that there is little evidence that correction has much effect on developing proficiency. In fact, Chaudron (1988) concluded that teachers frequently fail to correct errors, and the more often an error is made, the less likely a teacher is to correct it. This may reflect teachers' tacit understanding of learners' interlanguage development, such that they may only correct errors that they think learners are ready to eliminate.

Another hypothesis about the effects of formal instruction is that negotiation may be the most important aspect of classroom interaction. Negotiation in writing classes implies that closed tasks, which produce more negotiation and more useful negotiation, are likely to be more effective than open tasks where there is no predetermined solution, thus offering fewer opportunities for negotiation. An example of a closed task would be what Leki and I (Leki & Carson, 1997) called text-responsible writing, in that the writer is responsible for producing a written product that accurately reflects a particular content. Because the content is either right or wrong, the writer's representation of that content is discussable–explainable–negotiable. In an open task such as an expressivist essay, there is no predetermined correct representation and thus, less content is available for negotiation. The idea of error in closed tasks, then, includes much more than does the conceptualization of error in open tasks where the focus is less on content (i.e., content may be more or less adequate, but is rarely wrong) than on syntactic and rhetorical form.

I have only touched on a few relevant concepts in SLA theory that seem to me to be relevant to L2 models of teaching and learning writing, and I make no claim that an adequate SLA theory will eventually, or even should, include the acquisition of writing ability. Yet, models of teaching and learning writing must develop a perspective on acquisition that to date has not been adequately incorporated, and this has much to do with the lack of research on acquiring the communicative competence that underlies writing ability. We also lack an adequate explanatory theory that will account for the ways in which L2 writers, readers, texts, and contexts interact, the ways in which these factors may be defined and expressed, and also the myriad ways in which they differ. The goals of such a theory are ultimately pragmatic in that they provide a broader interpretive framework for composition researchers and practitioners than is currently available.

REFERENCES

Bialystok, E. (1978). A theoretical model of language learning. *Language Learning, 28*, 69–84.

Chaudron, C. (1988). *Second language classrooms: Research on teaching and learning.* Cambridge: Cambridge University Press.

Cumming, A. (1998). Theoretical perspectives on writing. *Annual Review of Applied Linguistics, 18*, 61–78.

Ellis, R. (1994). *The study of second language acquisition.* New York: Oxford University Press.

Friedlander, A. (1990). Composing in English: Effects of first language on writing in English as a second language. In B. Kroll (Ed.), *Second language writing: Research insights for the classroom* (pp. 109–125). New York: Cambridge University Press.

Gardner, R. C., & Lambert, W. (1972). *Attitudes and motivation in second language learning.* Rowley, MA: Newbury House.

Larsen-Freeman, D., & Long, M. (1991). *An introduction to second language acquisition research.* London: Longman.

Leki, I. (1991). Twenty-five years of contrastive rhetoric: Text analysis and writing pedagogies. *TESOL Quarterly, 25,* 123–143.

Leki, I., & Carson, J. (1997). "Completely different worlds": EAP and the writing experiences of ESL students in university courses. *TESOL Quarterly, 31,* 39–69.

O'Malley, J., & Chamot, A. (1990). *Learning strategies in second language acquisition.* Cambridge: Cambridge University Press.

Pienemann, M. (1984). Psychological constraints on the teachability of languages. *Studies in Second Language Acquisition, 6,* 186–214.

Shaughnessy, M. P. (1977). *Errors and expectations: A guide for the teacher of basic writing.* New York: Oxford University Press.

Schumann, J. (1977). Second language acquisition: The pidginization hypothesis. *Language Learning, 26,* 391–408.

14

Dangerous Liaisons: Problems of Representation and Articulation

Carol Severino
University of Iowa

Have you ever tried to clear up a misunderstanding between two friends? Then you know that acting the go-between to heal a rift is risky business and hard work. First, you have to know and understand both friends well enough to represent each one accurately. Second, you have to articulate each friend's position and the background and reasoning behind it in an advocatory way, although you might sympathize with one more than the other. You have to airbrush some *he saids* and *she saids* to eliminate hurtful overtones. You also do not want to come off two-faced—the mediator speaking with forked tongue. And you do not want your "liaising" to act as a safety valve that keeps your friends talking to you rather than to each other. Third, you have to know when to take yourself out of the picture. What happens if you liaise too much for too long? What happens if you distort your friends' positions, if you include injurious comments and connotations, sometimes because you yourself have not yet worked out those same problems with one or both of them? You could turn what was once a communication gap into a yawning communication chasm. The nightmare scenario is when they both say to you: "Oh, so she really thinks I'm a loser, huh? Sounds like you do too. The hell with you both." Your valiant attempts to bring the two together result in them growing further apart and in you losing two friends. That is why liaisons can be dangerous.

As a trainer and adviser of rhetoric teachers, as a writing center director, and as the Rhetoric-ESL liaison in my department, my professional liaisons are also dangerous. I am in the risky business of explaining one group, its positions, practices, and where it is coming from, to another. One reason for the constant liaising is that, structurally, the writing center and its tutors are in an automatic mediatory role between students and teachers and also between cultures. In academic parlance, the writing center is a contact zone; in everyday language, it can be a zone between a rock and a hard place.

As a liaison, first of all, I explain ESL students and American teachers to each other—often on the spot in a classroom, meeting, or office—lots of opportunities to open mouth, insert foot, and lose friends. I cannot possibly be personally familiar enough with all the international students and their cultures to explain them accurately and to know when a particular feature of a student's behavior or writing is cultural or individual or a little of both. Second, I explain to my colleagues and TAs that the argumentative rhetoric they know and love is not the only one that exists. By the same token, I explain to ESL students the features of Euro-American rhetoric that are confusing and harder to adapt to. Third, moving from teaching to scholarship, I explain the conventions of second language (L2) research to first language (L1) researchers and vice versa—all dangerous liaisons. I would like to explore each of these tightrope-walking explanatory tasks. First, the risky business of explaining ESL students to American teachers and doing it in an advocatory way that does not distort, stereotype, or patronize, so that the ESL students and American teachers will not say, "With advocates like you, who needs enemies?" Or "Kill the messenger."

Rhetoric TAs often ask me questions about the writing, and classroom and interpersonal behavior of ESL students in their classes. For example, why are there so many nonstandard features in my Vietnamese student's in-class writing if he's been in the United States since he was 11? Why does my Chinese student not write in complete sentences? Why is my Korean student's introduction unrelated to the rest of his paper? Why do my Malaysian students not participate in class discussions? Why does my Arab student miss appointments?

How to mediate in these situations? After a number of cultural gaffes in which I inadvertently stereotyped the student, the teacher, or both, and possibly exacerbated misunderstandings, I realized that I had to resist the temptation to start explaining and making speculative generalizations, especially tempting when both the teacher and I are rushed for time. I learned how to slow down. I now ask to see the pieces of student writing teachers are referring to. I read them carefully and ask the teachers questions.

It turns out that the Vietnamese student was writing in class rather than at home and made careless first-draft mistakes, although some of them seem to be transfer-type errors. A few of the Chinese students' sentences were missing *to be* verbs, but all of them are "complete"—by a less rigid definition of completeness I explained to the teacher. The Korean student's introduction, in her final draft, is an example of warming up to the controversial topic of bribery—preferable to confronting the issue head on and right away—a mini-lesson for the teacher in contrastive rhetorics. The Malaysian students are not participating in Rhetoric because the class is discussing Generation X, one of the most confusing course topics for ESL students, many of whom are mystified by the idea of slackers. In the case of why the Arab student missed appointments, I simply said I did not know. Indeed, I did not know whether it was cultural or individual, but I noted that she had also missed appointments in the Writing Center. In other words, the teacher should not take it personally. Just like the liaison does with teachers, teachers themselves should slow down and tactfully ask the students questions about their writing, their behavior, their perceptions, and their needs, and then listen carefully to the students' responses. As Currie (Chap. 3, this volume) and Leki (Chap. 2, this volume) remind us in their chapters, students, both nonnative and native speakers of English, have much to teach us teachers to enable us to teach them better.

By the same token, nonnative speakers ask me just as many questions about American teachers and students. Most of the time they ask these questions with curiosity or wonder, not moral judgement or criticism. Because many are guests in this country, they usually do not feel they have the authority or right to complain about us (I am doing some liaison-type speculative explaining here). Why do American students not read and study as much as we do, they ask? Why do some of them seem less than interested in getting to know us and making friends? On the other hand, why does my Rhetoric or Literature or Writing Center teacher sometimes act like my friend? International students also ask about what is confusing to them about American culture and language. Why do so many American couples live together before they marry? Why so many teenage mothers, so many single and divorced parents? Why do American families place their elderly in nursing homes? Why are they so interested in the sex life of their president? Why do they believe democracy is a cure-all? Why do they eat so much fast food and red meat? Why do they greet one another with "How are you?" but then seem uninterested in a response?

Again, it is tempting to answer these questions with generalizations. The reasons we became teachers in the first place is that we *like* to explain. Explaining is teaching. I, for one, find great satisfaction in playing Ms.-Know-it-All-Cultural Liaison and Contact-Zone Contact Person. I feel so important satisfying an international student's curiosity with my anthropological pronouncements as a critic of, even a gleeful traitor to, my own culture and as a praiser of and consort with theirs. "Oh," I explain. "Americans are impatient; they want immediate results. That's why they won't wait to marry to live together. In fact, that's also why they buy fast food instead of raw ingredients. Chinese people, like you, and even me, although I'm obviously not Chinese, are more patient and interested in the aesthetic experiences of cooking and eating." Then like the two-faced cultural traitor I am, after my morning writing center hours I will run over to Burger King for lunch.

In the long run, however, constant explanations about Americans may do more harm than good, just like constant explanations to teachers about their ESL students. In seeming to satisfy the ESL students' curiosity about Americans, habitual liaising might strengthen some of their prejudices against American culture and students and discourage them from asking these same questions of their American peers and teachers, thus preventing them from interacting and initiating and building relationships. They may come to rely on you, the liaison, for more explanations instead of leaving the safety of your relationship or the writing center and finding out for themselves—the same way that your maintaining the liaison role (or even the classroom researcher role) can discourage any student from negotiating with his or her teacher, or for that matter, can discourage your two friends from discussing their problems with one another instead of with you. A better role for the liaison is to prepare ESL students rhetorically, linguistically, and psychologically to ask these questions themselves. The student would want to know: What questions do I ask? In what order? How do I word them? What is the best timing, when should I ask these questions? How do I build my confidence to approach the teacher? After these issues are dealt with through role playing and rehearsal, like the state under communism, the liaison should wither away.

Another liaison role is explaining to Rhetoric professors and TA's what is often to them the bad news that the rhetoric they know and love—that of the strong central argument, topic sentences, and tight cohesion and coherence—is not synonymous with "The Only Proper Way to Ever Write." It is not the only rhetoric that exists in English and in other languages. The idea of contrastive rhetorics is easier to accept when studying comparative literature, periods and genres in literature, or feminist literature or rhetorics, but easier to resist when studying comparative student nonfiction, that is, student papers. That is probably because teachers are not studying these papers but evaluating and grading them according to a set of U.S. culturally-based criteria—the standards that Cumming (Chap. 15, this volume) refers to. As Hamp-Lyons (Chap. 8, this volume) emphasizes in her chapter, all assessment of writing is political.

Other professional mediating happens with research and scholarship. The more familiar liaison situation to me is when first language (L1) compositionists who love literature want to maintain good relationships with their literary colleagues. I was used to that liaison necessity from attending graduate school in an English department and from discussions at the Conference on College Composition and Communication. Yet I had never mediated between second language (L2) writing and literature until I coedited a book for MLA, *Writing in Multicultural Settings* (Severino, Guerra, & Butler, 1997). I wanted this book to discuss cross-cultural issues fully, not only from the limited L1 view of cultural diversity, which, as Belcher (Chap. 5, this volume) points out, emphasizes variation by class, race, and gender, but neglects nationality and language background. ESL scholars sent me their work, some of which confused the MLA series editors and acquisitions editors because it did not fit the MLA mold of theorizing and close reading. I was reminded that in the two communities, what constitutes research and knowledge is different and is presented differently, differences that go beyond MLA and the American Psychology Association (APA) style and have more to do with the contrastive rhetorics of the humanities and the social sciences. Some of the ESL articles for the book reported actual results of empirical research studies, one after another, leading to strings of citations. All of these studies and results and citations seemed foreign to the MLA series and acquisitions editors. I mediated by explaining where applied linguistics–ESL was coming from to MLA and vice versa to get the authors to "MLA-ify" their articles slightly. As the liaison, I had to persuade both parties to compromise a bit.

My most recent persuasion challenge was explaining ESL students and their needs, in fact, briefly reviewing the nature of L2 and L1 learning and writing, to our college administration. My local example is the following: The external review of our Rhetoric Department suggested that the Writing Center was overused by ESL students. The Dean asked us why so many of them use our Writing Center, draining energies and resources that could be used to help native-speakers. Shouldn't the Linguistics–ESL Department help those students, not Rhetoric and the Writing and Speaking Centers, which are not qualified to teach ESL students anyway and who have enough to do with 5,000 mostly native-English speaking first year students? Where do we begin to answer these questions? How do we unpack all the assumptions about language learning behind them?

After some brainstorming, some of the Rhetoric faculty found it useful to distinguish between ESL students, that is, those still enrolled in ESL courses, and nonnative speakers of English (NNS's), those who had already finished their ESL course work. Thus, we maintained that, in fact, we did not teach ESL students in the writing center, but nonnative speakers of English. After that rhetorical move, we had to refute the L2 version of the inoculation theory—that once students have taken their ESL courses, they have no more problems with English. The best refutation is what Leki (1992) did at the beginning of *Understanding ESL Writers*: get your audience to think of the writing problems they have in their L2s (e.g., to recall that paper on Impressionist painting in fourth year French that was returned covered with red marks). This move usually results in an epiphanal light bulb appearing over their heads, although then the light goes out and we have to try to light it up, again and again. Actually, responding to the L2 version of the inoculation theory is refreshing because in (Mother-Tongue) Rhetoric we usually face the L1 version—that once students have taken Composition or Rhetoric, they are inoculated and have no more writing, reading, or speaking problems in their native language. Both L1 and L2 versions come from the lack of a developmental perspective on language learning, in other words a misunderstanding, somewhat like the misunderstanding that drives two friends apart. As liaisons, we need to remind our colleagues that language learning and the improvement of rhetorical strategies, in L1 or L2, are lifelong endeavors, not one-shot deals.

We explained to the Dean that nonnative speakers may still encounter problems with strategies of academic rhetorics in English, especially if they differ from those of their native languages and cultures—strategies and features such as hierarchical organization, thesis formulation, providing enough relevant evidence to support the thesis, explicit connections between ideas, and formally citing authorities. To avoid exaggeration and misrepresentation, we pointed out that the native English speakers in and out of the center have problems with these same features. No English speakers, L1 or L2, are born knowing how to compose academic essays. As Grabe (Chap. 4, this volume) reminds us, the transmission of writing is cultural, not biological. Then we explained that NNS's also need help with idioms, idiomatic phrasing, two-word verbs, prepositions, and articles—features that are problematic long after ESL courses are completed, problems that do not mean students are slow learners or overly dependent on the writing center. Another liaison role in the writing center, we explained, is to help with understanding culture when the lack of cultural knowledge or its tacit nature to American teachers impedes progress on a writing assignment, for example, a Hindu student struggling to write about Christian symbolism and Joe Christmas as a Christ figure in William Faulkner's (1932) *Light in August*. (Here, the situation was a reciprocal one; as I explained to the student the life of Christ and Christian symbolism, the student explained to me the life of Krishna and Krishna symbolism.)

Our response to the observation that we in the Writing Center are not qualified to teach ESL students was to point out that because one-half of our lab teacher-training seminar practicum course is devoted to the liaison task of explaining ESL issues to the mostly American TA's working with ESL students, it can not be said that our writing center teachers are untrained, although there is always room for improvement. Our last point was to argue that an international writing center was in sync with the University's vision and mission of global education and cultural exchange. It took two writers, two drafts, and two faculty meetings to complete the response to the Dean. Apparently, these explanations were successful because, fortunately, no one has asked us to limit ESL enrollment in the Writing Center; ESL students still constitute 40% of our writing center population.

What are some liaison lessons we can pull from these examples? First, it would be better to help prepare nonnative speakers to be their own advocates and explainers, and then wither away, maintaining a role of support rather than liaison. The best case scenario would be ESL students organized in liaison committees, undergraduate and graduate, explaining, advocating for, and defending themselves and their courses, programs, and services through organizations like the Pan-Asian Student Organization, the TA's Union, or the Student Senate. Eliminate the native-speaker third party. Lose the liaison. As Smoke (Chap. 9, this volume) and Benesch (Chap. 11, this volume) demonstrate, nonnative speakers benefit personally and professionally from applying rhetorical strategies to represent themselves and articulate their needs.

Second, we need more rhetoric, composition, and writing center TAs who are international students, immigrants, or bilingual or nonnative speakers of English themselves. These teachers would not require such cultural and linguistic explanations because they have lived them. Instead, they would assume some of the burden of this explaining themselves.

Third, when you are in a situation in which you have to make explanations about culture or education, make sure you qualify them and that your audience comes away understanding those qualifications. Emphasize *some* and *sometimes*. Use Kaplan's (1988) terms of "cultural preferences" revealed with degrees of "frequency" (p. 10) rather than a discourse of fixed traits that always reveal themselves. The world is changing and the world's peoples are changing, too. Sometimes, it seems that they are changing places. More Japanese families are placing their elderly in nursing homes. More people from other countries are eating fast food as more Americans are eating tofu and vegetables and drinking tea. Third, do not be afraid to say "I don't know." Don't be afraid to refuse to be or stay the liaison. If a student is having a problem with an American teacher about the teacher's assessment of the student's work, encourage the student to go talk to the teacher, not to keep talking to you.

Fourth, when ESL students ask about what they have witnessed of American practices and rituals, ask them to write about those observations. Why defuse a potentially good writing opportunity with more explanation? For example, a Taiwanese graduate student in Linguistics, who is also a Chinese language TA, was studying the differences between American and Chinese conversational openers and bonding. In the Writing Center, I asked her to compose a dialog to illustrate what she had studied in her literature review—another way of working on the same material. Here is what she wrote—a dialog of missed communication and misunderstanding between two neighbors at a bus stop, Tzu-shin from Taiwan and Katie, from the United States:

Katie: How's it goin', Tzu-Shin?
Tzu-Shin: Have you eaten breakfast yet?
Katie: Sure, I just grabbed a bagel, some cream cheese, and some juice down at the Union Pantry. Say, how about those Hawkeyes? Did you catch Tim Dwight's touchdown?
Tzu-Shin: What is a touchdown? Who is Tim Dwight?
Katie: Oh, I'll have to teach you all about football some time. I'm on my way to vote in the local elections. Are you involved in politics in Taiwan? Are you affiliated with a party?
Tzu-Shin: I don't know very much about politics or parties. By the way, how's your job? Are you making big money?
Katie: My bus is coming. See you later.

Katie and Tzu-Shin could benefit from a temporary liaison to clear up their misunderstandings—to explain that Americans greet one another with the convention "How are you?" and Taiwanese with "Have you had your breakfast yet?," but neither wants or expects a long response. Taiwanese friends often, but not always, prefer to refrain from discussing politics, and Americans prefer to refrain from discussing their salaries. Then, once that is explained, Katie and Tzu-Shin can resume their relationship, without a third party's facilitation or interference. In most situations, like the Writing Center teacher, the ESL liaison's purpose is to work themselves out of a job. That way, the three of you will have a greater chance of remaining friends.

REFERENCES

Faulkner, W. (1932). *Light in August*. New York: H. Smith and R. Haas.
Kaplan, R. B. (1988). Cultural thought patterns revisited. In U. Connor & R. B. Kaplan (Eds.), *Writing across languages: Analysis of L2 Text* (pp. 9–22). Reading, MA: Addison-Wesley.
Leki, I. (1992). *Understanding ESL writers: A guide for teachers*. Portsmouth, NH: Boynton/Cook.
Severino, C., Guerra, J., & Butler, J. (Eds). (1997). *Writing in Multicultural Settings*. New York: MLA.

15

The Difficulty of Standards, For Example in L2 Writing

Alister Cumming
University of Toronto

This chapter focuses on standards. And why not? Everyone seems to be talking about them these days. Indeed, a reason for my focusing on standards is that numerous differing uses of the term have appeared in recent professional, scholarly, and public discussions. The popularity and ambiguities of this term make it worth examining closely. I do so here in respect to two recent, but very different, research studies that investigated standards for second language (L2) education in secondary schools: One was an international survey, and the other was a case study in two schools. Conducting these studies made me especially aware of four fundamental dilemmas that formulations of educational standards confront, particularly in respect to L2 writing: (a) defining the construct of L2 writing, (b) ascertaining what students have learned, (c) relating L2 writing to other abilities and modes of communication, and (d) accounting for variability among language varieties, people, and situations. These issues require considerable further research (in the scientific sense of standards), particularly as (essentially political) pressures to assert educational standards increase, and language educators are correspondingly held accountable for their implicit conventions of practice (as standards of professional culture).

These issues warrant clearer understanding, not only theoretically but also in terms of principles for educational practice (including curricula, instruction, and assessment) and to guide further inquiry in this domain. Standards can be helpful and are even necessary, but our limited knowledge and ambivalent professional consensus about certain aspects of L2 writing currently constrain people's ability to specify or use the idea of standards rigorously, systematically, or extensively. As a result, certain confusions tend to surround the specifications of standards rather than produce the kinds of clarification they should.

THREE SENSES OF STANDARDS

I want to focus on three senses of the term *standards*, each with a differing level of importance and conceptual basis. The first sense is associated with scientific research; it poses norms for empirical inquiry (e.g., validity or reliability). We need such standards to be able to assure ourselves that claims to knowledge arising from principled inquiry are true or credible. This expectation is commonly asserted in reference to, and is indeed often a criterion for, publication in scholarly or professional journals, the primary sources for documenting such knowledge. Similarly, in such educational matters as the assessment of students' L2 writing or evaluation of programs, scientific standards are also necessary to assure comparability, accuracy, and fairness across differing populations of learners, programs, institutions, or other contexts. This sense of the term *standards* is not particular just to science, but plays a larger role in our lives and societies in reference to (essentially political) conventions by which we abide, such as how we reference scholarly information (e.g., APA or MLA citation style), our adherence to standard time, or even the standard types of nuts and bolts basic to the construction of any building or device.

The second sense of standards is more avowedly political; it has arisen frequently in discussions of education in two ways. One sense, which I view as primarily positive, is in reference to specifying curriculum standards. In recent years there have been innumerable instances of professional associations or educational jurisdictions stipulating new sets of standards to define curriculum policy; to set clearer, more appropriate goals for student achievement or instructional practices or resources; or to bring different but related groups within a common, umbrella framework. Some relevant, noteworthy examples are Teachers of English to Speakers of Other Languages' (TESOL's) *ESL Standards* (1997, 1998), International Reading Association's (IRA's) and National Council of Teachers of English's (NCTE's) joint *Standards for the English Language Arts* (1996), or the Council of Europe's *Common European Framework for Language Learning, Teaching and Assessment* (summarized recently by Trim, 1998). Similarly, nearly every school board, university or college, and state or province in North America seems to have revised (and often re-revised) its curriculum policy since 1990, producing an astonishing, if not redundant, plethora of such standards (or frameworks, or benchmarks, or attainment targets, as they might also be known). The prominence of this sense of the term *standards* relates to trends such as increasing global interdependence, the public accountability of education and resulting outcomes-based curricula (see, e.g., Brindley, 1998; Torrance, 1995), as well as efforts to reform and make more uniform the highly decentralized organization of education in North America (in contrast, for example, to many other countries in the world, where school and even university curricula are tightly defined by centralized authorities, see Dickson & Cumming, 1996). But eminently positive senses associated with such moves to clarify and debate standards can be found in the ideas of educational philosophers, such as Dewey (1916, 1938) or Habermas (1984, 1987), who have advocated democratic conceptualizations of education and the need for public deliberations about them.

However, this sense of the term *standards* has also been used negatively (e.g., to talk about declining standards in education, often in reference to students' abilities to write). This negative connotation appears, in part because media reports often portray such circumstances negatively (i.e., as a problem that requires resolution, e.g., "the standards at our institution or in our educational system are falling"), but also because most perceptions of declines in literacy standards arise simply from the opening up of educational opportunities to more diverse populations than those who had participated in education in the past (see, e.g., Graff, 1994), so they are a condemnation of the diverse peoples coming to participate in education, but not of education practices per se. More implicitly, there is a negative aspect as well arising from the professional literature on education having tended to ignore the situations of linguistically and culturally diverse student populations (e.g., as Silva, Leki, & Carson, 1997, argued in respect to L2 writing). Moreover, there is, contrary to what numerous politicians are fond of proposing, no firm evidence that making curriculum standards more explicit actually has any impact per se on a society or its economy broadly (Levin, 1998, even argued there is a negative relation between the explicitness of such curricula and many countries' economic wealth; Germany, the United States, and Canada are obvious exceptions to any such trend).

The third sense of standards I wish to discuss is perhaps idiosyncratic (in that I have not heard other people discuss it much), although I think it highly germane. My thinking about this jelled while, as I should have been preparing this chapter, I happened to be listening to some jazz recordings by Keith Jarrett and by Shirley Horn, in which the musicians professed to be providing new renditions of old standards, that is, tunes (e.g., from Broadway musicals or popular radio) that have become traditional components of jazz musicians' repertoires since the 1970s or so. Looking ahead to points I describe in detail later, I propose that many of our ideas about standards of writing and related instructional practices are akin to these jazz standards. They involve implicit performance genres that each of us appreciates, from a common cultural tradition, as conventional expectations for students' writing or abilities, classroom activities, or teaching. Examples specific to L2 writing include genres such as the 30-minute argumentative essay (which has become a standard expectation for L2 writing assessment, Cumming, 1997), or various other types of writing tasks commonly assigned in university courses (e.g., as described in Berkenkotter & Huckin, 1995; Hale et al., 1996), or to extend the analogy, even certain routines of teaching, classroom activities, or beliefs associated with them, common to L2 writing instruction (Cumming, 1992; Shi & Cumming, 1995).

Many current views of standards related to L2 writing are of this order: they are implicit, culturally circumscribed, professional expectations (my third sense of standards, which admittedly blends together with certain aspects of the other two senses of the term). Correspondingly, as pressures come upon educators to specify curriculum standards (in my second, positive sense of the term), there is also a great need for more systematic research in standards (in my first sense of the term) to clarify what they really involve (in my third sense of the term) and to counter negative applications of this concept (i.e., in my second, negative sense of the term, or just ignorance). Put simply, we need to research and refine the standards of educational practice related to L2 writing, not only to better understand them and to know how to act on them but also to know how to be critically wary of certain political uses of this concept. As content as we may feel with our implicit beliefs about standard practices of teaching L2 writing, unless these are articulated, studied, evaluated, and justified, they are prey to confusions as well as political manipulations. Lest this all appear circular, let me move for the sake of exemplification to describing two of my recent research activities in which the idea of standards had particular, complex significance, specifically in respect to L2 writing. But I should acknowledge that my preceding remarks have only touched on some of the varied uses of the term *standards* now common in language education (e.g., see Davidson, Turner, & Huhta, 1997).

TWO CASES

The two cases I wish to discuss have contrasting perspectives. One involved an unusually global perspective, aiming to compare whole educational systems in numerous countries, and the other was very much a case study of a local context—a dozen language teachers in two secondary schools in Toronto. The global viewpoint appeared in a project I worked on for several years with colleagues from around the world: the International Association for the Evaluation of Educational Achievement's (IEA) Language Education Study (LES). Results from its first phase were published as Dickson and Cumming (1996), profiling policies for language education in 25 different countries. I discussed some of the project's history as well in Cumming (1996a) from my viewpoint as Chair of its Steering Committee. LES was organized through a coordinating center at the National Foundation for Educational Research in England and Wales, under the auspices of IEA, but the design and conduct of the project (and the standards it adhered to) involved collaboration among research coordinators from each of the 25 participating countries (as well as various people with whom they worked or conferred within their countries, and others in IEA's network). In this discussion the focus is on some of our ideas that never materialized (and probably now never will): plans that were drafted in proposals, but never funded, to survey students and their teachers in secondary schools in each of the participating countries through questionnaires about their curricula, instruction, and learning as well as tests of the proficiency the students had attained in L2 or foreign languages such as English, French, or German. As you might imagine, planning to study L2 writing from this truly global, comparative perspective raised many issues about the scientific, political, and cultural aspects of standards.

The more local context is one that several researchers and I (Cumming, Swain, Howard, Hart & Shi, 1999) at the Ontario Institute for Studies in Education (OISE) investigated in 1996, under funding fromthe provincial government of Ontario. We aimed to see how a sample of Grade 9 teachers of various languages (English Language Arts, ESL, and Core French) were starting to use the standards specified in a thennew (but since extensively revised) curriculum framework, mandated by the Ontario Ministry of Education and Training (1995). A brief synopsis of this study appears as Cumming (1996b), and more details appear in Cumming et al. (1999). The basic details are that we tried to document, through year-long case studies in two schools in Toronto, what language teachers were actually doing with the mandated standards in their classrooms and how the instructors and students perceived these. We found a variety of perspectives and influences on the utilization of these standards in these two schools, ranging from teachers who had never read the Ministry document, to teachers who said they had too many difficulties understanding its vague terminology to make use of it, to teachers who used the curriculum standards extensively to shape and direct their classroom activities (integrating syllabi, tasks, and student assessment in unique ways). The Ministry's *Language Standards* set specific outcomes for students to achieve in English and French at the ends of Grades 3, 6, and 9 in respect to specific aspects of writing, reading, listening, speaking, viewing, and representing, each demarcated by six levels of normative performance. We focused only on Grade 9.

I am considering these two circumstances because they each involved a complex intersection of the scientific, the political, and the conventional genres of educational activity (as well as key aspects of curriculum policy, instructional practices, and student learning and assessment). The juxtaposition of such concerns are probably why most discussions of standards in education appear: People propose new policies or reach new research insights, then to act on them they try to alter, or find they need to clarify better, the existing standards of educational practice. As such, much recent discussion about standards in education has been motivated primarily by concerns to reform education. However, in practice, as Stern (1983) warned, language educators some time ago, processes of educational change can produce a *levels confusion*. That is, knowledge or debate at one level of educational practice—be it foundational research or theory, curriculum policy, or instructional practices—tends to intermingle with, and be confused by, issues at the other levels. For this reason, it is worth trying to outline now certain points and sources of such confusion (which did abound in the two situations I describe later), focusing particularly on the issue of L2 writing (which was one prominent consideration, among other aspects of language learning and teaching, in both circumstances).

Specifically, I want to focus on four challenges or dilemmas that are fundamental to standards in L2 writing:

- defining the construct of L2 writing,
- ascertaining what students have learned,
- relating L2 writing to other abilities and modes of communication, and
- accounting for variability among language varieties, people and situations.

THE CONSTRUCT OF L2 WRITING

Every language curriculum framework involves, at least implicitly, some theoretical conceptualization of what L2 writing is. Unfortunately, as we all know, there is no generally agreed-on definition of this construct, let alone any substantiated model that is vying for this status. I know all too well myself, from having tried over several years to start to construct, with little empirical success, such a model in one setting (see Cumming & Riazi, 2000). Moreover, in recently reviewing the past 5 years' published research (in preparation for Cumming, 1997—having been asked by Grabe (personal communication, 1996) to state what "current theoretical conceptions of L2 writing are"), I was only able to affirm that research has recently highlighted the multidimensionality of L2 writing—from text analytic, composing processes, and sociocontextual perspectives—and distinguished the components (i.e., texts, writers, and contexts), the participants (students, instructors, policy makers, etc.), and basic educational functions (curriculum, instruction, and assessment) of L2 writing. These distinctions are useful, but they hardly form a theory or even much of a definition of what L2 writing is. This absence of explicit theories (and foundation knowledge or consensus), accompanied by an obvious complexity of situation from place to place, is probably a major reason why so many educational jurisdictions have taken it upon themselves to define, in their particular curriculum frameworks, what standards for L2 writing should be: If the experts cannot tell us, then we will have to define it ourselves. From the perspective of Stern (1983), however, this produces an inevitable disjuncture between the level of foundation knowledge (i.e., research and theory) and the level of curriculum policy (in which such standards are typically stipulated), with further complications at the level of instructional practices (which standards should practicing teachers follow? Those in curriculum policies? Those of theorists or teacher educators? Or just those in the textbooks and workbooks?). This approach leaves the specification of curriculum standards open to severe criticism from expert opinion as well as to the differing viewpoints of practicing educators. Moreover, it makes the concept of standards into a primarily political, rather than scientific, enterprise—and one often fraught with political tensions (see, e.g., Bourne, 1997; Moore, 1996, for accounts of language education reform in Britain and Australia, respectively, that highlight such tensions).

In planning LES, we recognized fairly quickly that there was no theoretical framework that could guide, in any standard way, an analysis of language education in 25 or so countries. As comprehensive as any published analysis of, for example, L2 writing (e.g., Grabe & Kaplan, 1996) might be, you cannot convince several dozen researchers from around the world that concepts defined solely by North Americans are valid or relevant for education in countries in Europe, Asia, and the Middle East as well, let alone sufficiently well articulated to analyze accurately and fairly students' achievements in education in diverse languages. So we decided we had to build an understanding of the relevant constructs (e.g., L2 writing) empirically in the course of the project: first by identifying and synthesizing existing curriculum policies (as are now described in Dickson & Cumming, 1996), then by conducting an analysis of curriculum documents from each of the 25 countries (which we started to do, finding a surprising degree of similarity among them), then to survey nationally representative samples of teachers to describe what they actually taught (all this prior to being able to design a survey of students about their learning and proficiency, then to field test and validate its instruments, then actually to conduct the study, its analyses, and to report findings). (Little wonder that funding did not materialize, although three larger, comparable studies of math and science education have been conducted, and a fourth is now being planned.)

This approach necessarily skirted around defining, in any scientific sense, what integral concepts like L2 writing are. But it would have produced empirically grounded descriptions of how L2 learning and teaching are practiced and how they vary, framed in terms of the conventional genres of educational practices (my third sense of the term standards, described earlier). This in turn would have allowed us to demarcate the domains in which the relevant constructs exist, along with their major, related variables (at least in secondary schools). But how can you convince people to fund this kind of research when you do not know precisely what the constructs are that will be surveyed or assessed? What patterns of variation in them might appear from one country to another, and indeed in regions or subsystems of education in countries? What aspects, for instance, of L2 writing are valued or practiced in certain countries or educational programs? Or what aspects are central to the construct across languages as diverse as English, French, or German? In sum, the inevitable circularity is that such questions cannot be answered very well, for the purposes of designing such research, without first doing a study like the one we proposed. On reflection, my impression is that we either have to admit that much of our knowledge and standards on such matters is severely limited, or we have to venture into doing research of a truly global scope and scale to try to clarify them, despite the expenses, efforts, and futilities that entails.

Looking at the construct of L2 writing in my other example situation, there was a different order of confusion about standards. The Ministry document neatly laid out sets of performance outcomes for students to attain in writing by the end of Grade 9 (e.g., in terms like, to cite just one among hundreds of similar phrases, "uses narrative and literary forms to integrate cultural and global experiences and issues; demonstrates clear control of form and purpose," Ontario Ministry of Education and Training, 1995, p. 59). The final pages of the document cited the practicing teachers who had contributed, together with Ministry officials, to prepare the framework, thereby declaring the theoretical foundation of the framework to be, in effect, a long-term committee decision (i.e., expert judgement on what constructs like L2 writing are and should be at this point in schooling). Two pages of references were cited in the framework, solely for "further reference" (pp. 112–113), rather than as any theoretical foundation. Several shortcomings related to core constructs were particularly evident to the teachers we interviewed and observed. First, the so-called standards focused solely on student performance, providing no guidance to teachers on how they might teach or organize their syllabi, and only a couple of the teachers we interviewed had received any formal orientation to how they might use it. Second, the framework was so large a document, expansive in its scope, and impenetrable in its terminology, and for most teachers we talked to, out of synch with the instructional practices they usually followed, that most had not bothered to read, let alone, begin to try to use it. Third, there were no published pedagogical materials or assessment instruments available that were linked to the curriculum framework, around which the teachers felt they could organize their instruction—except for Core French, in which, in fact the teachers were relying heavily on a new textbook series, as one happily proclaimed, "xxx [name of textbook] offers reading activities, grammar, everything the Ministry expects us to be doing with our students is there. As this is the first year we are using this program, we are sticking to it more closely than we might after we become more familiar with it." (teacher of French) The few teachers who did utilize the statements on student outcomes extensively did so in ways they uniquely devised, deciding themselves how to adapt them to organize units of study and for assessment, in ingenious, elaborate, but relatively ad hoc ways. For example, in respect to writing:

> I tend to do smaller and shorter projects. I assess what they do in class. I mark their writing. They have a folder which is assessed for its quantity, its process. . . . The evaluation is based on the guidelines. I ask them to choose from several paragraphs and polish it up. I will give some tests that I will mark on content and writing skills. I went through the outcomes and I put them on this sheet. I listed the outcomes. If I give a test, I give 6 for writing skill, 6 for understanding or comprehension, then 6. . . . There are 6 outcomes for the test. The marks will be entered into these columns. It's very painstaking. Getting the mark from the test or the writing folder into here and then a percent is very time-consuming. This is based on the Ministry Common Curriculum document. (teacher of English)

In sum, the Ministry had prescribed expected outcomes for students, but these had fallen far short of defining standards in terms of constructs for teaching or assessment that most of the teachers we interviewed thought they could readily utilize. The teachers' concerns about the curriculum framework did not center on its lacking a theoretical or scientific foundation, though some did query this (and I certainly would have—in my first sense of the term *standards*). Nor were they especially bothered by the Ministry's political agenda in aiming to specify what students' outcomes should be (my second sense of the term *standards*). But the teachers nearly were all perturbed by the curriculum framework's limited utility and lack of relevance to their own pedagogical understandings and practices as well as their current students' abilities or interests. (Or, alternatively, they went to great lengths, like the teacher quoted earlier, to create elaborate syllabi and assessment schemes that were so idiosyncratic that they literally defied the idea of *standards*.) That is, my third sense of *standards* dominated here. The teachers wanted to rely on standard tunes they knew how to play and knew would be appreciated by their relevant audiences. This does not reflect poorly on the abilities or capacities of these teachers in any way; indeed school-board administrators had referred us to these particular schools because they thought they had exemplary language programs. But this finding does say a great deal about how constructs, such as L2 writing, need to be defined in order to be accepted as standards by practicing teachers. Instead of focusing solely on students' behaviors (as the Ontario Common Curriculum and many earlier curriculum frameworks have, drawing on assessment models), curriculum frameworks need to address the knowledge, contexts, and interactions that conventionally exist, as culturally conventional standards (e.g., for constructs such as L2 writing), among students and teachers, and that are jointly constructed by them (as, in the past few years, many versions of language standards prepared by teachers' professional associations have in fact done (e.g., IRA & NCTE, 1996; TESOL, 1997; Trim, 1998).

ASCERTAINING STUDENTS' LEARNING

A key rationale for setting new standards in education has been to clarify what students achieve, or should achieve. Notoriously, though, this is a problem for L2 writing. Several widely used, holistic- or analytic-type assessment instruments may be adequate to make global evaluations of students' proficiency in L2 writing, but they are not sufficiently fine grained, comprehensive, valid, or relevant for educational purposes to determine specific achievements learners may make, for example, over the period of a course or program (Cumming, 1997; Polio, 1997; Raimes, 1990). Indeed, Bialystok (1998) recently charged that this limitation in valid assessment instruments constrains all aspects of L2 research and education. So, without valid instruments to assess students' achievements, for example, in L2 writing, how can educators be certain that students have learned anything in particular, or presume refinements in curriculum standards may be responsible for this? There is a major disjuncture in L2 education between curriculum standards and assessment standards.[1]

The interface between standards for curricula and for assessment was a major dilemma in planning LES. This centered on the distinction between general proficiency assessment and achievement assessment. Assessments of general language proficiency presume there is a global, universally valid construct to be assessed, such as L2 writing. Everyone we conferred with agreed that a primary purpose for LES would be to ascertain the proficiency in languages (e.g., English, French, and German) of students completing high school in each country, using a common yardstick or general proficiency measure. However, when we started to describe what this general proficiency measure might consist of, through sample-test specifications and prototype tasks, numerous problems surfaced.

People all wanted something slightly different, catering to the situation of students in their own countries or the curricula they followed. In effect, they wanted tests that would assess the particular achievements related to school curricula in each country as well as account for the opportunities that exist to use languages outside of school (both of which vary greatly from place to place). How, for example, could the proficiency to write English be compared among students in schools in England, Thailand, or Italy? Do their curricula not emphasize such different aspects of ESL writing, and students make such different achievements in it, that it would be impossible to design one test that could capture this variability, let alone fairly account for what particular students did have the opportunities to learn? Moreover, what about achievements in different languages or school programs in a country, where one language (e.g., English) might receive many more hours of instruction and be more widely used in a society, than another language (e.g., French or German)? A further problem was the domains that might be covered in the tests. Given the various genres that L2 writing, for example, entails, who is to say which genres should be sampled for testing in a way that allows students to validly demonstrate their proficiency (in a period of time that would not unduly interrupt their schooling): essay writing, letter writing, or summary writing? And how many samples of each type of writing are needed to ensure a reliable representation of each student's proficiency? These are problems not only of relevance to the curricula actually implemented in each country, but also of defining the construct of L2 writing and of techniques of assessment. The idea of standards surely cannot go so far as to expect universal standards for language curricula, or students' opportunities to learn, in domains like L2 writing. But without presuming some standard of uniformity, how could one reasonably compare them from country to country?

In the study in Toronto, the problem of validly assessing students' achievements seemed to have passed by the wayside, despite the focus of the new curriculum framework almost exclusively on student outcomes and, several years earlier (in 1993), the implementation of a province-wide test for Grade 9 students's writing, which set its own standards for achievement that were well received and conceived. Ironically, standards were declared but could not realistically be implemented or monitored (apart from those implicitly established previously through the province-wide tests). First, as noted previously, teachers were left to their own devices to assess their students' achievements, and these appeared to vary dramatically from class to class. Second, the teachers and students alike had profound difficulties understanding what the specified outcomes were or how they could act on them to determine students' achievements:

> The language that describes different behaviors is so subtle that they don't allow for an expression of difference. They show "limited mastery," or "some mastery," or "very good mastery." Those are vague terms. It's hard to see what they mean. (teacher of English)

> Not only are the guidelines and descriptors too complex, they also leave zones of transition unaddressed. You'll get something that is associated with level 1, 2, or 3 performance, but in between there should be a lot of filling. The jump between levels leaves gaps, too many grey areas. (teacher of French)

Despite these constraints on summative assessment, many teachers and students did appreciate the specification of standards for the purposes of formative assessments, clarification of ongoing student performance, or in designing instructional tasks. For example:

> He usually tends to come around after he hands out, like, a writing folder-submission . . . and writes out a mark on a paper. . . . It's better to know where you're at, if you could improve, if there's any chance that you could improve. Like on Tuesday he told us we have a chance to improve. So you focus on something and you're going to try to do it better. I think it's a good thing. (student of English)

> He always explains what is going to be on the test and how he's going to mark it. I feel it helps me know what to study. For the exam, he told us you need to know your predicate, for example, or your sentences, and you also need to know what theme, character, and plot is. So I didn't go home and waste my time studying, say, Greek mythology, when it wasn't going to be on the exam. So I knew exactly what to study so I can bring up my mark. (another student of English)

> I was trying to work on the target, "writing in a role", which happens to be L14 in the provincial language standards. . . . What I was looking for is, how were the students able to get into the role of Shakespeare? I was thinking in terms of the provincial language standards. And when I saw the assignment, I had been moaning over something to do. And I said, ah perfect! (teacher of English)

RELATING L2 WRITING TO OTHER ABILITIES
AND MODES OF COMMUNICATION

Who is to say that L2 writing is a distinct ability, in relation to other abilities (e.g., L1 writing skills, lexical knowledge, conceptual knowledge, etc.) or other modes of communication (e.g., reading, which a person necessarily has to do to be able to write)? We treat it as such, as one of the implicit standards of L2 teaching, curricula, and assessment, seemingly around the world. But as far I can tell, the only justification for this implicit standard is convention (which may be a standard in its own right, as I suggested near the beginning of this chapter).[2] The challenge this convention poses for standards relates closely to the issues described previously—of defining the construct of L2 writing and of ascertaining students' learning with precision and validity.

In designing LES, we were hard pressed to justify, by any rationale other than convention, our decisions to distinguish between writing, reading, listening, and speaking as core components of the tests, curriculum analyses, or student surveys we were planning. All representatives contributing to the design of the research unanimously agreed to make this distinction simply because it reflects the way in which language curricula are organized in their countries. At the same time, we all recognized that L2 writing, perhaps more than any other of the so-called language skills, entails numerous interrelations to other abilities and language skills. For example, recognizing that L2 writing relates closely to native-language literacy, we pondered whether we would also have to assess students' L1 writing to be able to partial out its effects on L2 writing performance (or run the risk of our results reflecting more L1 literacy than L2 proficiency). Likewise, we thought about integrated tasks, for example of writing and reading together, but realized this would compound our measurement problems, rather than resolve them because we had no construct definitions of how these skills interact with each other. Moreover, we decided we had to opt for direct tests of composition, for the reason they would reflect the kinds of communicative performance with extended discourse that people want to see language students achieve, but we had no firm ideas on how we might assess students' attainment of component skills in their writing, such as grammar and vocabulary (which many people contributing to the design of the study argued also needed to be assessed, because they featured in the language curricula in their particular countries). In considering matters of learning and instruction, we also realized that we might be able to document through surveys the aspects of, for example, L2 writing that instructors might teach, and students might practice, but we recognized that we would not be able to make much sense out of any correlations between these variables and results of proficiency tests (e.g., to attribute causality between teaching, practice, and achievement), given how imprecise our construct definitions were, our lack of theoretical models to specify what their interrelations might be, and the obvious situational variability throughout the world.

Comparable dilemmas appeared with the curriculum framework in Ontario, as they do elsewhere in our field. The Ministry documents gave no rationale for distinguishing between particular language skills, other than to state, "All language skills–listening, speaking, reading, writing, viewing, and representing–are equally important. They are interconnected, and the student's progress in one area influences and is influenced by development in the other areas" (Ministry of Education and Training, 1995, p. 6). Rather than justifying this theoretical premise in any way, the distinction between language skills was made more complex, and mysterious, by stressing the interdependence of each, presumably in ways that teachers and students themselves would have to define. A further problem, and one that probably plagues all efforts to prescribe student outcomes in a standard way, was the interdependence of different strands of the curricula and the expected levels of attainment. For example, French is taught in 3 different types of programs in Ontario: as Core French (a few hours per week, where French is a school subject), as Immersion (where more than 50% of school subjects are taught through French as the medium of communication rather than as a school subject), and in an Extended format (similar to French Immersion, but in which less than 50% of school subjects are taught through French as the medium of instruction, along with some instruction in French as a subject). The curricula, time devoted to studies in the L2, and students' achievements are so radically different in each of these program types that the Ministry recognized it had to devise completely unique sets of outcome specifications for each to reflect the realities of curricula and student achievement alike, though this decision runs counter to any absolute idea of standardization, even for this one language.

VARIABILITY

So many of my preceding observations have mentioned variability that it is worth considering it a unique challenge. In many respects, the idea of standards stands in opposition to the idea of variability. People develop standards to overcome ad hoc, unintended, or unwanted variability. But at the same time, in specifying standards one is obliged to account for variability, as an integral component of standards (rather than to hide it under of the carpet of single norms). This is the great potential benefit of standards for minority aspects of education like L2 writing. But in the process of specifying standards, minority concerns need to be foregrounded, and to do this, research, theorization, and evaluation are necessary to identify and account for the sources and patterns of variability.

LES tried to confront the enormous variability in language education throughout the world, with the aim of starting to make comprehensive, empirical sense of it. On the one hand, the obstacles to this goal are numerous. People vary so greatly in their uses of languages as to defy standardization or comparisons among varieties of them. For example, in designing proficiency tests, which variety of a language should be used in test materials or scored in students' performance: British, American, South African, or Australian English? Or local standards common to countries such as Hong Kong or the Philippines, where English is also widely used but with different standards? It may be as Klein (1998) claimed, based on several large-scale comparative studies of adults' L2 acquisition in Europe, that the idea of languages are themselves convenient fictions and that we all use relatively unique subvarieties of them in various contexts. Likewise, the aspects of language performance valued in particular societies, or even subcultures, vary so greatly that it may be impossible to set universal standards for the purposes of comparison, apart from those established in a particular society. This was a conclusion reached in the IEA Study of Written Composition (Purves, 1992), which preceded LES by about a decade, focused on mother-tongue writing. Similarly, education systems vary greatly, both between and within countries, undermining the value of summary data at a national level, unless it accounts in some way for the extensive variability that also exists within regions or program streams or in the status of particular languages in a country. Even the ages and other characteristics of students at specific grade levels vary greatly between and within countries, making decisions difficult about which populations of students to sample and compare.[3]

On the other hand, if these sources of variation are not identified, with systematic and empirical rigor, then how are we to know reliably about them? How can we claim to have any standard, broad-based knowledge, for example, about L2 writing? Or is that a goal that could ever realistically be realized? The question that arises in view of such multiple sources of variability is not so much whether there should be standards, but rather how can standards be framed to account for and illuminate the major, relevant variables? Uniform standards may be misleading because they imply a single standard has been proclaimed paramount (amid other standards that are probably competing for this status). Perhaps multiple standards are what we should expect? Otherwise, we always have to ask critically, which or whose standard, and why?

A notable example of this dilemma appeared in our study in Toronto. As I alluded to previously, the Ministry framework presented different outcome statements for the two official languages of Ontario (English and French), accounting principally for differences in programs for teaching French (but saying virtually nothing about ESL or the various Aboriginal languages that are taught in some schools in Ontario). But our research uncovered an undesirable effect of the curriculum standards on perceptions of ESL students, particularly in the school with a comparatively lower socioeconomic situation, where about 60% of the students were either in ESL classes or had previously taken them. The English Language Arts teachers were, on the whole, the ones who were utilizing the new curriculum framework, seemingly because they or their colleagues had been involved integrally in its development and the provincial testing, which correspondingly reflected the standards and practices common to this domain of language teaching:

> The English teachers are the first to pick up the provincial standards. They can slip into it more easily than others, not because they are more progressive, because they certainly are not. It's because they've dealt with some of these

in a little different way with [their involvement in] the Ministry testing. They have worked with the kids with them, and assessed work in their classes with the scales. (Vice-Principal in one school)

Teachers in the English program have been evaluating in a very continuous way for a long time, so the writing folders, the portfolios, writing processes— all of that—has been very much a part of the English program. Our English program is really solid and progressive, innovative, but grounded in really good teaching, good literature, and a good balance. (Vice-Principal in the other school)

Perhaps because the Ministry's outcome statements featured only the English Language Arts curriculum (providing no expected outcomes for ESL students), some of the English teachers expressed visibly prejudiced opinions about the ESL students in their classes, judging them to be unprepared for the standards specified. Indeed, they used the Ministry standards as justification for this perception and as a basis for excluding certain students from the mainstream curriculum:[4]

In grade 9 you get students who have ESL problems. It doesn't take very long to find out who has reading and writing problems. If they are serious, they can be referred to the ESL Department or to Special Education. (teacher of English)

I think there is a strange philosophy about ESL. That is, they stay in ESL for a couple of months, then they integrate into the regular program. My belief is that it's done much too soon. So I have students who can actually speak very well, but they can't read a book, and their spelling is awful. It's obvious that they're coping with something much too big for them. (teacher of English)

As I remarked previously, when considering educational standards we always have to ask critically, which or whose standards, and why?

SUMMARY REMARKS

I may have dwelt too extensively, for a volume focused on L2 writing, on matters that pertain to education broadly. But the issues discussed here are vital now for all of us working on L2 writing, particularly at this point in history, when a relatively large body of information and concepts about L2 writing have accumulated, and sufficient commitment to the topic is evident to support a specifically focused journal and conferences. So, the first of several points worth reiterating, by way of summary, is that all of us working on L2 writing need to strive to establish how our knowledge and interests fit with those of education more broadly, and can inform them usefully.

Perhaps the subtext of this chapter is an appeal for a more broadly educational perspective on studies of L2 writing, to complement the influences of text linguistics, cognitive psychology, and critical pedagogy that have already shaped some of the key ideas about L2 writing. One aspect of this is awareness about issues like educational standards. This point was underscored by a recent survey (Center for Applied Linguistics, 1998) of foreign language teachers in the United States, which found that only half of the teachers sampled said they were aware of either national or state language standards. In turn, people working in other aspects of education need to be aware of the knowledge, particularly about variability, we do have from our perspectives on L2 writing.

Nonetheless, it is obvious that we need to know, research, and theorize more about the construct of L2 writing from all perspectives. What exactly is it, what are its integral components, and how does it interact with other language skills and human abilities? And how are standards about it set, for example, as norms in particular sociocultural communities? These questions are prior to our being able to identify, with any rigor or confidence, whether people have learned to write more proficiently in an L2. This is of vital concern to all of us, as it is to other educators who rely on our knowledge and views. To be able to ascertain learning validly, much research and development needs to be done in the area of L2 writing assessment. But without seminal and comprehensive definitions of the construct of L2 writing, how do we even know we are all talking about the same thing? Indeed, some of my colleagues working on LES would define foreign and L2 writing as different constructs (because they involve different populations of students in different types of educational programs), although that is not a perspective I could agree to, given the many shades of difference between situations where a language is, or is not, widely used in local communities or as the medium or subject of instruction. But where is the evidence to support this perception, or the contrary one? (I presume it is waiting for a point in history when LES' surveys, or something like them, might be undertaken.)

Third, there are many gaps in our knowledge about the implicit standards guiding educational programs for L2 writing. If, as suggested earlier, we view standards in a very broad sense and recognize their value in clarifying our activities then many of the conventions, practices, and criteria routinely guiding L2 writing require scrutiny and extensive research, not only to describe or recognize them better but also to know how to act on them productively. Similarly, to be useful for education, the idea of standards has to be expanded (as many have already started to do) to encompass, not just statements of proficiencies for students to attain but also the joint construction of curricula among teachers, learners, specific social contexts, and relevant subject matter. If we do not come to see things this way, we will be missing a big part of the educational picture, and we are bound to confuse levels of educational phenomena in discussing them.

Finally, we have to be cognizant of variability. This is just as true at an international level as it is locally. Although the focus of L2 writing research has recently been expanding beyond contexts in North America and northern Europe, it has scarcely developed an international perspective, let alone a cross-lingual one. Published ideas and standards about L2 writing are still based largely on studies of young adults learning English in North American universities or colleges, although studies of diverse bilingual children and of adolescent or adult learners of English in Japan, the Netherlands and Germany have recently also come to the fore, as has research on learners of French in Canada, Belgium, and France (see reviews in Cumming, 1998; Grabe & Kaplan, 1996). But this is not much of an international or cross-lingual perspective, nor is it sufficient for us to claim we are aware of the many sources and patterns of variation that no doubt exist in regards to L2 writing. How can we expect theories of L2 writing to be comprehensive, let alone standardized, with so little of the relevant phenomena documented, let alone compared in any systematic way? At the local level, we have to be wary of prejudices that feature in curriculum standards, or indeed any discussions of education that presume a monolingual norm when we know that extensive multilingualism and cultural diversity feature in all of our societies. This is a topic in need of ongoing research and lobbying in all curriculum situations. Standards without accompanying research are futile assertions that proclaim norms rather than aim to recognize the variable realizations of education, peoples, and societies.

ACKNOWLEDGMENTS

I thank Peter Dickson, Howard Russell, Razika Sanaoui, Merrill Swain, and Tony Silva for helpful comments on an initial draft of this chapter.

ENDNOTES

1. Some hope for resolution of this dilemma—given sufficient funding, research, and professional development—appears in the example of the Certificates for Spoken and Written English for adult immigrants settling in Australia, where a national ESL curriculum for several years has been defined to combine closely: (a) specific competencies for learning, which in turn (b) prescribe the syllabi, materials, approaches, resources to be used for learning and instruction, and likewise (c) specify assessments of competencies that students achieve (see Bottomly, Dalton, & Corbel, 1994; Burns & Brindley, 1994). But various limitations on such standards and their validity and utilization do exist (see Brindley, 1998). A related point, articulated

by Peter Dickson in discussing this chapter with me, and no doubt thinking of circumstances in England, is that a preoccupation with curriculum standards (excessively influenced by political and pseudo-scientific considerations) can lead to an unbalanced view of education, conceiving of standards in absolute, rather than relative terms, with assessment serving as an instrument and reference point, however inappropriate, for establishing these norms and for developing curricula and fashioning pedagogy.

2. Interestingly, the instantiation, although probably not origin of this convention in L2 education seems to have arisen from Carroll's skills model of L2 proficiency, which was developed for and utilized in the only two other studies of languages that IEA has sponsored (Carroll, 1975; Lewis & Massad, 1975). These were both analyses of French and of English, respectively, in secondary schools in countries where these languages were distinctly foreign, thereby avoiding the complexities of having to account for students' uses of the languages outside of school contexts (see Cumming, 1996a).

3. We opted in LES to consider the end of compulsory schooling as a comparison point across educational systems, as numerous other IEA studies had previously done, but that too poses great variability between countries, both in terms of students' ages and the number of years of schooling they have had. Moreover, the resulting student populations are affected by attrition rates, which likewise vary distinctly from country to country.

4. It is worth noting that although we had initial meetings and interviews with several ESL instructors, and did our best to recruit them for our research, none of them opted to continue their participation in our study, perhaps for the reason of such implicit biases against ESL programs they may have perceived in the curriculum framework.

REFERENCES

Berkenkotter, C., & Huckin, T. (1995). *Genre knowledge in disciplinary communication: Cognition/culture/power.* Hillsdale, NJ: Lawrence Erlbaum Associates.

Bialystok, E. (1998). Coming of age in applied linguistics. *Language Learning, 48,* 497–518.

Bottomley, Y., Dalton, J., & Corbel, C. (1994). *From proficiency to competencies: A collaborative approach to curriculum innovation.* Sydney, Australia: National Centre for English Language Teaching and Research, Macquarie University.

Bourne, J. (1997). "The grown-ups know best": Language policy-making in Britain in the 1990s. In W. Eggington & H. Wren (Ed.), *Language policy: Dominant English, pluralist challenges* (pp. 49–65). Amsterdam: John Benjamins.

Brindley, G. (1998). Outcomes-based assessment and reporting in language learning programmes: A review of the issues. *Language Testing, 15,* 45–85.

Burns, A., & Brindley, G. (Eds.). (1994). Special Issue of *Prospect, 9,* 2.

Carroll, J. B. (1975). *The teaching of French as a foreign language in eight countries.* New York: Wiley.

Center for Applied Linguistics. (1998). *National K-12 foreign language survey, 1987–1997: Fingertip facts.* Washington, DC: Center for Applied Linguistics.

Cumming, A. (1992). Instructional routines in ESL composition teaching. *Journal of Second Language Writing, 1,* 17–35.

Cumming, A. (1996a). IEA's studies of language education: Their scope and contribution. *Assessment in Education, 3,* 201–214.

Cumming, A. (1996b). Grade 9 teachers' use of language standards. *Research in Ontario Secondary Schools: A Series of Brief Reports, 3,* 2. Peterborough, Ontario: OISE Trent Valley Centre. Http://www.oise.utoronto.ca/field-centres/fcentres.htm#10

Cumming, A. (1997). The testing of writing in a second language. In C. Clapham (Ed.), *Language testing and assessment*, (Vol. 7 of 8), D. Corson (Ed.), *Encyclopedia of language and education* (pp. 51–63). Dordrecht, The Netherlands: Kluwer.

Cumming, A. (1998). Theoretical perspectives on writing. *Annual Review of Applied Linguistics, 18*, 61–78.

Cumming, A., & Riazi, A. (2000). Building models of adult second-language writing instruction. *Learning and Instruction, 10*, 55–71.

Cumming, A., Swain, M., Howard, J., Hart, D., & Shi, L. (1999). *Language teachers' utilization of language standards*. Manuscript in preparation. Toronto: Ontario Institute for Studies in Education/University of Toronto.

Davidson, F., Turner, C., & Huhta, A. (1997). Language testing standards. In C. Clapham (Ed.), *Language testing and assessment* (Vol. 7, pp. 303–311). D. Corson (Ed.), *Encyclopedia of language and education* (pp. 303–311). Dordrecht, The Netherlands: Kluwer.

Dewey, J. (1916). *Democracy in education*. New York: Macmillan.

Dewey, J. (1938). *Experience and education*. Toronto: Collier Macmillan.

Dickson, P., & Cumming, A. (Eds.). (1996). *Profiles of language education in 25 countries*. Slough, UK: National Foundation for Educational Research.

Grabe, B., & Kaplan, R. (1996). *Theory and practice of writing: An applied linguistic perspective*. New York: Longman.

Graff, H. (1994). Literacy, myths and legacies: Lessons from the history of literacy. In L. Verhoeven (Ed.), *Functional literacy: Theoretical issues and educational implications* (pp. 37–60). Amsterdam: John Benjamins.

Habermas, J. (1984). *The theory of communicative action*. Boston: Beacon Press.

Habermas, J. (1987). *The theory of communicative action*, Vol. 2. Boston: Beacon Press.

Hale, G., Taylor, C., Bridgeman, B., Carson, J., Kroll, B., & Kantor, R. (1996). *A study of writing tasks assigned in academic degree programs*. (TOEFL Research Report 54). Princeton, NJ: Educational Testing Service.

International Reading Association & National Council of Teachers of English (1996). *Standards for the English Language Arts*. Newark, DE: IRA and Urbana, IL: NCTE.

Klein, W. (1998). The contribution of second language acquisition research. *Language Learning, 48*, 527–549.

Levin, H. (1998). Educational preformance standards and the economy. *Educational Researcher, 27*(4), 4–10.

Lewis, E. G., & Massad, C. (1975). *The teaching of English as a foreign language in ten countries*. New York: Wiley.

Moore, H. (1996). Telling what is real: Competing views in assessing ESL development. *Linguistics and Education, 8*, 189–228.

Ontario Ministry of Education and Training. (1995). *The common curriculum: Provincial standards–languages, grades 1–9* (field test version). Toronto: Author.

Polio, C. (1997). Measures of linguistic accuracy in research on second language writing. *Language Learning, 47*, 101–143.

Purves, A. (Ed.). (1992). *The IEA study of written composition: Education and performance in fourteen countries*. Oxford: Pergamon.

Raimes, A. (1990). The TOEFL test of written English: Causes for concern. *TESOL Quarterly, 24*, 427–442.

Shi, L., & Cumming, A. (1995). Teachers' conceptions of second-language writing instruction: Five case studies. *Journal of Second Language Writing, 4*, 87–111.

Silva, T., Leki, I., & Carson, J. (1997). Broadening the perspective of mainstream composition studies: Some thoughts from the disciplinary margins. *Written Communication, 14*, 398–428.

Stern, H. H. (1983). *Fundamental concepts of language teaching*. New York: Oxford University Press.

Teachers of English to Speakers of Other Languages (TESOL). (1997). *ESL standards for pre-K–12 students*. Alexandria, VI: Author.

Teachers of English to Speakers of Other Languages (TESOL). (1998). *Managing the assessment process: A framework for measuring student attainment of the ESL standards*. Alexandria, VI: Author.

Torrance, H. (Ed.). (1995). *Evaluating authentic assessment*. Buckingham, UK: Open University Press.

Trim, J. (1998). European perspectives on modern language learning: Contributions of the Modern Languages Project of the Council of Europe. *Language Teaching, 31*, 136–151, 206–217.

Author Index

Subject Index